Contemporary British poetry and the city

MANCHESTER
UNIVERSITY PRESS

Contemporary British poetry and the city

Peter Barry

Manchester University Press
Manchester and New York

distributed exclusively in the USA by St. Martin's Press

Published by Manchester University Press
Oxford Road, Manchester M13 9NR, UK
and Room 400, 175 Fifth Avenue, New York, NY 10010, USA
http://www.manchesteruniversitypress.co.uk

Distributed exclusively in the USA by
St. Martin's Press, Inc., 175 Fifth Avenue, New York,
NY 10010, USA

Distributed exclusively in Canada by
UBC Press, University of British Columbia, 2029 West Mall,
Vancouver, BC, Canada V6T 1Z2

British Library Cataloguing-in-Publication Data
A catalogue record for this book is available from the British Library

Library of Congress Cataloging-in-Publication Data applied for

ISBN   0 7190 5593 8 hardback
        0 7190 5594 6 paperback

First published 2000

07 06 05 04 03 02 01 00   10 9 8 7 6 5 4 3 2 1

Typeset
by Helen Skelton Publishing, London
Printed in Great Britain
by Bell & Bain Ltd, Glasgow

To M and T from me

Contents

Acknowledgements

Earlier versions of chapters and parts of chapters have been used as follows: parts of Chapter 1 were given as a paper at the conference 'Postwar Anglo-American Poetic Relations' at the English Centre, London University, 9–12 July 1998; parts of Chapter 3 were given as a lecture to Oxford University Summer School, 30 July 1998; part of Chapter 5 was given as a paper to the Philosophy Society, University of Brighton, 27 April 2000; versions of Chapter 6 have appeared in the *Cambridge Quarterly*, autumn 1999, and in *Liverpool Poetry* (ed. Stephen Wade, Liverpool University Press); versions of Chapter 7 were given as a paper at the conference 'Space and Place: The Geographies of Literature' at Liverpool John Moores University, 11–13 April 1996, and at 'British and Irish Poetry in the Making', at the University of Salzburg, 30 October–2 November 1996. Expanded versions of the two papers appeared in the published proceedings of these conferences: *Space and Place: The Geographies of Literature*, Liverpool John Moores University, 1998, and *British and Irish Poetry in the Making*, ed. Holger Klein et al., Stauffenburg Verlag, 1999. A version of Chapter 8 appeared in the *Yale Journal of Criticism* (Johns Hopkins University Press), Spring 2000. I am grateful for the invitations to speak, the opportunities to discuss, and the permissions of reprint.

Part 1
Mapping

1 Introduction

Poetry's occlusion of the urban

An academic book needs a thesis which can be simply stated in a couple of sentences and then used as currency in academic exchange and debate. For even if it achieves profundity in every line, using the high-theoretical discourse of its day, a book's real life can only begin when readers bring it down to earth and put it into circulation by mentioning it, citing it, and even – when all else fails – quoting from it.

The simple thesis of this book, then, is that contemporary poetry is in trouble. A prime indication of the extent of the trouble was the withdrawal of its poetry list by Oxford University Press (OUP) at the end of 1998, on the grounds of its insufficient profitability.[1] Another symptom, which will be familiar to those who teach contemporary poetry at universities, is the comparatively low take-up of poetry courses at degree level whenever they are optional. In January 1998 the Council for College and University English (CCUE) published the results of their survey of what is taught on English degrees in Britain. Of the seventy-six university-level institutions which filled in the questionnaire, only nineteen said that contemporary poetry was compulsory for their students – fifty-one said it was optional and six said it was both (depending on programme of study, presumably). For purposes of comparison, it should be stated here that Victorian fiction is compulsory at thirty institutions, and that the most compulsory topic of all is literary theory, which is obligatory at forty of them, more than twice as many as require study of contemporary poetry. That, I think, gives us a context: the status of contemporary poetry on the university syllabus is somewhat precarious in relation to all forms of fiction, and particularly so in relation to literary theory.

The symptoms of poetry's trouble are obvious enough, really, but
what are the causes? A major one, I believe, is that poetry lacks
'street-cred', or to be more specific, *street*-cred. In other words, the
experience which is explored in contemporary poetry is too seldom
that of cities. Poetry has plenty of *country-lane*-cred, and *farm-and-
meadow*-cred, thanks to writers like Seamus Heaney and Ted Hughes,
poets undoubtedly distinguished in talent, but relatively narrow in
range. The latter's career, indeed, presented us with a seemingly
endless procession of animals which went on for over thirty years. His
last book won all the available prizes,[2] but the unique circumstances
of its publication, and the sensational nature of its subject matter,
mean that poetry in general can draw no comfort from this fact.
Unless we can re-associate poetry with the city then we may have to
accept its contemporary near-demise, its dearth, at least, if not (just
yet) its death. The overwhelming association of poetry with nature
and the countryside, is, I would maintain, a significant factor in its
decline. Because it can often seem to have little to say to 'anyone
brought up with television' (in Ian Gregson's words)[3] – meaning
anyone under fifty – poetry is not often chosen when people have a
choice (of which book to buy, which course to take, which book to
read in bed, and so on). After a couple of decades of this we can look
forward to a time when no press at all will be able to maintain and
promote a *list* of contemporary poets (quite different from basking in
the reflected glory of one or two stars). Breaking the automatic link
between poetry and the countryside, between poetry and 'nature', may
therefore contribute a little to keeping it in circulation, and perhaps
even to broadening its appeal. In the progress of modernism, Ezra
Pound famously said, the first heave was to break [the hold of] the
pentameter. The second was to challenge the dominance of Georgian
subject matter, especially its anachronistic ruralism, and in this area
the outcome of the modernist struggle has been less clear-cut. The
point made above about '*re*-associating' poetry with the city is made
advisedly, for there was a vigorous tradition of urban poetry in the
eighteenth century which flourished until the immense prestige of the
Romantics fused poetry and 'nature' in the public mind as if for ever.[4]
Monroe Spears, in his classic *Dionysus and the City: Modernism in
Twentieth-Century Poetry* (OUP, 1970) sees the Augustan period as a
high point in this regard, with 'excellent urban poetry, chiefly satirical
or parodic, and usually in "imitation" of a Roman model – for
example the "City pastoral" or "town eclogue" of Swift and Gay, or

the epistles and dialogues imitating Horace done by Prior and Pope, and Johnson's "London", done in imitation of Juvenal' (p. 74). He continues:

> But English poetry since the mid-eighteenth century offered few examples of successful rendering of the City. There were occasional brilliant exceptions: Blake's visionary 'London', Wordsworth's Westminster Bridge sonnet ... James Thomson's overwrought 'City of Dreadful Night', Henley's vividly realistic 'In Hospital' and 'London Voluntaries'; but in general the poets regarded the city as something alien, and they were not interested in writing about it. (p. 74)

The poetic avoidance of the subject of the city is very marked, then, in the major nineteenth century canonical poets: a 'bald street' will glimmer in Tennyson as a correlative of grief (*In Memoriam*, poem 7), but generally the city is absent from his work, and the preferred locations are classical or medieval: Browning, likewise, wrote elaborate poetic costume mono-dramas set in Renaissance Italy, and Arnold, whose life and work as a schools inspector revolved about the most mundane British towns and cities, similarly avoided that reality in his poetry. Even the Oxford on which he remained fixated mainly consists of the surrounding hills, or of colleges glimpsed romantically in dusky light from afar. In the twentieth century, as Spears points out, the city for Yeats is a place to escape from, away from the 'pavements grey' to a Lake Isle, a mystical Byzantium, or an idealised image of eighteenth-century Dublin. Indeed, Yeats's exclusion from the modernist foundational quartet of Eliot, Joyce, Pound and Woolf is partly on these grounds, for the others were conspicuously urbanists, and it is impossible to be a modernist while so completely occluding the city. (Other grounds for Yeats's exclusion would include his 1865 birth-date.) While the Irish poets of the 'Celtic twilight' (including Joyce himself as poet) and the English Georgians continued the apparent poetic interdict on the city, modernism brought it briefly back to the fore, with its epicentre in Eliot's *The Waste Land*, and though the modernist high-tide receded in the 1930s, the most prominent poets continued to feature the city overtly. The poets of the 1940s, however, especially those associated with the 'New Apocalypse', again pick up the Romanticism which always entails the eclipse of the city, and in the 1960s the best-known voices were Hughes and Larkin, the former exclusively rural in subject matter, describing a daily round of experience and reflection which a first generation Romantic poet would have thought odd in emphasis and expression, but unexceptional as regards subject matter, for they are set in a world without cars, phones or television.[5] Larkin's work is a little more difficult to categorise in this regard: it is pervaded by a strong sense of urban space, and though specific locations in the city of Hull have been identified, Larkin seems to take pains to make the poems 'urban-generic' rather than 'urban-specific', avoiding the use of street names or place names. Thus, specific places in Hull are referred to generically ('The Infirmary' or 'the cemetery'), rather than by their proper names. In this way, he tries to give his locations that quality of generalisability which seems to be felt as not inhering 'naturally' in cities. This book, then, re-asserts and attempts to re-establish the necessary connection between poetry and the urban.

Linguistic pastoralism

Yet ruralism, of course, lies very deep within our culture, suffusing the very words we use, and it would be foolish to desire or attempt to eliminate it. Indeed, one of the things which first set me thinking about poetry and cities was, paradoxically, noticing the prevalence, some years ago, of rural metaphors in academic and commercial life, and then beginning to speculate about the significance of the widespread liking for this kind of vocabulary. At universities, for instance, the complex degree schemes then coming into being had (and still have) what are called 'pathways' (not, let's say, 'A-roads' or 'motorways') which map out available choices for students. A subject area is called a 'field' (and will have its 'field leader'), and modules may well be grouped into 'bundles', an image which evokes stoops of hay or straw stacked for harvesting (these items feature in Edward Thomas's well-known poem 'Adlestrop', the very heart of twentieth-century 'meadow-cred' poetry). When finance was discussed at faculty meetings we heard of 'pump priming' and 'seed-corn funding'; there was talk of the available 'pot of money', and if there was a surplus it had to be 'salted away'. When difficulties were encountered we were urged to 'grasp the nettle' or, of course, to 'take the bull by the horns'. The use of this kind of vocabulary constitutes a shadowy, wishful adumbration of rural life in the quintessentially urban milieu of the large company or university.

Many other areas of professional life, no doubt, manifest a similar preference for a linguistic register in which the rural is heavily marked. Indeed, the more remote we become from the rural, the more its nostalgic pull is felt. Of course, the countryside evoked in this kind of language belongs to a vanished period – an anachronism, almost, even in Edward Thomas's own day. It is a countryside divided by fences and hedgerows into a patchwork of five- or ten-acre fields in which mixed farming is the norm, the farms having been in the same family for generations, each still employing ten or fifteen people from nearby villages. Not, in other words, the countryside of today, in which a highly mechanised, two-thousand acre, mono-crop agri-business may well employ no more than a single non-family worker. The villages in which the farm workers of the idealised rural past used to live now have rows of gentrifed houses and cottages, usually with names containing the word 'Old' (The Old Rectory, Smithy, School, Dairy, Post Office and so on), a row of evacuated linguistic signifiers, in which, again, the ghost or adumbration of a vanished community can be glimpsed.

Yet the curious thing about this preferred ruralised vocabulary was that it was never seen as an affected, self-conscious retro-style equivalent to turning up for work in a hacking jacket and green wellies. On the contrary, it had an air of modishness, of down-to-earth, straight-talking, clear-thinking practicality. When we used it we invariably felt rather pleased with ourselves, for in talking this way academics and administrators implicitly reject an alternative academic register, one which would be inescapably urban, which is to say Latinate, overtly 'learned', and containing a high number of abstractions. In terms of an age-old rhetorical trope, we were implicitly rejecting the inherent corruption and deviousness of the city, and associating ourselves with the innate goodness and honesty of the countryside. Hence, our preference for metaphors with a rural flavour seemed to highlight a more general and widespread desire to occlude the city.

Yet for my own part, I was also conscious that the emotive pull which the countryside had for many was actually exerted in my own case by the idea of cities, as I came to recognise from a series of small incidents. For instance, when teaching poetry I had a 'starter' activity which I sometimes used in class. I would ask students to circle the word or phrase in the text which seemed to encapsulate the emotional impact which the whole poem or section of the poem had upon them. On one occasion we were looking at the 'fire-watching' section of

Eliot's *Four Quartets*, the part where the speaker, during the London
blitz, meets the 'familiar compound ghost' and with him 'trod the
pavement in a dead patrol'. Doing this exercise alongside the class, the
word I circled myself was 'pavement'. Thinking about this later, I
realised that it is a word which conjures up the most mundane aspect
of the urban, and at that moment I realised that I must, in a way, be
fixated on cities, unsurprisingly, perhaps, since I have lived in cities
virtually all my life, and not among lakes or hills.

Cities in process

Another significant moment in the process of recognising the topic
and deciding to write this book was that of returning in adult life to
visit the urban streets in which I had been brought up, and happening
to go there when demolition was actually in progress. The sunny
air that day shimmered with a film of brick-dust, and an old lady
appeared in the doorway of the only house in the street still inhabited
(rather than bricked up). She called across to a child playing on waste
ground, which should have been several streets away, except that
the streets between no longer existed. I walked into abandoned
terraced houses and picked up items from the debris in the backyards
– a technical manual on photographic exposure, and the wing of a
Sunderland Flying Boat from an Airfix kit – I had made the same
model myself as a child, and my fingers recognised the familiar Braille
of its tiny plastic rivets. I also picked up a fixture-list for the Low
Hill & District Darts League, which had my uncle's name written on
it. Years later I realised how strange it was that these houses had not
been properly cleared out before the people moved – I had gone
into back bedrooms, and found them still partially equipped for
hobbies like carpentry or photographic enlarging. The houses, in fact,
seemed to have been abandoned in a hurry, as if at the approach of an
invading army.

This emblematic scene imbued in me a strong sense of how cities
are places of continual loss and change: the change is often long-
threatened – some of my childhood friends lived in streets over which
the threat of demolition and re-housing hung for more than a decade.
But in the end, as I now realised, it must have been sudden. At primary
school (as I recall it now) a classmate caused consternation by
announcing that the Corporation were going to knock down a house
in every street in Liverpool. We all went home worried that the

selected house might be ours. The announcement was in fact true – a house in Every Street was indeed being demolished – but now, in adult life, it was as if the inchoate fears evoked by that childish joke of long ago were being realised – the Corporation really did seem to be knocking down not just a house in Every Street in Liverpool, but every street in Liverpool.

The realisation that the cityscape which had seemed so immutable was actually just like stage scenery and could be swept away when finished with, did much to stimulate my sense of the city as a place of peculiarly fraught interaction between the personal, the social and the political. But while there are plenty of voices to mourn (or oppose) the imposition of change on the countryside (the loss of hedgerows, the dearth of songbirds, the closing of village schools and shops and so on) the even vaster scale of change imposed on cities in the 1960s and 1970s went generally unmourned. It was therefore a revelation to come upon the work of Birmingham poet Roy Fisher, especially his long poem *City*, and find that the kind of contradictory feelings of loss and resentment which I had had that day were articulated in contemporary poetry, not in a dirge-like lament (for what could be the point of that?), but in an inventive, supple medium of verse which combines the lyrical and the documenting impulse. Roy Fisher is a kind of laureate of the urban-prosaic, for me the quintessential city poet, and I use him in this book as a presiding figure. Likewise, the peculiar feeling I had that day, of looking across streets that were no longer there and finding that there is 'more sky than there used to be', was powerfully expressed in another contemporary poet strongly identified and identifying with a single urban locale, namely the Belfast poet Ciaran Carson, whose poem 'Clearance' captures the air of unreality that such scenes have to those who know how they 'ought' to look:

> The Royal Avenue Hotel collapses under the breaker's
>   pendulum:
> Zig-zag stairwells, chimney-flues, and a 'thirties mural
> Of an elegantly-dressed couple doing what seems to be the
>   Tango, in Wedgewood
> Blue and white – happy days! Suddenly more sky
> Than there used to be. A breeze springs up from nowhere[6]

The day after I visited the remains of my home district in Liverpool I went down to the river to look at the then derelict and redundant

Albert Dock, which had simply been abandoned to the tides, another strangely shocking sight in a city that had for so long boasted of its more than seven miles of enclosed docks. It was evening and the tide was out, revealing a vast expanse of uneven mud stretching across the dock, with dregs and runnels of dirty water following the retreating tide. How could the city live, I wondered, when its maritime life-blood was draining away? In fact, the port is more profitable today than ever,[7] but like those agri-businesses, it is almost completely mechanised, and there are said to be fewer deep-sea ships left in the Merchant Navy today than there used to be shipping lines. The Albert Dock, though, has been born again and is now the hub of a major tourist attraction, demonstrating the amazing power of a single innovative building or complex to start the revitalisation of a whole city. Whereas the gigantic but uninspired demolition and 'redevelopment' projects of the 1960s and 1970s merely accelerated inner-city despair and decay, a single imaginative building by a world-renowned architect can have a seemingly magical effect on the confidence, and then on the economy, of a whole region. Hence, for instance, the dramatic Ferensway project by Norman Foster and Terry Farrell in the centre of Hull, with a boulevard running diagonally through the complex 'roofed with a glass javelin 280 metres long and 30 metres broad at its widest'.[8] Apparently-terminal decline, then, can be swung round, not by attracting new industry, but by attracting a major architect – by art, in fact. But this is merely to acknowledge the hard economic fact that today the leisure, education and culture 'industries' drive our employment economy as coal, steel, shipbuilding and railways once did. In other words, as we might say in old Marxist terms, the 'superstructure' now sets the pace, not the 'base'. In cities like Hull and Liverpool a vigorous 'poetry scene' attracting national attention was a significant part of the cultural energies which helped to re-invigorate the sense of local worth and identity as traditional industries collapsed. Perhaps poetry even helped to pave the way for subsequent economic revival in the post-industrial cityscapes of the 1990s. Indeed, we might almost be tempted to believe that Auden was wrong (in his elegy on the death of Yeats), and that perhaps sometimes poetry *can* help, at least, to make things happen. For me, at any rate, this book has been one way of succumbing to that temptation.

Am I, then, offering what amounts to a new arraignment of contemporary poetry, similar in some regards to that made by A. Alvarez in the famous introductory essay, subtitled 'Beyond the

Gentility Principle', to his 1962 Penguin anthology *The New Poetry*?
Alvarez, it will be remembered, accused modern British poetry of
turning away, with genteel distaste, from 'modern horrors' like 'the
concentration camps' or 'the hydrogen bomb', and from the 'contem-
porary anxiety' which might suggest that these horrors somehow
acted out the repressed psychological wishes of many. He is often cari-
catured as having advised British poets to ape the verbal histrionics of
American poets facing psychological breakdown. But the accusation
actually has a much more general basis, and he explicitly denied
suggesting that 'modern English poetry, to be really modern, must be
concerned with psychoanalysis ... I am not suggesting, in fact, that it
must be anything. For poetry that feels it has to cope with pre-deter-
mined subjects ceases to be poetry and becomes propaganda' (p. 27).
His aim, really, and it is mine too, was to express a sense of frustra-
tion that the British often seem to want their poetry to be much more
purely recreational, and – yes – escapist, than they allow their contem-
porary art, music, or indeed, fiction to be. What I *am* noting, then, is
a curious failure on the part of a very large number of poets to engage
with one of the major facts of contemporary life, which is the fact of
the city. I don't mean, of course, that poets should offer wisdom, or
solutions, or even coherent analysis of the urban present. Even just
being there, from time to time, would count. If this amounts to an
'indictment' (grandiose term), then it must be applicable 'cross-
zonally', that is, to all of the realms of contemporary verse which I
identify in the 'map' of contemporary poetry outlined below. It is
certainly not a criticism from which avant-garde 'outer-marginal'
poets would be exempt.

Mapping the 'zones' of contemporary poetry

Until the late 1980s contemporary British poetry was usually mapped
as a stark oppositional polarity, with a conservative (that is, anti-
modernist) *mainstream*, which is implacably opposed to the excluded,
embattled and experimental *margins*. But recent writers seem to agree
that there has been a loosening up of this fundamental division. A
'new consensus' emerges in books by Gregson, Kennedy, O'Brien and
Robinson[9] which see a change taking place in poetry and its reception
since the mid-1980s; in the opinion of these writers we have had
'cross-fertilisation' (as Gregson calls it); or 'New relations' (as
Kennedy says); or 'Deregulation' (in O'Brien's words); or 'Instabilities'

(in Robinson's view), between formerly disparate types of verse, and this process has upset and superseded the old embattled positions of the 1970s. Of course, this new consensus is not universally accepted: for example, the older model is adhered to by Bush and others[10] whose 'Dissent' from the margins (by poets like Eric Mottram, Barry McSweeney, Bill Griffiths, etc.) contrasts sharply with the loosening-up process implied by the keywords used in the book titles of the other four authors listed – 'dialogue', 'refashioning', 'deregulation' and 'instability'. The end-product of the 'dialogue' and 'deregulation' between formerly polarised kinds of poetry is that there is a wide-spread preoccupation on the part of poets of all persuasions today with more-or-less 'experimental' explorations of such things as: linguistic registers, implied voices, varieties of narrative technique and viewpoint, ways of using metaphor to undermine the 'real', and various ways of using myth. In consequence, the kind of poetry which once seemed ubiquitous now seems quite rare – that is, the kind in which a straightforwardly autobiographical speaker muses on aspects of his/her love-life or domesticity or ruminates on relationships with god and nature (or even God and Nature). To imagine that the anxious or celebratory meta-poetries of the deconstructed subject are still the *exclusive* preserve of an always-excluded avant-garde is simply to be twenty years behind the poetic times.

Yet I would like to suggest that the situation today is actually more complex than either the consensus model of Gregson, Kennedy, O'Brien and Robinson, or the dissenting voice of Bush. For it would be naive, on the one hand, to imagine that the old divide between mainstream and margin has simply been 'Berlined' – that the wall between them has been toppled, giving us an 'end-of-history' world of recent poetry. What has happened is that, yes, there has been a change, and these authors, in their different ways, are right to identify it. But the new situation is that there are now *more*, not fewer, zones and divisions than before; yet they are also *more fluid*. A 'zonal map' of contemporary British poetry may be a simple way of representing this new situation. In the map, contemporary poetry is divided into four notional 'zones': the four zones, and suggested names for them, are shown in Figure 1.1.

The map can be glossed as follows: Zone 1, the Inner Canonical, is where the 'H' poets reside – Heaney, Hill, Harrison, Hughes – names which would probably be recognised by the average reader of the *Observer* or the *Independent*, or the average professor of English.

Zone 1: *Inner Canonical* (e.g. Heaney, Hughes, Larkin, Hill, Harrison)
Zone 2: *Outer Canonical* (e.g. Raine, Fenton, Adcock, Muldoon)
Zone 3: *Inner Marginal* (e.g. Edwin Morgan, Roy Fisher, Denise Riley)
Zone 4: *Outer Marginal* (e.g. Levi Tafari, Iain Sinclair, Aidan Dun)

Figure 1.1 Zonal map of contemporary British poetry.

A crucial defining feature of Zone 1 poets is that there exist *individual* books about them from major commercial and academic presses – Faber, Macmillan, Routledge, OUP, and so on. At any given moment in the history of poetry, I would say, there is only room in the inner-canon for about five poets, who are nearly always male poets. There is, of course, two-way traffic between the inner and outer canonical zones, though it is in slow motion when compared to inter-zonal traffic elsewhere on the map. At present, for instance, Geoffrey Hill may be losing his inner-canonical place to Paul Muldoon. Nor does conferment of any office give automatic inner-canonical status – Andrew Motion, for instance, in spite of his Laureatship, is still unambiguously outer-canonical as we enter the new millennium.

Zone 2, the Outer Canonical, contains very familiar names, and these too are poets who are published by major presses – Faber, OUP, and so on. Generally speaking, there are no monographs from major presses on single figures from this zone, but there are articles on them in mainstream academic journals. Indeed, this is almost their defining feature from the viewpoint of the literary scholar – they are poets who have *articles* rather than *books* written about them. It should be added that the zonal map has geographical variations within the British Isles. In Scotland, for instance, Edwin Morgan is a major inner-canonical figure, whereas elsewhere he has a reputation as an 'experimentalist' in 'concrete' and 'visual' modes (based on much-anthologised pieces like 'The Computer's First Christmas Card' and 'The Loch Ness Monster's Song').

Zone 3, the Inner Marginal, contains names which may not be familiar, even to people who take an interest in modern poetry or are involved in teaching it at schools or universities. These poets *may* occasionally be published by high-profile presses like OUP, but usually only in late career: you *may* find them on the shelves of a good high-street bookstore if this is the case, but otherwise not. More often, they are confined to less well-known imprints. From the academic viewpoint, the defining feature of poets in this zone is that placing articles on a single such figure in a mainstream, generalist journal may well be difficult: editors will have trouble thinking of suitable referees, and will doubt whether interest in them is sufficiently wide.

Zone 4, the Outer Marginal, finally, is an altogether colder region, the orbit of Neptune and Pluto, if we were to use the analogy of the solar system. Poets in this outer-marginal zone may be published by regional presses, or presses in which they themselves have a hand, and they will not be found on the shelves of the major bookshops, since they are outside the major distribution networks.

A number of significant factors should be mentioned: first, the 'Inter-zonal' poet seems to me an important new phenomenon, especially those situated somewhere within Zones 2 and 3 of the map; typical inter-zonals are the poets discussed by Kennedy under the chapter heading 'British Postmodernism' – John Ash, Peter Didsbury and Ian McMillan. In some ways these poets are 'experimental' enough to have been banished to the small-press 'exclusion zone' if they had been working it the 1970s. Yet they have been able to enter this vital 'inter-zone', which gives access to high-profile 'outlets' such as literature festivals, local and national radio, *Poetry Review*, residencies, and reviews in national broadsheets and the *Times Literary Supplement*.

A second significant factor has been the many changes in the publishing 'infrastructure' of poetry, notably the growth and immense energies of Bloodaxe Books, the archetypal 'inter-zonal' press, and by far the largest publisher of contemporary poetry in Britain, operating in the crucial territory which covers Zones 2 and 3, which is where the older separate spheres of the 'Mainstream' and the 'Exclusion Zone' come into contact with each other. Bloodaxe has promoted the reputations of poets like Ian Duhig and Ian McMillan, whose status is representative of the 'instabilities' etc., already mentioned. Indeed, it is also generally true that if the major division between 'Mainstream' and 'Exclusion Zone' no longer holds, then this is also partly due to technological developments and economic changes which have meant that the categories of 'large' and 'small' press are much more blurred now (and the most important distinctions concern methods of distribution, advertising and sale, rather than production). Furthermore, the period of fluidity and instability has corresponded with a decline in the output or status of the 'large presses' (like Faber, OUP and Secker) which dominated the 1970s. Typically, these presses have tended to turn their main attention to modern rather than contemporary poetry, or to the production of re-issues of out-of-copyright 'classic' poets, mainly for the academic market.

I want to mention briefly some tentative generalisations about poetry in the 3–4 inter-zone, because these poets are strongly represented in this book. First, poetry in these zones is often 'Non-Experiential', by which I mean that it obviously isn't just the voice of a 'unified subject' recording and musing upon personal experience. Instead, it may conflate several subjectivities, inter-cutting between them, or present a *melange* of voices which seem un-anchored in any conceivable actual personage. Second, the poetry concerned is often notably 'Language-Centred', in the sense that shifts and inter-cuts in linguistic register are strongly foregrounded by this absence of definable speakers, consistent attitudes, or identifiable events. Third, this kind of writing is often 'Overtly Politicised', deeply implicating poetry in the making of statements which are feminist, or anarchist, or green, or pacifist or Marxist. Fourth, writing of this kind is often densely 'Content-Specific', in the sense that it has worked into it substantial data of a scientific, technological, historical or mythical kind. In combination, these features make many demands on the resources and commitment of poetry readers, and yet, surely no more so than many works of contemporary art, music and fiction. Typically, the kind of urban poetry discussed in this book will be larger-in-scale than the average published poem. In most books of poetry the notorious forty-line limit imposed externally by the organisers of many poetry competitions is self-imposed by authors upon themselves, with most of the poems being lyrics closer in length to around twenty-five lines. By contrast, the urban scale often seems to demand a formal-correlative of the poet, though this may result in the use of composite forms (like Edwin Morgan's 'Glasgow Sonnets', for instance).

In general, I have discussed in this book poets from all the 'zones' except the Inner Canonical, omitting these on the grounds that plenty of discussion about such major figures is already in print. This has meant that much notable urban poetry is left out, such as: the Belfast which has an always carefully circumscribed presence in Heaney's work; the Hull which suffuses Larkin's urban world, though without ever emerging into full focus; the Hull of Douglas Dunn's brilliant 1969 debut volume *Terry Street*, a paradigmatic 'city' collection, and one which first made me realise that the kind of terraced streets I discussed earlier are just as 'poetic' as lakes or daffodils. Equally exemplary, but omitted on the same grounds, is another major

paradigmatic urban poem, Tony Harrison's 'V', and the Leeds of his
startlingly original (and expanding) collection *From the School of
Eloquence*.[11] I have left out this Zone 1 material because I am not
trying to write a history or a general survey of modern urban poetry.
Rather, my desire is to extend the range of what is generally known
about and discussed of contemporary urban poetry, so as to bring
about a shift in our general conception of contemporary poetry. Like-
wise, when urban poetry from other zones has already received fairly
widespread recognition I have not included detailed discussion of it.
Hence, though Roy Fisher's *City* is the archetypal (near) contemporary
urban poem, and crucially influential on my own view of this topic, I
have not discussed it closely in the Roy Fisher chapter, but have
preferred to write in detail on Fisher's more recent material, and have
suggested a structural formula which gives an overview of his urban
writing over a period of nearly forty years. In the discussion through-
out the book I have deliberately mixed together poets from different
zones in order to embody the notion of 'deregulation', rather than
adopting what would be the self-defeating tactic of grouping 'outer-
zonals' together and treating them as a generic group.

Women poets and the city – Denise Riley

There is one omission, however, which I should discuss at greater
length. Where, in this examination of contemporary poetry and the
city, are the women poets? The question is both quite easy and quite
difficult to answer. The easy answer is that I have favoured poets
whose representations of the city are what I call 'urban-specific' rather
than 'urban-generic' and this means, among other things, that the city
appears in the poetry as an external, denoted reality which is
referred to using the names of specific streets, buildings, neighbour-
hoods and districts. I have found, however, that this seems not to be
the way that women write about cities: more common with women
poets is an appropriation and internalisation of geography, so that it
represents and embodies such things as states of mind, and structures
of feeling.[12] This might be expressed in formulaic terms by saying
that for many women poets geography is 'always already' psychic
geography, place is already space. Naming public spaces, like streets,
squares, and locales is an act which proclaims ownership and identifi-
cation, and it may be that poets who are women feel less confident
of such ownership, and are therefore less likely to name hotels, pubs,

workplaces and public buildings than male poets. This 'internalised geography' is the situation I illustrate in the case of Deryn Rees-Jones, whose work is discussed in Chapter 5. For her, words like 'geography' and 'map' are typically used of the body. Likewise, an essay by a woman poet and academic promisingly (from my point of view) entitled 'The Paper City' is not about an actual city but is an enquiry into the mental writing space and processes of women poets.[13] The same writer has an essay in *Kicking Daffodils: Twentieth-Century Women Poets*[14] on 'Scottish Women Poets and the Topography of Tongues', but again the 'topography' here is not, in the main, literal topography, and in so far as it *is* literal it is mainly rural and regional rather than urban. The section of the book in which this essay appears (which is called 'The Politics of Place') does not include material on cities, and the tendency towards an internalised concept of geography is partly indicated, for instance, by the presence of the key word 'room' in the title of an essay on Northern Ireland women poets, which is '"From Room to Homesick Room": Women and Poetry in Northern Ireland'. Generally, women poets seem not to use the kind of external geographic specifics which are the mainstay, almost, of several of the male poets I discuss, and they are less likely to have the kind of chronotopic (relative) fixity of viewpoint which is another of the prerequisites of the kind of writing I mainly examine here. This amounts to saying that the women poets tend to be more radical in technique, which in turn tends to rule out the direct representation of place.

I can illustrate both this and its problems, by commenting on a poem from Denise Riley's *Mop Mop Georgette* (Reality Street, 1993) which is entitled (with a strong ironic charge in the present context) 'Knowing the Real World'. It opens fairly straightforwardly in the mode I call 'urban-generic', identifying no particular place, but vividly evoking the urban through impressionistic, subtle lighting-effects:

A yellow glow slips from the brick houses.
Some steely clouds swell up over them.

One afternoon hour burns away until a rust-
coloured light sinks in towards evening

or any time at all when I fall straight through
myself to thud as onto the streaked floor of

a swimming pool drained out for winter, no
greeny depths but lined in blackened leaves.

Here, just when it is all set up nicely in the first two stanzas, in urban-
generic mode, and with a single identifiable chronotope (the poet
towards evening, let's say, standing at the window and looking out
across the rooftops), suddenly that implied viewpoint is dissolved – 'or
at any time', the poet says – and we are dropped (as we at first think)
into another scene (the drained, leaf-strewn swimming pool in winter).
This would be tricky, but manageable, one scene being fast-faded into
another, a kind of cinematographic trick which is a fairly familiar
avant-garde technique. But a second look shows that this is a misrep-
resentation of the text, for the fall is not from one scene to another,
but 'straight/ through myself', in other words, from exterior space
which we hold in common with the poet, to an inner, psychic space
which we don't. The next line seems to revert to the outer scene set up
in the first two stanzas ('Then the cold comes to tighten the air'), and
the remainder of this couplet (the fifth in the poem) views the scene
from the room, the room as a spatial concept being of very frequent
mention in women's poetry, representing a private geography in which
the self is, by preference, located, rather than in the public geography
of the streets: 'In my room/ I can hear cars and the snow flying around
the street'. At this point I feel I again know where we are: I have re-
identified a chronotope, even though I don't quite understand what
happened (that 'falling straight through') between the two geogra-
phies. I see a clear dichotomy between the public space outside and the
private, the latter being both literally that of the room in which the
speaker is situated, and the inner psychic space of the mind. But with
the next couplet this careful orientation collapses yet again:

I am not outside anything: I'm not inside it either.
There's no democracy in beauty, I'm following

human looks. Though people spin away, don't
be thrown by their puzzling lives, later the lives

secrete their meaning. *The red sun's on the rain.*
Where do I put myself, if public life's destroyed.

This isn't the end of the poem (there are another five couplets), but it's enough to illustrate the kind of difficulties generated in the writing of women poets about space. First, there is a kind of denial of the efficacy of any kind of normative locatory process at all ('I am not outside anything: I am not inside it either'). Then in the second couplet there is a sense of the constant urban flux of the bewildering 'multitude of strangers' who pass by, which all writers on the city testify to, seeing it either as exhilarating, as Whitman does in the New York of *Leaves of Grass*, or (more often) as faintly nauseous, as Wordsworth does, writing of London in *The Prelude*, or Baudelaire, writing about mid-century Paris in *Les Fleurs du Mal*, or Pound in the Paris of his 'In a Station of the Metro', where the endless flux of pale faces suggests the faintly neurotic image of damp petals stuck to the bough of a tree; or indeed Eliot in *The Waste Land*, where the crowds of City office workers crossing London Bridge are seen as the souls of the dead flocking into Hades. Novelists, in general, seem better able to cope with the flux of faces: Virginia Woolf, sitting on a London 'omnibus' (as she called it) in the 1920s, would imagine plots and stories to fit the characters seen around her. Riley seems to be writing about this flux of strangers when she says 'Though people spin away, don't/ be thrown by their puzzling lives', apparently confident, like Woolf, that meanings will emerge ('later the lives/ secrete their meaning'). Is it a coincidence that both the writers resisting the nauseous panic reaction, and instead taking this more confident 'long view', are women? Of course, I don't know the answer to this. The final line quoted is a question, though it is without a question mark, and it speculates about the relationship between the private self (or selves) and public space, public identity ('Where do I put myself if public life's destroyed'). As far as I can tell, this isn't a question which particularly troubles the male writers I look at: they move through ravaged urban spaces – London's derelict docklands in Ken Smith's poems (Chapter 3), Liverpool in the 1980s riots in Robert Hampson's *Seaport* (Chapter 5), ruinous places where 'civic dialogue is discontinued' in Iain Sinclair's London outskirts (Chapter 6) – without ever doubting where they should put themselves. Riley's poem, then, seems to contain a much more radical series of doubts about place and identities than are encountered, by and large, in contemporary male poets. All this is only a very limited explication of a single poem, but it is indicative of the kind of difficulties I constantly encountered when looking at poetry by contemporary women within the ambit of this topic of the city. Undoubtedly there is a book to be written about the city and contemporary women's poetry, but I had to conclude that tackling this topic adequately is beyond my range.

What follows is divided into two main sections. The chapters in the first section (Mapping) are fairly broad in scope, while (with the exception of the final chapter) all those in the second section (Local Specifics) each concentrate on poetry associated with a particular city. Within the first section: the first part of Chapter 2 discusses the tendency for cities to be constructed negatively in poetry, placing this fact within the context of the widespread cultural denigration of cities; the second part looks at some ways in which aspects of contemporary life tend to deconstruct the absolute distinction between city and country, and at reflections of this situation in a contemporary poet and a poet-essayist. Chapter 3 sets out three ideas which are used to structure much of the discussion of poetry throughout the book, these being; first, what is called here 'double visioning', second the Bakhtinian notion of the chronotope, and third a distinction between 'setting' and 'geography'. Chapter 4 considers some of the ways in which contemporary poets have represented the 'inner city', in the usual 'social' sense of this term, meaning the deprived and run-down areas of cities, and what they reflect of our inequitable social structure. This section is placed near the start of the book in order to counteract the possible charge of 'urbanism', a coinage intended to designate a tendency to idealise the city, analogous to the 'pastoralism' which idealises the countryside. In the second section (Local Specifics) poetries associated with the cities of Hull, Liverpool, London and Birmingham are considered in successive chapters, using, developing and supplementing the ideas introduced in the Mapping section. The final chapter mainly considers how poets have responded to the pervasive urban phenomenon of rapid de-industrialisation since the 1970s, using an 'inter-city' focus like that of the 'Writing the inner city' chapter. These two chapters 'bracket' the loco-specific 'intra-city' chapters which make up the core of the book, and thereby link the two major sections together.

Notes

1   See the many reports of this event in the British national press in late 1998 and early 1999, such as 'Minister attacks dons as "barbaric"', *Independent*, 4 February 1999, p. 11.

2 Hughes's *Birthday Letters* won the Whitbread Poetry Prize, the Whitbread Book of the Year Award, and the T.S. Eliot Memorial Prize.

3 See Gregson's polemical article 'An exhausted tradition', *New Welsh Review*, No. 27 (Winter 1994), pp. 22–3.

4 See, for example, *Eighteenth-Century Poetry: An Annotated Anthology*, ed. David Fairer and Christine Gerrard, Blackwell, 1998. The section 'Urban Description' contains poems by John Philips, John Gay, Jonathan Swift, John Dyer, William Cowper, Anna Seward, and Mary Robinson.

5 Of course, the Hughesian countryside is anything but easy and comfortable – its escapism is not of the pastoral order. Indeed, Terry Gifford, in his book *Pastoral* (Routledge, 1999, p. 137), notes Hughes's fondness for reading, to audiences of urban schoolchildren and university students, his poem 'February 17th' (a protracted and gory 'anti-pastoralist' poem about a stillborn lamb which is decapitated by the farmer in an attempt to save the mother). Gifford has witnessed (as I have) people fainting during the reading of this poem.

6 Originally in Carson's collection *The Irish for No* (The Gallery Press, 1987; Bloodaxe, 1988) and reprinted in his *The Ballad of HMS Belfast: A Compendium of Belfast Poems* (Picador, 1999).

7 'The Mersey Docks & Harbour Company has brought wealth back to the port, taking pre-tax profits from £800,000 in 1984 to £46.7m by 1998', *Independent*, 27 October 1999, p. 12.

8 See *Independent*, Review, 16 August 1999, p. 10.

9 The relevant books are: *Instabilities in Contemporary British Poetry*, Alan Robinson, Macmillan, 1988; *Contemporary Poetry and Postmodernism: Dialogue and Estrangement*, Ian Gregson, Macmillan, 1996; *New Relations: the Refashioning of British Poetry, 1980–1994*, David Kennedy, Seren, 1996; *Deregulated Muse: Essays on Contemporary British and Irish Poetry*, Sean O'Brien, Bloodaxe, 1997.

10 For an expression of this 'dissenting' view, see, for example, *Out of Dissent: Five Contemporary British Poets*, Clive Bush, Talus, 1997; *Contemporary British Poetry : Essays in Theory and Criticism*, ed. James Acheson and Romana Huk, State University of New York (Albany) Press, 1996. See also the following recent anthologies, with their introductions: *Conductors of Chaos: A Poetry Anthology*, ed. Iain Sinclair, Picador, 1996, and *Other British and Irish Poetry Since 1970*, ed. Richard Caddell and Peter Quartermain, Wesleyan University Press, 1998.

11 The 'School of Eloquence' sequence was first published in 1978 as a series of eighteen extended sonnets, that is, sonnets thickened up to sixteen lines and consisting of four quatrains. Harrison treated the School of Eloquence material as an 'open book', as I would call it, freely extending the sequence and adding to it. So in 1981 he published *Continuous: 50 Sonnets from 'The School of Eloquence'* (Collings). By 1984 when the

first edition of Harrison's *Selected Poems* was published by Penguin, the 'School of Eloquence' material had expanded to sixty-seven sonnets. The second edition of the *Selected Poems* expanded the 'School of Eloquence' to seventy-eight sonnets.

12   In this book my interest is in what Gillian Tindall, in the preface to *Countries of the Mind: The Meaning of Place to Writers* (Hogarth Press, 1991) calls 'the specific real place' before it has been 'so entirely subsumed by what it comes to represent that it cases to be identifiable place at all' (p. ix). I should record here a general debt to the attitudes and approach of this writer.

13   The essay is by Helen Kidd in *New British Poetries: The Scope of the Possible*, ed. Robert Hampson and Peter Barry, Manchester University Press, 1993, pp. 156–80.

14   Ed. Vicki Bertram, Edinburgh University Press, 1997.

2 'The roads to hell'

Thinking with cities

> The roads to Hell were paved;
> that much we could deduce.
> The rest was guesswork.[1]

So writes Ian McMillan at the start of a poem called 'Responses to Indus-trialisation', his point being that paved roads are city roads, and that those are the ones that lead to Hell. There is, of course, a note of irony in his lines, a certain mocking of the academic's attempts to package the 'real' world into neat parcels of ideas, for the title of the poem is also the title of an Open University 'foundation' course. This notion of the intel-lectual 'foundation' envisages the gradualist, orderly acquisition of knowledge, with areas of specialist expertise rising on a generalist infra-structure, a notion which begins to look quaintly archaic in our increas-ingly 'digital' age of wall-to-wall on-line databases. McMillan's poetry, in fact, often concerns his bitterly angry responses to *de*-industrialisation, in particular that of the South Yorkshire coalfields during the 1980s, and his work has a pervading sense of how poetry not only makes nothing happen, as Auden's elegy on Yeats famously asserts,[2] but is also powerless to *stop* anything happening. This wry sense of the limitations of poetry crystallises towards the end of this short poem in a reference to a book by Donald Davie, another 'poetic' Yorkshireman, whose *Purity of Diction in English Verse* had appeared in 1969. As McMillan remarks, 'Purity of diction is one thing, but/ it brings us to now.' What McMillan registers here, and in much of his writing, is poetry's awkward relationship with the urban everyday. McMillan himself might seem to represent an enviably 'integrated' and 'engaged' kind of poetry – he has a strong Yorkshire regional identity, is poet-in-residence at Barnsley Football Club, official poet to the 'Northern Spirit' railway company,[3] and presenter of the literary parodies show *Booked* on BBC Radio 4. This kind of poetic integration with urban life has its price, of course, but my initial point is simply that it is rare. More frequently, the poet, when *in* the city, is not *of* it, for the inner eye (or ear) is elsewhere, a rural elsewhere with the daffodils, for instance, or mentally hearing the lake water lapping, while pacing 'the pavements grey' of a city which is fastidiously screened out of the poem. It cannot be accidental that the two poems referred to here (Wordsworth's 'Daffodils' and Yeats's 'Lake Isle of Innisfree'), are among the best known in the language and indeed are emblematic for many of poetry itself (they used to be drummed into children at school by rote learning). Yet they teach a willed act of looking away from the city and have a persona who instead projects an eidetic image of a rural idyll.

The well-known saying to which McMillan's lines refer tells us that 'The road to Hell is paved with good intentions'. It's a familiar remark, but it is easy to miss the way it associates cities with Hell, for a paved road can only exist in a town or city. The notion of 'paving' evokes (at the material level) the built-up area, water mains, sewers and phone lines, and beyond that the day-to-day business of planning committees and urban councils; the large-scale movement of goods and people, the network of commercial, industrial and residential districts – in other words, the familiar urban environment in which most of us live. The road to hell, that is to say, is not a country lane with its picturesque twists and meanders, but one which is heavily trafficked and knows where it is going, which is to the devil. The phrase 'the road to hell' is part of the traditional mental framework which sees the countryside as nature, the work of God, and the city as culture, the product of 'Man', and hence always suspect, part of a scenario in which Sodom and Gomorrah, the infamously wicked 'cities of the plain', become the covert (and hence, of course, thrilling) archetypes of all cities.[4]

Such attitudes are outmoded, but they are still culturally pervasive. They persist in contemporary poetry to a surprising degree, not least in the fact that there is a strong tendency for poets to use imagery which constructs the craft of poetry itself as a rural pursuit. For instance, in a famous early poem, 'Digging', Seamus Heaney dedicates himself to poetry while seeing his father ploughing, and envying the skill and sureness involved. He despairs of ever acquiring such physical self-possession, but all is not lost, for:

> Between my finger and my thumb
> The squat pen rests:
> I'll dig with it.

(The last line has to be stressed '*I'll* dig with *it*'). Here the locus of poetry is identified as rural, for unlike that of the road to hell, this is *un*paved ground – you cannot dig in the tarmac of cities. Heaney's metaphorical equivalents for the crafting of a poem are ineluctably and unthinkingly rural – digging, planting, and ploughing – rather than urban.[5] What, indeed, would an urbanised metaphor for poetic activity look like? It is an indication of the extent to which we have internalised the rural that the question is quite difficult to answer. Yet not impossible. For instance, writing poetry could have been imaged as drawing up blueprints, laying foundations, erecting a framework and so on, which would envisage the making of a poem in terms of a large-scale building operation. But this is speculative. Let's get text-specific: the North-East poet Barry MacSweeney, in his sequence *Hellhound Memos* (The Many Press, 1993), uses an 'urban' implement as a metaphor for the act of writing, in contrast to Heaney's spade which digs the rural earth. The implement in question is the oxyacetylene torch which is used for metal cutting in heavy industries like shipbuilding and repairing, and shipbreaking. He writes:

> I don't care what the damage is. Or the waste.
> I enjoy the flames. I can scorch a line, a beautiful
> blue and true line through the hull of your lives
>
> and must say I like it better so. I adjust my visor
> accordingly. Cut, cut, cut. It's my dark, dark memo,
> almost a badge. I groove in the magenta heat.
>
> (Conductors of Chaos, Picador, 1996, p. 227)

MacSweeney's implement is masculinist and phallic, to be sure ('I lean/ into it. I don't erect headstones', the lines continue), with the poet appropriating the female function of engendering life, but Heaney's rural metaphor for writing is gendered too – digging is what fathers do in Heaney's world, not mothers – and in Heaney's poem the pen, notoriously, also sits in the hand 'snug as a gun', opening up a set of phallic and onanistic associations which are heard elsewhere in Ulster poetry.[6] Furthermore, MacSweeney's urbanism doesn't imply any abnegation of the 'natural'. On the contrary, he associates his written lines with the lines of rain that fall relentlessly from the urban sky, for this poem ends 'I come down like slate-grey rain. That's all. No God available.' By contrast, the 'blue heavens', which he typecasts as rural, are associated with myth and fairy-tale, with a never-never land – 'Hosanna those/ sky-blue heavens in the fairy tales. I deliver.'

Yet the relative unlikelihood of a poet selecting this kind of urbanised or industrialised metaphor to represent the act of poetic composition is, I think, apparent, and indeed, poets often go further and see the poetic imagination itself as ruralised, as existing at a remote distance, and removed from the bustle of city of life. In fact, if the poetic imagination is seen as cognate with thinking itself, then the view is frequently expressed that you need to go somewhere other than cities in order to do it. Thus, Derek Mahon's 'A Disused Shed in County Wexford' ('One of the most influential poems of the period', says Sean O'Brien, introducing Mahon in his anthology *Poetry from Britain and Ireland after 1945*[7]) begins with this:

> Even now there are places where a thought might grow –
> Peruvian mines, worked out and abandoned
> To a slow clock of condensation,
> An echo trapped for ever, and a flutter
> Of wild-flowers in the lift-shaft,
> Indian compounds where the wind dances
> And a door bangs with diminished confidence,
> Lime crevices behind rippling rain-barrels,
> Dog corners for bone-burials:
> And in a disused shed in Co. Wexford

'Peruvian mines', 'Indian compounds', 'lime crevices behind rain barrels' – thoughts grow, it seems, a long way from cities, a long way from the (presumably un-rural) places where poets work as 'a reviewer, a scriptwriter and a university teacher' (O'Brien's introductory note on Mahon, again), and far from the city where (it seems probable) this sentiment was expressed in verse. It is not, it should be stressed, that Mahon's shed is magically outside history and politics, so that his liking for it would constitute some kind of pastoral political evasion; on the contrary, the shed is 'Deep in the grounds of a burnt-out hotel', apparently abandoned 'since civil war days', and providing mute testimony of killings and strife. Presumably plenty of urban sites would testify just as starkly as this shed on behalf of the 'Lost people of Treblinka and Pompeii', that is, the victims of Holocaust or natural catastrophe, but the rural location seems to be chosen almost instinctively, as we might say, as seeming to have greater resonance, depth, or pathos than the urban. Now, it is no part of my purpose to deny the immense power of this poem, and it is clear, too, that part of that power resides in the oblique representation of its subject which the rural location precisely facilitates. Nevertheless, the poet seems to feel that the notorious sites of urban conflict and suffering – Stalingrad, Dresden, Hiroshima, Beirut, Belfast – are somehow less *generalisable*, more difficult for the non-local reader to identify with, than the rural, which, even when locally specific, as in the title of the poem, seems to remain more readily available for generalised emblematic appropriation. Indeed, this is perhaps generally true of the way we perceive the urban and the rural in literature. Thus, the Paris depicted in Balzac's novels 'takes the lid off France under the Bourbons', and Dickens's London 'exposes the injustices and complexities of Victorian society' – such remarks are commonplace in literary histories. But their local and chronological exactitude is remarkable, for they pin down the significance of these literary works to particular dynasties and epochs ('Bourbon' France, 'Victorian' Britain). By contrast, Hardy's Wessex peasants are often said to be 'universal' emblems and representations of 'human nature' or 'human suffering'. If Hardy's novels had been set mainly in Bournemouth or Brighton these universalising claims would not have been made nearly so frequently. The city, then, is commonly seen as locally and temporally specific, whereas the countryside is taken to be timeless and generic.

But whatever the reason (and it is easy to imagine several), Ulster poets, especially, seem prone to conceiving of a place apart as the making-place of thought, and hence of poetry, rather than a place within the flux. Thus Heaney has his 'Door into the Dark', a 'place of regress', which is a highly localised, compacted reservoir of personal myth and memory: but in so far as it can be 'placed' anywhere specific it is a stable door, or the door to a blacksmith's shop, and hence yet another antithesis of the urban, just like Mahon's shed. And another major contemporary Irish poet, John Montague, whose Brooklyn infancy 'was full of the rumble of trains' (*The Figure in the Cave and Other Essays*, Syracuse University Press, 1989, p. 2), and who subsequently lived in Dublin, Paris and San Francisco, nevertheless takes his poetic bearings from rural Garvaghey, where he lived for seven years between the ages of four and eleven, and whose Gaelic name, in translation, gave him the title of his third collection, *The Rough Field* – that rural metaphor again. Like Heaney, Montague's conceptualisations of poetic composition are in terms of ploughing: he speaks in the title essay of *The Figure in the Cave* of when '*The Rough Field* was being ploughed or excavated' (p. 10), and of his writing generally in terms of 'ploughing rough ground' (p. 18). Likewise, he values especially the moment when his French neighbour, passing on his Massey-Ferguson, recognises what the poet does as work, no less onerous than his own, with a 'mixture of respect and complicity' (p. 19) and calls out a greeting to the poet at his desk, asking him how *his* work is going. This moment is a useful supplement to the well-known Heaney poem just discussed, a kind of Oedipal fantasy of 'parental' respect and approval, in which the parent acknowledges how right the child had been, all along, in wanting to be (say) a rock star, and concedes that such work is just as 'real' as what Daddy does in the office. The metaphor of fields and ploughing by which writing is designated seems very 'natural', but what of all those effaced cities in the Montague's life? We might well feel sympathy with his first wife, whom he quotes as remarking (after seeing a section of his latest rurally focused work-in-progress) that 'there has been enough cowdung in Irish poetry' (p. 10). The remark might be taken as an equally valid critique of British contemporary poetry. My point is, then, that this succession of rural places and activities evoked in trying to conceptualise the poetic act strikingly divorces poetry from the urban.

Another example of the placing of an explicit demarcation between thinking and cities is seen in another major contemporary poet of wide influence, the Welsh poet R.S. Thomas, whose 'Fugue for Ann Griffiths' (in *Welsh Airs*, Seren, 1987) contains the lines:

> A nineteenth century
> 　　　　calm;
> that is, a countryside
> 　　not fenced in
> by cables and pylons,

> but open to thought to blow in
> from as near as may be
> to the truth.[8]

Here again, the countryside is the locus of thought; it is 'open to thought to blow in' and the indices of the urban (the cables and pylons) interfere with it, threatening to fence it in, and, by implication, interfere with poetry itself. Thomas's influence on younger poets is as powerful as Heaney's, and that of both was deplored by Ian Gregson in a polemical article (already mentioned) in *New Welsh Review* (no. 27, Winter 1994, pp. 22–3) when he wrote that the 'biggest influences on young poets in Wales seem to be R.S. Thomas and Seamus Heaney – important figures in themselves, but products of comparatively static rural cultures whose preoccupations are largely irrelevant to anyone brought up with television'. All this is surprisingly consonant with the attitude to the city seen in the first-generation Romantic poets, with the Coleridge who, in 'Frost at Midnight', presents himself as brought up 'In the great city, pent 'mid cloisters dim', where the resulting feeling of imaginative confinement, inherent in the word 'pent', is sharply reminiscent of Thomas's pylons and cables which fence him round and prevent thought from blowing in. Indeed, there has been a renewed poetic occlusion of the urban even in post-war poetry, representing in this regard a regression from the 1930s, when the city featured prominently in the work of Spender, Auden and MacNeice. Furthermore, making it do so was one of the ways in which they asserted their modernity, and perhaps also their modernism, against the Georgian poets of the previous generation. In the post-war period the anti-urban feeling among major poets continued, so that, for instance, Dylan Thomas's writing fled from the urban and industrial landscapes of South Wales to greener represented pastures, while the Movement's rejection of modernism also seemed to involve a rejection of at least the urban aspect of modernity, so that the city retreated again from poetry.

It is one of the purposes of this book to show that the view expressed by Heaney, Mahon, Montague and Thomas (that the urban, in effect, disables poetic thought) is not by any means universally held by contemporary poets. A striking exception to a prevailing 'ruralism' is the Birmingham poet Roy Fisher who says starkly and straight forwardly of his home city that 'Birmingham's what I think with'. And while he now lives in the Staffordshire countryside, his poetry continues to explore the urban, reversing the more usual scenario of poets who live in the city, working as reviewers, university teachers, and so on, but whose work more-or-less occludes the city, and draws on sources of imagery which seem predominantly rural. Thus Fisher, sometimes called a 'neo-modernist', uses a city to think with, just as Joyce used Dublin, Pound used Washington, Rome, London and Paris, and Eliot used Boston, Paris and London. This book, then, examines contemporary poets who, in their different ways, use cities to think with, remaining relatively untempted by the doors into the dark, the disused sheds, the men on tractors and the unfenced countryside.

Dissolving the urban?

Yet the ancient dichotomy between country and city, whose persistence I asserted just now, has, of course, been transformed in the present century. An extreme view would be that it no longer has much validity at all, as John Barrell and John Bull assert in the introduction to their *Penguin Book of English Pastoral Verse*:

> The separation of life in the town and in the country that the pastoral demands is now almost devoid of any meaning. It is difficult to pretend that the English countryside is now anything more than an extension of the town'.[9]

In one sense, of course, they are right: the thatched cottage glimpsed from the train or motorway, which seems to embody the essence of the rural, is probably linked to the rest of the world by phone, fax, TV, e-mail and internet, and in this sense its occupants are as much 'of' the city, even if not 'in' it, as those of Hackney or Toxteth. Indeed, it may well be one of those electronic prisons in which those who work digitally 'from home' (not '*at* home') confine themselves in voluntary house-arrest. If (as Roy Fisher says in a text which will be discussed later) country is now merely an island within a continent of city, then the culture of cities is no longer confined to cities. Rather, all of us live in an urbanised environment (digitalised, on-line, image-bombarded) and mere physical location is less and less a determinant of way-of-life. Indeed, the absolute distinction between country and city had already been fundamentally altered by the start of the nineteenth century, when William and Dorothy Wordsworth lived at

Grasmere, 'cut off', it might seem, in the Lake District and living in conditions in some ways little altered from medieval times (stone-flagged rooms lit by candles and oil-lamps, home-cooked, locally caught or grown produce, dependence on traditional herbal remedies to cure ailments, and so on). Yet culturally their lives were in many ways distinctly 'modern'; they had available, for instance, regular timetabled, cross-country travel (by stagecoach), and a daily postal service which deposited mail for collection at a 'post-office' in the town a few miles away, bringing them newspapers, journals published in London and Edinburgh, and extensive correspondence – in other words, facilitating their active membership of a public domain of educated secular discourse, which in previous ages would have been found only in a few large cities and university towns. One reading of the situation, then, is that the town/country dichotomy has progres-sively been eroded for many generations, and is now virtually mean-ingless.

But we might go further and ask whether it was ever anything more than a conventional commonplace or construct which never truly reflected social reality, for the countryside can never be wholly 'nature' nor the city wholly 'culture'. For one thing, to equate the former with nature is to merge it with the notion of the wilderness, with the realm of the sublime rather than the picturesque, since most of what we see is the product of gradualist processes over many hundreds of years which have produced the 'landscape plotted and pieced – fold, fallow, and plough' which Hopkins praises in his poem 'Pied Beauty'. Roy Fisher goes further and explores the notion of the 'industrialised coun-tryside', where the presence of mines and quarries produces the effect of an obviously 'worked' landscape which does not differ essentially – only in degree – from the city (see Chapter 8). In addition, there have been large-scale acts of human intervention, like the deracination of the massive southern forest, of which Highgate Woods in North London is the last surviving remnant, and the deforestation of the Wirral, 'the wilderness of Wirral', as it is called in the medieval poem *Sir Gawain and the Green Knight*, a notorious bandit hide-out in medieval times because of its inaccessibility. And just as the country-side is partly a synthesis and a construct, so too must the city incor-porate the given features of the landscape. Roy Fisher, again, writes about his native city of Birmingham as a necessary collusion with the natural, and even its eventual industrial character (as a centre of metal manufacture) is partly determined by the fact that it was remote from any major river, so that all its goods had to be shifted by cart or pack-horse, leading to a concentration on the production of light-weight metal objects, like brooches or belt-buckles, which could be easily transported. By the time of the Renaissance it had become what a booklet of 1938 (published to mark the centenary of the municipal charter in 1838) called an 'industrial village', already well on its way to becoming an industrial town: Leland, visiting in 1538, recorded that 'a great part of the town is maintained by smiths' and Camden, fifty years later, described it as 'echoing with forges'.[10] Hence, Cowper's assertion that God made the country and man made the town has never been entirely true: rather, the theological and ontolog-ical polarisation of the two (into the work of God and the work of 'man', into 'nature' as opposed to 'culture', and so on) disguises the fact that one of the most common environmental phenomena of the past few hundred years has been the gradual modulation of the one into the other, with the city incorporating the shapes of ancient fields and land contours into its own layout, and perpetuating in its street names the titles of former landowners, or the sites of now-vanished landmarks.

This ubiquitous process of assimilation and incorporation is exam-ined by Gillian Tindall (who has written several key books on culture and cities, and on literature and place) in *The Fields Beneath* (Paladin, 1977), which is about the growth and development of the London district of Kentish Town. Tindall vividly delineates the process of continual progressive overlay by which cities are formed, a process which has been of vital interest to several of the poets discussed in this book. She pays particular attention to the fate of rivers and water-courses in built-up urban environments, for the one natural feature which towns and cities found it difficult to absorb were the streams and rivers, which often suffered pollution and degradation in the process of urbanisation, and in extreme cases (like that of the Fleet River in London) became open sewers, and were then bricked over, or diverted into culverts, often with periodically disastrous consequences. Tindall notes the tendency for the 'lost stream' then to be idealised and romanticised, made in memory into 'the archetypal playground of lost childhood, lost innocence' (p. 26). Hence, these 'lost' watercourses are invested with large amounts of our cultural baggage, becoming the symbolic icon of a lost pre-industrial Eden. She quotes from William Morris's *Earthly Paradise*:

Forget the spreading of the hideous town
Think rather of the packhorse on the down,
And dream of London, small and white, and clean,
The clear Thames bordered by its gardens green. (p. 27)

And she adds (writing of the Fleet) a remark which can also be used to describe the kind of significance which vanished, buried, or polluted rivers often assume in cities:

The river, having disappeared below ground, had ceased to be a perceived fact but had become a myth, a mysterious presence, an embodiment of all that civilisation has lost. (p. 27)

Urban poets have frequently endowed urban rivers with this kind of significance: for Pope in *The Dunciad*, for instance, the despoiled and cloacal Fleet is a correlative of the city's moral and spiritual decline. In the twentieth century Eliot in *The Waste Land* uses the Thames in exactly the same way, contrasting its present polluted state, littered with 'empty bottles, sandwich papers,/ Silk handkerchiefs, cardboard boxes, cigarette ends' (lines 177–8) and sweating 'oil and tar', (267) with its earlier manifestation as the 'sweet Thames' of the Elizabethan period, when it is a kind of embodiment of an energised spirit of place, presented in heightened imagery of rippling light, water, and sound – 'The brisk swell/ Rippled both shores/ Southwest wind/ Carried down stream/ the peal of bells/ White towers' (284–9). Lost or polluted rivers are also used extensively by poets such as Allen Fisher, Roy Fisher, Aidan Dun, Ciaran Carson and U.A. Fanthorpe.[11] Recently, Andrew Motion, too, has used this kind of material, for his poem 'In a Perfect World', written for the 1999 TUC Conference, is in the tradition which I call elsewhere in this book 'London Ambulatory' writing. It records a specific riverside walk ('I was walking the Thames path from Richmond/ to Westminster', it begins), imbuing it with a 'state-of-England' spiritual and cultural significance.[12] The ambulatory eye notes the riverside evidence of industrial decline ('the smoke-scarred walls// of a disused warehouse'), much as Roy Fisher does on a similar walk in Birmingham, and also takes in the point where the polluted River Wandle (one of London's 'lost' rivers) discharges into the Thames ('The mouth of the Wandle stuck/ its sick tongue out and went.'), this being the river which Pope in *The Dunciad* had described as the 'blue transparent Wandalis' and had contrasted with the spoiled and degraded Fleet. The river, then, is often a potent synthesis of the notion that both country and city are merely different kinds of 'worked landscape', both being always vitally 'in process'. Indeed, the image of the river, as used in contemporary urban poetry, often highlights the inter-penetration of the two categories 'country' and 'city' and brings into focus the often-painful cultural contestations involved.

Another way in which the categories of 'urban' and 'rural' inter-fuse each other is seen in the contemporary process whereby demolition and 're-landscaping' can bring back into existence the 'fields beneath' the urban streets, so that a lost ruralism is re-asserted within a long-established urban setting. This is seen, for instance, in 'inner-city' housing projects which abnegate recognisably urban styles (terraces, 'town-houses', flats and apartments) and instead offer 'villagey' clusters of small semi-detached houses, all with 'vernacular' architectural features (pitched roofs, gables, dormer windows and individual gardens) and yet within walking distance of city centres. Such schemes seem to reject the very idea and ideal of the city altogether (by implication associating it with the urban social hell of 'Cowperesque' thinking). They want to be 'in' the city but not 'of' it, so they try to evoke the ambience of (say) a Cotswold village or a Cornish fishing hamlet. The signs of this kind of 'anti-urbanist' think-ing are the throwing up of incongruous grassy knolls, the planting of saplings in protective cages, and above all, the building houses in would-be convivial rural huddles rather than urban rows. Clearly schemes like this are a panicky over-correction of the modernist 'high-rise' error.[13] If the city is taken to be a text (as in a currently dominant architectural metaphor), then such places might be read as inappro-priate extended quotations. Built in the wrong place, the irregular clusters of houses (unlike the straight terraced streets which they replace) provide too many dark corners which can quickly become the setting for muggings, drug dealing and sexual assaults.[14] In other words, the 'rural' values which are pined for are not, of course, imported with the picturesque rainhoods over the front doors and the variegated roof lines.

A further way in which recent conditions tend to break down the older absolute distinction between 'town' and 'country' is the growth of 'out-of-town' shopping centres on which both places (the notional 'town' and the notional 'country') quickly become dependent for their major needs. The designation 'out-of-town' is itself a denial of the city/country dichotomy: these centres are not said to be 'in the country' – they are just 'out of town', so that the designation tells us where they are not, rather than where they are. Indeed, their location is often given as a *direction* rather than a *destination*, specifying roundabouts and motorway exits, for instance. The effect is to suggest somewhere which is neither city nor country, nor indeed anywhere precisely definable in pre-existing terms, but simply a generic local abstraction. Given the powerful forces of homogenisation which have been at work now for several decades – the same chain stores in every high street, the elimination of local architectural features and land-marks in comprehensive 'renewal' schemes – these suburban generic spaces are perhaps typical of the locale in which many of us now spend significant parts of our time.

The embodiment of this ideal of the suburban generic space might be taken to be the chic, 'state-of-the-art' Bluewater shopping centre, positioned 'half an hour up the A2' from London in a highly treated, fantasised rural setting of fuschias and wooden-decked, glass-enclosed eateries.[15] It is a place which can satisfy diverse and distinctly metro-politan tastes (providing a sushi bar, Calvin Klein, Waterstones, bonsai trees, Pret-à-Manger, aromatherapy oils, conceptual architecture and so on). Bluewater is different from the urban covered shopping complexes built on cleared 'brown-field' sites in the 1970s and 80s, the Arndale centres, for instance, with their clinical 'modernist' look, like Manchester's, which till recently had a massive, blank, tiled exterior, and constituted an enormous bulk which became, as Bill Bryson remarks in *Notes from a Small Island*, an impassable closed citadel after dark, requiring pedestrians to make lengthy detours to get beyond it. Bluewater is also different from a later phase of this kind of complex, a phase in which the scale was more human, and the fabric incorporated some postmodernist 'retro' elements, such as art-deco style fibreglass statues and perhaps a row of 'Georgian' shop-fronts and facades, not, of course, as they really are now in British towns, but in their idealised form, with picturesque bow windows, and strangely unspoiled by modern fascia and plate-glass. (Several such were probably demolished to make way for the structure which now incorporates their simulacra.) Bluewater, by contrast, is massive but not modernist: pinnacles and granite-facing are favoured; plate glass is used, but in combination with wooden decking; the structure itself is part of the experience, offering, not just a shopping trip, but a form of entertainment, with playful elements, 'allusions' and 'quotations'.

It's a new kind of space, not just (as in the 1970s and 80s) the old kind of thing canopied, or 'pedestrianised' or horizontally stacked or otherwise 'made over'. Clearly, it would make no sense to call such a place either urban or rural, since its defining characteristic is that it is an interface between the two which becomes a significant third dimension. Rather than offering a 'masculine-gendered modernity' (as it is called in Nan Ellin's *Postmodern Urbanism*, Blackwell, 1996, p. 244), that is, a place rigidly zoned like a conventional city with separate places for work and leisure, day and night, rich and poor, this is 'feminine or un-gendered postmodernity', which is to say that it is a 'trans-zonal' space (natural lighting, with trees and flowers, but these are glass-enclosed streets without weather). Hence, this is a Barthian *texte-lisible* which you have to interpret, and which has its ambiguities, like a literary text, rather than using the 'open-mapping' of the old-style city, with its commercial district, its shopping areas, its industrial zones and so on. It is, literally as well as metaphorically, a multiply inscribed place, with ponderous quotations built prominently into the fabric (one of them – from Kipling – ends 'out of the spent and unconsidered earth, the cities rise again'). It is, in fact, one of the characteristic spaces of our times, one which defies easy definition, confronting the 'readable city', with a text-in-cipher. It offers (at least to those accustomed to something more conventional) a spatio-temporal (h)interland, an open-ended chronotope which is like an Escher print, with one plane opening unaccountably into another, within an overall framework which disturbs our basic framing concepts, though not gravity and three-dimensionality, as with Escher, but rather such guiding dichotomies as 'traditional', 'modern' and 'postmodern'.

Poetry and the urban dissolve – Paul Farley

What, we may wonder, might contemporary poetry make of such places? Does it anywhere register the kind of reactions and feelings I am trying to describe here? Well, the contemporary poet Paul Farley (who won the Forward Prize for the best first collection in 1998 with *The Boy From the Chemist is Here to See You*, Picador) has a poem which may be seen as delineating an analogous experience, an encounter with ambiguous urban space which the percipient cannot (literally) 'place', and hence cannot work out how to behave in. In his poem 'Not Fade Away' he draws upon the pop-music lore and iconography which is an important element in his work, imagining a resurrected Buddy Holly arriving at some such ambiguous locale, having mysteriously survived the plane crash which killed him:

> A cornfield deep in drifts. I walked an hour
> without moving. The outskirts of a town
> that felt, with all its ploughed streets and neon,
> like stepping from a page.

Entering this suburban generic hinterland (of which Bluewater is merely an extreme example) nearly all of us become to some extent disoriented Van Winkles, revenants from another age (though this is part of the intended 'effect', of course). Thus, Farley registers the sense of cultural dislocation which places like the Bluewater centre can create. We stumble in from a different age, or rather, from a different geography, and try to decode its conflicting and congested signs (like ploughed streets juxtaposed with neon). For the figure in the poem, the signs remain defiantly opaque, and in the end he retraces his steps to the crash site and re-inserts himself into the wreckage:

> ... Carefully
> I ease myself back down among the wreck's
> ice-dusted cache – the dials the crew misread,
> the Bopper's dice and Ritchie's crucifix -
> and wait for history.
>
> (*The Boy From the Chemist is Here to See You*, p. 46)

Here the emphasis on reading and misreading, and the discarded grand narratives suggested by the dice, the dials and the crucifix give a pessimistic view of the possibility of cultural re-assimilation. The Holly figure is irredeemably trapped in the timewarp of his own moment, like a modern Ancient Mariner who merely bores the world-weary clubbers with his hammy, glittering eye, and his improbable and relentlessly chronological tale, and is eventually given the bum's rush. Bluewater, of course, *might* have time, somewhere in its shopping-as-entertainment complex, for a tragically born-again Holly, but only as a 'look', or perhaps as a style for a themed fast-food outlet ('Nosh 'n' Roll'?). Nobody would *really* want to know (just as nobody in the post-*Hamlet* world would really want to sit through poor Horatio's pious attempts to absent himself from felicity a while and re-tell Hamlet's story).

The persona in Farley's intriguing poems is often suspended between two different urban worlds in this way. His 1970s Liverpool is haunted by the ghost of its own 1950s past (a reviewer noted the 'premature nostalgia' for one still in his early thirties). His Holly figure lives in two dimensions, as does the window cleaner in 'Laws of Gravity' (winning poem in the 1995 Arvon International Poetry Competition) who is perched 'a hundred rungs above a fifties street', stranded in the past, that inaccessible country where they do things differently. The poem ends (its simple, well-made lines descending the page like the careful steps of the window cleaner with a hangover):

> There are no guidebooks to that town you knew
> and this attempt to build it, brick by brick,
> descends the page. I'll hold the foot for you.
> (*The Boy From the Chemist is Here to See You*, p. 8)

There are many unexpected doors in Farley's poems which suddenly open into this other country. In 'Treacle' the opening of a tin of this substance triggers a sensuous regress to this country of the past. The poem begins 'Funny to think you can still buy it now,/ a throwback, like shoe polish or the sardine key./ When you lever the lid it opens with a sigh/ and you're face-to-face with history'. 'Breathe its scent', the speaker urges us of the black liquid 'something lost from our streets// like horseshit or coalsmoke', and the stuff is seen as 'the last dregs of an empire's dark sump'. I don't know if this is the kind of thing which should be condemned as what Sean O'Brien calls 'the easy nostalgic recital of brand names and defunct commodities deployed as a means of evading the present' (*Deregulated Muse*, p.191). The streets conjured up by 'horseshit' and 'coalsmoke', and the murky connotations of the phrase 'dark sump' of empire, do not constitute a nostalgic image of the past, and indeed, we seem to be dealing with the other side of O'Brien's dichotomy, the process whereby 'the self reaches into and identifies itself, wholeheartedly if never quite with a finished coherence, in concrete realities'. The distinction between 'nostalgia' (easy or not) and 'reaching into the self' is one which will be relevant to several of the poets discussed in this book, many of whom evoke an urban past in ways which it is superficially tempting to identify as nostalgic. In Farley and other poets, the semiotics of these 1950s streets of the past, signified settled and very fine demarcations of occupation, rank and status, in a finely graded progression from the basic, flat-fronted terraced house to the five-storey Belgravia mansion. Even the individual terraced streets, densely packed and looking indistinguishable from each other in an aerial photograph, all had their rankings and a specific social reputation. Such obsessively stratified, 'open-mapped' urban networks reflected a class system of similar rigidity and complexity, just as post-zonal suburban generic spaces like Bluewater register the desire for a commercialised democracy of leisure.

Moral anxieties and the urban dissolve

Changes of the kind represented by Bluewater have come about in concert with the switch (noted in Nan Ellin's *Postmodern Urbanism*) from 'a culture of production to one of consumption' (p. 244), a transition which has, in often dramatic ways, altered the character of the cities discussed in this book. Where the older means of production required massive concentrations of material resources in a relatively small number of urban centres, the culture of consumption is quite different: the centres of material production are much more dispersed than hitherto. High-tech electronic components are best manufactured at places with easy access to rail and motorway networks: the important growth industry of 'call-centres' is provincially and regionally based, since supposedly customers find northern voices and accents more friendly and re-assuring than southern ones.[16] These commercial forces are inherently decentering and devolutionary in character.

A contemporary poet and essayist who has frequently discussed issues of this broad cultural kind in relation to poetry and cities is the Welsh writer John Barnie, whose 1989 essay collection *The King of Ashes* (Gomer Press, 1989) includes the essay 'The City and Nature' which raises concerns which are later developed in his prose-and-poetry sequence *The City* (Gomer, 1993), and in *No Hiding Place: Essays on the New Nature and Poetry* (University of Wales Press, 1996). Barnie's point in 'The City and Nature' is that modern conditions have very much eroded any absolute distinction between country and city. But his emphasis is different from that of Barrell and Bull, for his is a *moral* anxiety about the growing pervasiveness of urban values. Since 1851, he reminds us, over half the British population has lived in cities, and, he says, most of us cannot trace our families back to a pre-urban past beyond this, but 'the great problem is how to live with the fact of cities and the urban mentality ... without it leading to a civilisation so divorced from the reality of nature that it destroys the environment of the earth, on which we and all life depend' (p. 95). For this important poet and contemporary humanist thinker, then, the idea of the city still represents a threat to the species, even though Barnie is very far from any simplistic identification of 'nature' with rural goodness and integrity. It is a stance which is at base ethical and ecological, viewing cities with anxiety and suspicion, registering their tendency to coarsen our responses and induce superficiality and philistinism.

Barnie's concern is that the worst aspects of the urban mindset are no longer confined to cities, but are all-pervasive, a kind of cultural toxin contaminating what had been a reservoir of alternative values: 'Differences still exist, of course, between city and country, but less and less as urban values play a part in rural life, so that increasingly it is possible to talk of the "city" not merely as a place but as a state of mind which may exist anywhere' (p. 93). By contrast, in the eighteenth century what was perceived as vice was given a very specific urban localisation: sexual promiscuity, in Vanbrugh's *The Country Wife*, emanates from central London, with its epicentre in Drury Lane, and drunkenness and degradation in Hogarth's print 'Gin Lane' is pin-pointed to the same locale by the inclusion in the background of a local landmark, the distinctive ziggurat steeple of Hawksmoor's church of St. George's, Bloomsbury. To escape 'vice' of this highly localised kind was relatively easy – you had merely to stay in the countryside, away from the metropolitan sources of contamination. Increasingly, from the eighteenth century onwards, the growth of the city – especially London – was seen as something 'monstrous' (Defoe), as a massive infected blister festering on the countryside (Cobbett's 'Great Wen'), as vomit, disease, or defecation – George Cruikshank's well-known 1829 engraving 'London going out of Town or The March of Bricks and Mortar' shows London as an army invading the countryside, with a fusillade of bricks being spewed from a volcano-like brick kiln at defenceless and retreating haystacks, cows and trees. Diagrams charting the growth of London in the nineteenth century show a black, cancerous-looking stain spreading ever wider. Today, ironic allusions to London as 'the Smoke' see it as a source of infection, as in the days of the killer smogs, and traffic-flow problems are imaged in terms of a diseased body, so that the capital is said to be 'choked' with traffic, with its major arteries 'clogged', and so on.

Barnie's concern is with the moral counterpart of all this perceived physical corruption. Just as the medical authorities in some major

nineteenth century provincial cities believed that the typhoid infection
was air-borne rather than water-borne, so Barnie seems to see a conta-
gious moral emanation from cities, borne on the broadcasting
airwaves, and not requiring physical contact to pass on its contagion.
The only change from the eighteenth-century attitude, then, is the view
that you don't actually have go to the metropolis to be corrupted by it
– you can be infected in the comfort of your own living room. The
infection is a form of urban alienation, (what Nan Ellin, in *Postmod-
ern Urbanism*, calls – quoting Julienne and Mandon – 'an urbanity
which touches all sectors of activity', p. 246), summed up for Barnie
by the growth of a pervasive element of 'virtuality', by which he means
the widespread growth of an urban 'spectatorial' attitude which tends
to reduce all experience to some form of 'viewing' – modern design,
he suggests, heightens this effect, so that for example, the tinted,
sealed-off windows of high-speed trains, and the inaccessible open-
deck space of modern 'super-ferries' reduces landscape and seascape to
a virtual-reality moving picture which we watch while seated. Thus
the real increasingly becomes representation, an 'effect' which is
'produced' like a scene in a play. Though radically changed and recast,
then, the distinction between country and city is by no means entirely
superseded.

So the city has changed, then, both as a concept and as an actual-
ity, and new locations exist which problematise the old dichotomies.
The countryside, of course, has changed too. The birds to which the
Romantic poets wrote their Odes are now endangered or rare
species;[17] the numbers of songbirds are in sharp decline, and 'all the
birds/ Of Oxfordshire and Gloucestershire', which were heard from
the stopped express in Edward Thomas's 'Adlestrop' are not what they
were. Neither, of course, is anything else mentioned in this rural-iconic
poem which for many people is the very quintessence of poetry – for
instance, those picturesque, conical stacks of hay – the 'haycocks dry'
– are everywhere replaced by enormous wired cylinders of hay which
are dumped out by industrial-scale machinery: the meadowlands
packed with wild flowers (the 'willow-herbs', and the rest) have
vanished. Likewise, the woods and hedgerows from which Hughes's
Crow took wing have been removed in the interests of volume-yield
and productivity, and the pool in which his pike swam is long gone,
'deep as England' though it might have been. The countryside evoked
in poetry, then, is often a 'virtual reality', a nostalgic construction
whose mere evocation accuses our urban reality of inauthenticity,

much as the Virgilian country farm of the *Georgics* arraigned the values of the imperial city of Rome. But it is part, too, of a whole panoply of iconography which we begin to absorb in the first months of life, when we are surrounded with brightly coloured pictures of cows, sheep, horses, duck-ponds, hay-stacks, barns, cottages and farmhouses. Poetry strives to collude with this neo-Georgian pastoralism, and one result is a widespread desire to revisit what is left of it, resulting in its increasing over-use. Even Wordsworth, a hundred and fifty years ago, had to campaign to prevent the building of a railway to Keswick in the Lake District, to satisfy the demand for easy access to the wilderness, which (paradoxically) his own poetry had stimulated. The demand, of course, is entirely predictable, for if we assert (as Wordsworth did in his way) that thoughts can indeed only grow in such places, then naturally the attainment of 'fulness of being' will require our going there fairly regularly. As Jonathan Bate reminds us in *Romantic Ecology* (Routledge, 1991, p. 42) Wordsworth's best-selling book by far in his own lifetime, and the first to reach a fifth edition, was his *A Guide to the Lakes*. In the 1840s he opposed the building of the Kendal to Windermere railway which would have helped tourists to satisfy the taste which this book (and, of course, his poetry) had stimulated. The tourists would probably have been mainly from Manchester, the nearest major city, and had it been built it would have protected the Lake District (an irony which Bate points out) from the cars and coaches which now threaten it. Our present notion of 'nature' is crystallised by the Romantics, as is the perceived association between poetry and nature: I mean by this the widely held assumption that 'nature' is the natural subject of poetry. To make this association is, in the end, to collude with the view cited at the start of this section, that you cannot think with cities.

Notes

1 Ian McMillan, *Selected Poems*, Carcanet, 1987, p. 26
2 The precise assertion is that 'poetry makes nothing happen: it survives/ In the valley of its saying where executives/ Would never want to tamper'. The lines occur near the end of the second section of 'In Memory of W.B. Yeats', in *W.H. Auden: Selected Poems*, ed. Edward Mendelson, Faber, 1979, pp. 80–3.
3 See the *Independent*, 15 July 1999, p. 1, 'Rail firm puts poetry into locomotion'.
4 'God Almighty first planted a garden', says Bacon in *Of Gardens*. 'God

the first garden made, and the first city Cain', says Abraham Cowley in *The Garden*, Essay V, and 'God made the country, and man made the town', asserts William Cowper in *The Task*, Book I. line 749. If they had needed it, these writers could have found a source for the sentiment in Varro's '*Divina natura dedit agros, ars humana ædificavit urbes*' (Divine Nature gave the fields, human art built the cities), *De Re Rustica*, iii. 1. But the point is that the thought is commonplace and no source is needed for it. (*Familiar Quotations: A Collection of Passages, Phrases, and Proverbs Traced to their Sources in Ancient and Modern Literature*, John Bartlett, 9th edn, Boston, Little, Brown, and Company, 1901)

5 In his influential *Honest Ulsterman* review of Heaney's 1975 collection *North*, fellow poet Ciaran Carson criticises Heaney for a kind of mystique of the spade; what is dug up (from the Jutland bogs and elsewhere) is taken as explicating the present – 'The spade is no longer a spade, it becomes elevated to the status of a deity', Carson writes, so that in the end Heaney becomes 'an apologist for the "situation", in the last resort, a mystifier'. The original review appeared in *The Honest Ulsterman*, 50 (Winter 1975), pp. 183–6. Substantial sections of it are reprinted in *The Poetry of Seamus Heaney*, Icon Critical Guides, 1998, pp. 84–6.

6 In Tom Paulin's early poem 'Settlers', for example, a company lorry clandestinely used for Protestant gun-running by night has its bonnet still warm to the touch when the workers arrive in the morning. The activity is pervasive but not remarked upon: instead 'He stores a warm knowledge on his palm.// Nightlandings on the Antrim coast, the movement of guns/ Now snug in their oiled paper below the floors/ Of sundry kirks and tabernacles in that county.' (Blake Morrison and Andrew Motion, *The Penguin Book of Contemporary British Poetry*, 1982, p. 116). Here hands, guns, snugness, and onanistic overtones collocate, as in the Heaney passage, and they do elsewhere in early Paulin, for instance in 'Under the Eyes', where a judge is 'Shot in his hallway before his daughter/ By a boy who shut his eyes as his hand tightened' (Morrison and Motion, p. 117).

7 *The Firebox: Poetry from Britain and Ireland after 1945*, Picador, 1998.

8 I am indebted to my friend and former student Dr Chris Morgan for this example. 'Fugue for Ann Griffiths' is reprinted in *R.S. Thomas, Collected Poems, 1945–1990*, Phoenix, 1995, p.470.

9 Quoted by Terry Gifford in *Pastoral*, Routledge, New Critical Idiom, 1999, p. 3.

10 Details from *A Short History of Birmingham*, Conrad Gill and Charles Grant Robertson, City of Birmingham Information Bureau, 1938, p. 14.

11 For Carson see the prose section 'Farset', pp. 47–9 in *Belfast Confetti* (Bloodaxe, 1990). For Fanthorpe see her poem 'Rising Damp' (a prize-

winner in the 1980 Arvon Poetry Competition) in her *Selected Poems* (Penguin 1986), pp.42–3, also reprinted in *Thames: An Anthology of River Poems*, comp. Anna Adams, Enitharmon Press, 1999. In the preface to this volume Iain Sinclair writes that the 'river is the essence of the great poem of the city; constant, changeable, sluggish and swift' (p. 7).

12 The poem was first printed in the *Guardian*, 8 September 1999, p. 7. Another poem by Motion, entitled 'Fresh Water', is on a similar theme and is written in a similar manner, using a kind of relaxed, prose-like, long-lined blank verse *terza rima*, and included in the *Thames* anthology (pp. 56–60) detailed in the previous footnote

13 As the epigraph to his last book *Englishness and National Culture* (Routledge, 1999) Antony Easthope quotes Raymond Williams's remark, which seems apt to the case: 'When in doubt, the English imagine a pendulum.' That is, they move to the opposite extreme of the position or practice they have just rejected.

14 An example of this kind of misreading of the urban text was the Radcliffe Estate, off Everton Road, Liverpool, which was built in the 1970s 'as an echo of a Cornish village; instead it was a maze of dark passages and complicated walkways'. It was empty and derelict by the mid-1980s. See *Liverpool: It All Came Tumbling Down*, Freddy O'Connor, Brunswick Printing and Publishing Co., 1986, p. 44.

15 Bluewater, near Greenhithe, between Dartford and Gravesend in North-West Kent, England, opened in March 1999 and is Europe's Largest Shopping Centre. It is built on a 240-acre site, at a cost of £1.12 billion. As part of 'the entertainment experience' it has three 'leisure villages' incorporating restaurants, cafes and a multiplex cinema. It is surrounded by parkland which includes a network of waterways, seven lakes, and a million trees and shrubs. Its website publicity claims that 'with a variety of retail, leisure and catering opportunities, Bluewater aims to offer visitors a complete day out in a safe, pleasant and high quality environment'.

16 See the *Independent on Sunday*, 29 November 1998, p. 7, 'Britain learns to love a scouse accent'.

17 In the past twenty-five years, for instance, there has been a 75 per cent decline in the number of skylarks (*Guardian*,'Leader', 4 September 1999, p. 21).

3 Three urban tropes

Urban 'double visioning'

What kinds of thinking, then, *can* be done with a city? One kind is what I will call 'double visioning', which I will identify in a number of contemporary poets, but will illustrate here in an earlier poet. Double visioning arises from the tendency of cities to foreground time and change, whereas the countryside, in spite of the changes just referred to, primarily connotes (when used as a cultural signifier) timelessness and continuity. Since the most evident change in the countryside is seasonal and cyclical, its paradoxical emblematic status is that it is often perceived as not changing at all, providing a model of stability in the midst of flux. Thus, when Hardy, overwhelmed in 1915 by a sense of the old international order crumbling, wishes to suggest that there exists a consoling element of guaranteed continuity which is rooted, permanent and beyond threat of change, the images he uses (in 'In Time of "The Breaking of Nations"') are inevitably rural ones. He cites the ploughman ('a man harrowing clods'), the burning of 'heaps of couch-grass', and the 'maid and her wight' who pass by in this almost pathologically stilled, enervated and somnambulistic rural setting (ploughman and horse are 'half asleep as they stalk', the grass has 'thin smoke without flame', and the young couple 'come whispering by'). The whole atmosphere suggests a scene in which time is dragging to a halt, as if the clock were about to come to a standstill at ten to three, as in another of these rural-iconic poems, Rupert Brooke's 'The Old Vicarage, Grantchester' written (in Berlin) a few years earlier, and also evoking, in its more tongue-in-cheek way, this same enervated atmosphere, with much about sleep, slumber and dreams. Keats's 'Ode to Autumn', another poem I would place in the rural-iconic category, also has the same motifs of slumber, enervation and the seductive fantasy of time frozen and suspended into a 'cold pastoral'. The rural, then, is frequently associated in our culture with timelessness. No wonder we are told in the Bible that we have here 'No abiding *city*', rather than no abiding farm, or village. So whereas the cultural-essence of the village is its very 'abidingness', the city much more readily collocates, in poetry and otherwise, with notions of transience. In Shelley's 'Ozymandias' (to take a random instance) the notion of the transience of earthly glory is conveyed in the image of the once great city which has now entirely disappeared, except for the fragment of statue in the sand, and the inscription which registers the absence of the city which once was its setting.

By contrast, in the city the fields are now buried beneath the streets, leaving perhaps merely a verbal trace in an apparently inappropriate street name (like an 'Orchard Road' in a drab inner-city environment), or perhaps in an odd bend in a road whose building line follows the course of a now-vanished stream. The 'double visioning' simultaneously perceives both the built-up present and the inscriptions upon it of a pre-urban past. In another of her books, *Countries of the Mind: The Meaning of Place to Writers* (Hogarth Press, 1991), Gillian Tindall quotes Karl Marx to the effect that all cities are haunted by the ghosts of their former selves, and the haunting partly consists of the prevalence of such verbal and topographical echoes of the past.[1] What I am calling 'double visioning' is the attainment of a multi-layered chronological perspective which typically superimposes one historical period upon another, so that the viewed entity becomes radically trans-historical. A classic example of 'double-visioned' poetry about London is seen in the nineteenth century in the work of James Thomson ('B.V.'), not in the much-cited 'City of Dreadful Night', but in a piece called 'Sunday at Hampstead', where a mundane present scene is 'pierced' by the viewer and then overlaid with a series of scenes which take place on the same spot at remote periods in time. Thus, Thomson uses a 'palimpsest' technique which sees through the present and back through geological ages:

> This is the heath of Hampstead,
> There is the dome of Saint Paul's;
> Beneath, on the serried house-tops,
> A chequered lustre falls:

And the mighty city of London,
Under the clouds and the light.
Seems a low set beach, half shingle,
With a few sharp rocks upright.

The speaker and his female companion, wage-slaves ('donkeys') enjoying their Sabbath leisure release their usually caged (or 'pent') imaginations to contemplate the scene. Sunday inverts the social structure ('On Sundays we're Lord and Lady'), and more than this, they seem to rise above creation and view it with divine indifference ('Would you grieve very much, my darling,/If all yon low wet shore/ Were drowned by a mighty flood-tide,/ And we never toiled there more?'). Four couples have agreed to meet on this spot and then have tea together, watch the sunset and tell stories. Five stories in all are told, each set ten thousand years before the previous one, but in the same place, which is the place where they are now seated. The first begins 'Ten thousand years ago ... This place where we are sitting was a wood', and the tale concerns 'four naked squaws' and 'four tall naked wild men'. The women await the return of the men from hunting, then cook wild boar and 'cowered/ Until their lords had finished, then partook', after which they all crept into their cave and slept. In the second story 'From where we sit to the horizon's bound/ A level brilliant plain was spread all round ... high as your knee/ Aflame with flowers'. Out of this tropical landscape (complete with palm-trees) ride four swift horsemen, splendidly attired: they reach the camp and the women who have been waiting for them prepare the evening meal. In the third 'Where we are sitting rose in splendid light/ A broad cool marble palace', with broad terrace gardens stepping gradually down to the sea. Four giant figures arrive in a silken-sailed galleon and embrace 'the glorious women' who have been waiting for them. In the fourth story the place where they sit 'Was in a sea a hundred fathoms deep': four mermaids sit beneath the coral rocks awaiting 'four mermen from out the deep-sea dells'. A calamitous rumour has reached them from above that they are to be 'All disinherited from the great sea': the tail which enables them to swim so easily is to 'split into an awkward double limb,/ And we must waddle on the arid soil'. In the fifth and final story 'four lovely girls' are on Hampstead Heath and with three youths are listening to a fourth 'Discoursing history crammed full of truth ... And monstrous grimy London lay beneath'. We'll all be mermaids in ten thousand years he tells them, and, further, the evolutionary cycle will re-mix the sexes ('We'll all be men and women turn about'). The conclusion is 'The ring is round, Life naught, the World an O;/ This night is fifty thousand years ago'.

My contention about highly-staged, apocalyptic, writing of this kind is that there is something characteristically urban about it. It requires an educated awareness of the facts of evolution, and of geological and climate changes, to provide the driving force, and the promulgation of this kind of thinking depends upon essentially urban institutions, such as printing and publishing houses, learned societies, museums, public lectures and at least post-elementary systems of education. This is not to say, of course, that there is any correlation between being urban and being educated and intelligent: on the contrary, the point is that thinking of the kind exemplified by the poem does seem to require access to forms of knowledge which require an urban infrastructure for their dissemination. Second, a metropolitan setting of unprecedented growth in which a 'natural' landscape is transformed within a generation, as with London in the late nineteenth century, is the essential backdrop to such writing. The eyes which look down on the city and envision its transmutation are urban eyes which see this process in miniature as a daily fact. Beyond this, the urban elements in the vision in Thomson's poem would include the professed 'free thinking' of the protagonists (they are 'Too grateful to god for his Sabbath/ To shut its hours in a church'), and the liberalism which enables these young couples to spend the day in unchaperoned freedom, imagining a time of polymorphously perverse, unfettered sexuality, even if gender relations as such seem to remain conservatively unchanged and unchallenged. Thomson's poem will serve, then, as a convenient, if gaudy, illustration of a 'palimpsestic' way of seeing diachronically, perceiving through the city several layers of time, several epochs, simultaneously. This is the first of three important urban poetic tropes I wish to introduce here.

'Setting' and 'geography'

The second trope is the poet's option of using either 'setting' or 'geography' (or a combination of these) in their work. In the twentieth century, the best-known 'London' poem is T.S. Eliot's *The Waste Land*. The poem uses urban *geography* rather than just an urban *setting*. 'Setting', in this sense, is *generic*, evoking a generalised impression of the urban or the metropolitan, while 'geography' is *loco-*

specific, giving a rendition of specific cities, and often signaled by using the names of actual streets, buildings or districts. This 'redundant specificity' gives a cartographic precision, rather than just urban-generic, atmospheric details. Thus, Eliot frequently names actual streets, all of them radiating from St Mary Woolnoth in Lombard Street, which marks his place of work at Lloyds Bank from 1917 to 1925. His poetry moves from the urban-generic of the early poems (such as 'Preludes', 'Rhapsody on a Windy Night', 'Portrait of a Lady' and 'Prufrock') to the loco-specific of *The Waste Land*, and then on, in *Four Quartets*, to a mode which seems to combine the two, for the scenes of the London Underground in *Burnt Norton*, and the 'dead patrol' of the air-raid warden in the London blitz in *Little Gidding* avoid the use of local names, but are specific enough in their details to be unmistakably this one city. In *The Waste Land* the reader needs to know the precise social status of such places as Richmond and Kew, not as places of residence, but as destinations for day trips, for the Metropolitan Underground Railway had made such places easily affordable out-of-town trips for shop assistants or clerks. Thomson's 'wage donkeys' were no longer confined to places like Hampstead Heath which they could reach on foot. Likewise, the social difference between the Canon Street Hotel and, say, the Dorchester crucially underpins an important motif in the poem.

To appreciate an 'urban-generic' passage, the reader typically needs a pictorial imagination and some knowledge of the poetic tradition, for the relevant 'co-texts' – which is to say the texts on which the poet has drawn, and which a reader might profitably know about – are 'non-secular', that is, literary material, for a literary tradition in the representation of the metropolitan city in poetry had grown up since the nineteenth century, and Eliot sees through the eyes, the words and the images of (for example) Thomson's 'The City of Dreadful Night' and the French poetry of Laforgue and Baudelaire. Such matters are analysed in detail in excellent books like Robert Crawford's *The Savage and the City in the Poetry of T.S. Eliot* (Clarendon Press, 1990), which undertakes the 'forensic tedium' (as Crawford calls it) which is necessary to unravel these and other sources. In the case of urban geography, by contrast, the 'co-texts' are (from the literary point of view) 'secular', which is to say non-literary, and including material like guide books, books containing data on local history and geology and similar materials.

Generally, the urban-generic is 'soft focus' – it tends to emphasise atmospheric effects, providing a kind of 'subjective correlative' for the mood of the speaker or the nature of the business in hand: it is often key-noted and de-noted in literature by a characteristic emphasis on 'moody' lighting effects[2] – here in *The Waste Land* 'the brown fog of a winter dawn', 'the violet hour', and so on. By contrast, the loco-specific is 'hard focus', in that it tends to use actual street names, actual bus numbers, the names of actual shops, and so on. It may also use a knowledge of the way parts of the city are 'coded' as safe or not safe, genteel or not genteel, etc., by its inhabitants. So whereas the urban-generic is predominantly 'pictorial', the loco-specific is often much more 'diagrammatic'. The urban-generic is likely to be 'coded-in', meaning that it depends primarily on the resonances and conno-tations of the terms and concepts used in the text, and on received cultural practices within the closed economy of literature, such as the use of image-patterns, allusions or defamiliarisation effects. These elements, or 'coded-in' details, can be translated into Barthian terms as corresponding to the *Semic Code*, the code which concerns the way connotations crystallise into theme. By contrast, loco-specific passages are likely to be 'coded-out'; in other words, they are likely to refer out beyond the text to prior knowledge of the social and cultural signifi-cance of particular localities. Or, as Roland Barthes might have said, the *geography* factor is part of the *Cultural Code*, the one which gestures beyond the text to aspects of extra-textual knowledge. For convenience, these various features distinguishing the use of setting and the use of geography are summarised in Figure 3.1.

In *The Waste Land* Eliot's only escape from the hated commercial 'unreal city' of the present is via the past, to a London which is cere-bral, intellectual and imagined. This other London is 'over-mapped' onto the 'unreal city' of the London-present – he *looks* at the Thames, for instance, but he *sees* 'Elizabeth and Leicester beating oars', giving the kind of urban 'double visioning' already discussed. The other London becomes the 'psychic geography' through which he walks, eclipsing the contemporary physical geography. For Eliot this other London has a very specific cultural matrix, and it is accessed via the many post-Reformation churches in the City of London. In fact, few medieval churches survive in the City, largely because eighty-six out of a total of one hundred and seven were destroyed in the Great Fire of 1666. Fifty-one of these were rebuilt by Wren, and in addition an Act of Parliament in 1711 commissioned the building of another fifty new churches, of which twelve were actually built. These were the first

Setting	Geography
urban-generic	loco-specific
pictorial	diagrammatic
atmospheric/soft-focus	hard-focus
coded-in	coded-out
Semic Code	Cultural Code
literary co-texts	'secular' co-texts

Figure 3.1 Setting and Geography: summary of characteristics.

churches actually built as Anglican, rather than being medieval buildings which were originally Catholic. For Eliot these new buildings embody the enlightened Anglican theocracy of John Donne and Launcelot Andrewes, which he so much admired. Many were built on very restricted and enclosed sites, so they required large windows with clear, rather than stained, glass to avoid perpetual gloom. The fashion of the time was for a balcony-tier running round three sides of the building, and the effect is often more like a theatre than a conventional church. The main 'stage' is the pulpit rather than the altar (which is often just a simple communion table), so the emphasis in these post-Reformation churches is on discourse and enlightenment rather than ritual and mystery. All this exactly suited Eliot's temperament, and these orderly and serene interiors seemed to him an embodiment of that rational and secure belief which was for him the essence of the early seventeenth century. This is for Eliot the brief window between the darkness of the Middle Ages, and the disastrous 'dissociation of sensibility' of the 1660s, which, Eliot says, wasn't caused by the Civil War, but was caused by the same causes as those which caused the Civil War – a *nice* distinction. In this early seventeenth century interval, religion, reason and culture seem to Eliot to be in equilibrium and harmony, and this vision is encapsulated for him by the interiors of these churches by Wren, Gibbs and Archer.

I have dwelt on *The Waste Land*, the most familiar example of modern urban poetry, because it provides another convenient paradigmatic example of 'double visioning' and of the distinction between setting and geography. Approaching the poem in this way involves relating it directly to Eliot's 'outer' life (where he worked, the churches he slipped into at lunch times, and so on), and this presupposes putting aside the tired formalist aesthetic which would proscribe the making of such 'external' connections and insist on seeing the perceiver in the poem as always merely an implied 'persona'. As a reading *practice* this proscription has long outlived its demise as a reading *theory*, to the detriment of poetry. Writing about representations of the city in poetry presupposes a degree of literary realism in the writing discussed, and I must acknowledge here the difficulty such presuppositions can raise. In the next section I will focus on the Bakhtinian notion of the 'Chronotope', using examples from a variety of poetic sources – Ian McMillan, Andrew Motion and Bill Griffiths.

Chronotopic approaches

One of the problems in writing about contemporary poetry and cities can be usefully highlighted by using Mikhail Bakhtin's notion of the chronotope. Bakhtin defines the chronotope as a 'formally constitutive category of literature', expressing 'the inseparability of space and time (time as the fourth dimension of space)', where 'time ... thickens, takes on flesh, becomes artistically visible', and 'space becomes charged and responsive to the movements of time, plot and history'.[3] The chronotope, then, is the specified or deducible moment and place in which events, as we say, *take place*, an idiom which might be called inherently chronotopic in outlook. In realist fiction the chronotope is always clear and defined, and its being so is inherent in the very notion of realism. Non-realist fiction allows for chronotopic 'out-takes', for periods of 'dreamtime' or 'walkabout', when chronotopic rigidities are suspended, as in adventure stories, or fantasy tales, or sequences like the *Just William* books when the hero is suspended for ever at the age of eleven. This is so even when the 'extemporal hiatus' in which his adventures take place is inserted into the 'real-time' period of the Second World War (in the book called *William and A.R.P.*). What this suggests is that even the extemporal hiatus of the magical tale or the fantasy adventure story exists in a *definable* relationship to real times and places, the relationship consisting of the clear understanding that 'true' temporality and location have been suspended for the duration of the story. In fiction, that is to say, readers always know where and when they are.

   In traditional 'first-person' poetry which dramatises the subjectivity of an individual speaking persona – a category that pretty well comprises most of the lyric tradition – a generally similar situation applies. When Hopkins writes 'I wake and feel the fell of dark not day' the utterance has a straightforward chronotopic fixity: he is reflecting upon a recent event (a troubled night spent wrestling with religious doubts), which he is now about to relate for us. It is clear when the event happened (recently) and where it happened (in his bedroom). Likewise, in the Romantic period, a tight chronotopic specificity became the norm, as in Wordsworth's 'spots of time' passages in *The Prelude*, or the locationary precision in Coleridge's 'Conversation Poems', where both the time and place of the moment of reminiscence, and the precise details of the recalled scene are given (as in 'Frost at Midnight', for instance). This kind of specificity had replaced the tendency to much greater vagueness of chronotope in the poetry of the previous age, where the act of reflection itself, and the rendered landscape both tend to be more generalised.

In contemporary poetry the situation is quite often chronotopically fixed in this 'Romantic' way too. Thus, to confine myself to poems in Ian McMillan's *Selected Poems* (Carcanet, 1987), we have openings like these: 'It is almost nine o'clock. The women/ are taking the children down to school' ('Form without Implicit Moral', p. 31) or 'An hour before a poetry reading in Telford/ and I'm nervous as I always am' ('What Really Happened to the Buffalo', p. 56). Poems which begin with this kind of chronotopic specificity can, of course, subsequently go walkabout, slipping into the surrealist dreamtime of an extemporal hiatus – that, indeed, is the characteristic trajectory of a McMillan poem, and indeed of a major stratum of contemporary poetry. But the chronotopic fixed point remains in place for the duration of the poem, for the surrealist effect is peculiarly dependent on layers of fixity against which bizarrely juxtaposed events or objects can be perceived *as* bizarre – thus, the *baguettes* in a Magritte painting have to fall slantwise from the sky against the background of an ordinary urban street, and the effect would not be surreal if they were arranged in the same pattern against a completely abstract (that is, a chronotopically neutral) background.

In modern poetry the moment of reflection sometimes is and sometimes is not 'chronotopically anchored' in the way it is in the Coleridgean 'Conversation Poem'. In the case of Auden, Alexandra N. Leontieva argues in 'The Chronotope of W.H. Auden's Poetry: A Bakhtinian Approach',[4] the reflection is detached and floats in an unanchored 'great time': in 'In Memory of W.B. Yeats', for instance, the voice speaks as if in public and from 'on high', giving a privileged overview. As M. K. Spears puts it (in *Dionysus and the City*, OUP,

1970) at such moments Auden 'uses the City symbol explicitly, exten-
sively' (p. 82): he cites 'Memorial for the City' (p. 83), and the volume
Nones (p. 84), and Auden's discussion of 'the City and related
symbols' (p. 85) in *The Enchafed Flood* and in the section of *The
Dyer's Hand* called 'The Poet and the City'. But such use of the city as
'abstract concept or conscious symbol' (p. 90) – the urban-symbolic,
as we might call it – is a mode which I will, generally, exclude from
separate consideration, though as a layer in a triple approach to the
city – urban generic, urban-specific, and urban-symbolic – it is clearly
of some significance. By contrast, in Auden's '1 September 1939' the
chronotope of the reflection is tightly anchored to this date (the
chronos) and to 'one of the dives/ On fifty-second Street' (the *topos*).
It is clear (or, at least, I should make it clear that this is my belief) that
neither poem would work if their chronotopic circumstances were
transposed. I am keen to discuss poets who write about the city in
ways which are different from those of the Yeats elegy, where the cities
which feature in the poem are merely metaphorical abstractions (as in
'The squares of his mind were empty,/ Silence invaded the suburbs').
Rather, it is the chronotopically anchored writing like that of '1
September 1939' which interests me, where the 'Faces along the bar'
are those of an actual place, even though this place remains available
for the kind of 'high appropriation' of the idea of the city which we
get in the Yeats poem. The two modes are not mutually exclusive, and
'1 September 1939' contains the other kind of writing too, as when,
for instance, the commuters come out of the subway 'From the conser-
vative dark/ Into the ethical life'. Describing the dark of the subway as
'conservative' and the light in the street above as 'ethical' obviously
transforms the actual city into a symbolic network.

    Yet the notion of Englishness, which is implicit in Auden's elegy on
Yeats, and in much of his early American work, is often constructed
without any reference to cities at all. As Judy Giles and Tim Middle-
ton say, in their anthology *Writing Englishness, 1900–1950: An
Introductory Sourcebook on National Identity* (Routledge, 1995), 'In
the ideology of Englishness the English town or city has never carried
the same positive connotations as the English village or countryside …
The city in this period is reconceptualised as the site of modernity; it
is the centre which pulls in exiles and émigrés and which provides the
context in which individuals and groups can break from established
patterns of culture' (p.194). Here the city is associated with dispossess-
sion and rupture (exiles, émigrés, breaks with established patterns),

and yet with a kind of irresistible magnetism which 'pulls in' people, as if against their will. This is exactly the image of the urban which features in another Auden poem of the same period, 'The Capital', which ends with a memorable image of the city as a vortex of dynamic energy and excitement, radiating its hypnotic lure across the country-side:

> But the sky you illumine, your glow is visible far
> Into the dark countryside, the enormous, the frozen,
> Where, hinting at the forbidden like a wicked uncle,
> Night after night to the farmer's children you beckon.
>
> (*Selected Poems*, pp. 78–9)

With its typical emphasis on muted and subtle light, this is strong urban-generic writing, powerful enough to over-ride the potentially bathetic feyness of the wicked uncle. When these helpless ones ('children') are pulled in they will join the 'malicious village' where political exiles plot their return to power; or be swallowed by the industrial hinterland; or lose themselves in the hedonism of little restaurants 'where the lovers eat each other'; or live lives of wage-slave drudgery as urban 'donkeys', where 'the lonely are battered/ Slowly like pebbles into fortuitous shapes'. What these exiles will not have is the pleasure Coleridge envied his brother, of bringing up his children 'in the same dwelling where his father dwelt', ('To the Reverend George Coleridge', line 5), and being buried ultimately with kinsfolk and rude forefathers in a village churchyard which re-assembles a community of the dead immediately adjacent to that of the living. For the people cited in the poem, deracination and translation to a metropolis (which is a decentred agglomeration of 'villages' and 'quarters') is the norm, but the poem makes no attempt to mime this condition by fracturing and dislocating its own continuities, providing instead a chronotopic stability, a counter-modernist poetic space which can be navigated with far greater ease than is the case with, say, *The Waste Land*.

The real problem is, though, that a great deal of contemporary poetry is really *without any identifiable chronotope at all*: what we have is the equivalent (to revert to the Magritte example), not just of arranging the loaves against an abstract pattern, *but of arranging one abstract pattern against another*. And then another, and another, and another. Thus, it may well not *usually* be clear who is speaking and in which circumstances or location, and the writing may well be so contrived as to deconstruct all these categories (those of 'who', 'speaking', 'circumstances' and 'location'), making those questions precisely the wrong ones to ask. For instance, the 1980s mode of 'secret narrative', as practised by Andrew Motion and others, set out to do precisely that. A prototype poem in this mode is 'Open Secrets'.[5] Here, the two opening stanzas are placed inside speech marks and relate an incident concerning 'father', 'Florrie' and 'McDermot'. In the final stanza a narrating 'I' confesses that he made this up 'prolonging my journey home to you', and then elaborates the narrative further, insisting that 'He was never/ myself, this boy' (that is, McDermot, who features in the narrative), but admitting that 'if I tell you his story/ you'll think we are one and the same.' The poem ends by saying that *both* are hiding in fictions 'which say what we cannot admit to ourselves'. The result of all this is (among other things, and to put it mildly) to defy any kind of chronotopic precision. All the same, there is a scenario of *some* kind in Motion's poem which stays still for long enough to allow the reader grounds for sustained speculation about it (somebody is telling a story and its content is implicated in and complicated by the fact of his own failing relationship with whoever he is prolonging his journey home to).

But the property of standing still long enough for the reader to get some kind of fix on the scenario depicted is, to repeat, unusual in much contemporary poetry. One distinct kind, for instance, makes constant use of what I call 'phrasal imagery', or 'end-stopped imagery', or 'flick imagery', in which there is a rapid 'flick' throughout the poem from one image to the next, each apparently 'end-stopped', and without any evident continuity with adjacent ones, and each consisting of little more than a phrase. These features, for instance, give the characteristic John Ashbery effect, as at the opening of 'They dream only of America' (in *The Tennis Court Oath*):

> They dream only of America
> To be lost among the thirteen million pillars of grass:
> 'This honey is delicious
> *Though it burns the throat.*'
> And hiding from darkness in barns
> They can be grownups now
> And the murderer's ashtray is more easily –
> The lake a lilac cube.[6]

Of course, it is possible to recuperate these details through imposing some kind of 'narrativisation', but the primary reading experience is that the grammatical discontinuity between one line and the next intensifies a whole repertoire of discontinuities (of style, viewpoint, event, and so on). Generally speaking, such features make for some difficulty in enlisting the verse under the heading of 'city poetry', and given that these are the features of some of the most exciting of contemporary poetry, it follows that the bias of this book is towards a relatively conservative kind of writing which holds an identifiable scenario – a definable chronotope – to the fore long enough to enable the reader to begin to identify landmarks.

Coping with chronotopes –
Bill Griffiths's *The Book of Split Cities*

These difficulties will arise even when a poet is explicitly dealing with the kind of urban materials in question here, for example, the Bill Griffiths collection *The Book of Split Cities* (Etruscan Books, 1999), a work of some ninety pages in three parts ('The Trauma of the City', 'The Middle City' and 'The University'), with an introduction by Iain Sinclair. Griffiths's professed 'London' identity (he was one of the three poets in the Paladin 'Re/Active' anthology *Future Exiles: Three London Poets*, 1992) make him impossible to ignore in this context. But the challenges to the reader are extreme, requiring some perhaps desperate recuperations: for instance, I see in the 'Historium' section of 'The Trauma of the City' a strong vein of mocking intertextuality with Eliot's *The Waste Land*, as Griffiths insists on the actual brutal- ity of Eliot's idealised Elizabeth the First. Thus, we get a guide's patter as mummified fragments of Gloriana are displayed:

> *Don't be scared!*
> *The one and lovely famous maxi-vestige of Gloriana*
> *Yes the very Virgin who*
> *burned the adventurous at their stakes,*
> *the Golden Astraea who exhibited*
> *the bowels and limbs of the out-mouthed*
> *– so, will She talk to us today?*
> *Will She say something …?*
> *And these are real pearls. Note.*
> *This her tanned skin that permitted genetic reconstruction.* (p.10)

The penultimate line here seems to echo Eliot's 'Those are pearls that were his eyes, look', and on the following page he mocks the awestruck Eliot staring up at the 'Ionian white and gold' columns of Wren's church of St Magnus Martyr, insisting that these are merely the architectural correlatives of the ruthless Roman imperium:

> This room of lofty columns
> icy-white and curly-gold
> is dedicated to Rome from Whom alone the proper
> sense of our being just and fair – not only right
> that is, but capable of seeing when one is wrong
> and adjusting the future accordingly so as not to be criticised
> but to show correct.
> that is the legacy of the myth of the beloved imperial ruler;
> (p.11)

So the architecture which struck Eliot with its '*inexplicable* splendour' is all too explicable to Griffiths – it is frozen ideology, interpellation made concrete, the artistic means by which (in Althusser's terminology) we interpellate ourselves as just and rational beings. I am conscious that when the poem 'slows' as it does at these points I can recuperate it, as here with the intertextual parallels. But I am also conscious of not being able to do this for large proportions of it, though the most difficult bits are often the prelude to the sections where a specific and clear-cut chronotope suddenly opens up. Thus, in 'The Horse Whisperer' section of 'The Middle City', comes this:

> What! horse wheats meats
> control song heart
> for ease of breed and eat
> not pose or pay but the grey of
> continual directions ...
> the metrical bowel's
> stress on regularity
>
> say gless
> say garage
> say Chomley.

Here there seems to be a paralleling of the control of a horse by a rider and the metrical control of verse, with the possible implication of something unnatural in both processes. But the difficulty then dissolves as the poem enters into a fully developed anecdote (lasting two pages) of an incident during the miners' strike in the 1980s when a picket was pursued into a supermarket by a police officer on horseback. The sudden clearing of the chronotopic horizon provides some (I think necessary) relief to the reader, and the formula is a powerful one, consisting of 'a-chronotopic' sections which build a densely textured mesh of phrasal images interwoven with narrativised, chronotopic out-takes. I am enough of an academic reader to expect that the latter would provide broad thematic clues which would help in decoding the former.

If the most progressive contemporary poetry is only semi-chronotopic (MacMillan, Motion) or has only an intermittent chronotopic grounding (like Griffiths) it follows that, in spite of its aspired, zonal catholicity, this book needs to make relatively conservative choices of 'target' poets, since the more a poem moves towards the a-chronotopic, the less it can convincingly be said to be registering a city, especially as regards the topographic specifics of 'geography'. This, again, will partly account for the relative absence of women poets, since a great deal of women's poetry eschews 'geography' (perhaps as representing spaces still coded as predominately masculine) and moves decisively towards the a-chronotopic.

Notes

1 The words quoted from Marx refer to 'the soft veil of nostalgia that hangs over unbanished landscape' (p. 144), meaning the sense of the abiding presence of the rural ground on which the city is built. The 'nostalgia' is viewed positively by Marx, as stimulating a desire to improve present conditions and so bring back that imagined golden age.

2 The founding text of the urban generic mode is perhaps the poem 'Le Crepuscule du Soir' ('Dusk') in the 'Tableaux Parisiens' section of Baudelaire's Les Fleurs du Mal (1861).

3 See Mikhail Bakhtin, 'Forms of Time and Chronotope in the Novel,' The Dialogic Imagination: Four Essays by M.M. Bakhtin, ed. Michael Holquist, trans. Caryl Emerson and Michael Holquist, University of Texas, pp. 84–258. The summary is quoted from 'Bakhtin's Definition of the Adventure Chronotope and the Phenomenon of The X-Files Fan Fiction', University of Bergen, Norway.

4 Master's degree thesis, Department of English, University of Bergen, Norway, 1996.
5 Andrew Motion, *Dangerous Play, Poems 1974–1984*, Penguin, 1984, p. 11.
6 John Ashbery, *Selected Poems*, Paladin, 1987, p. 33.

4 Writing the inner city

The term 'inner city' has an ambiguity which is worth exploiting. On the one hand, it suggests a process of personal negotiation with a city, a selective interiorisation of the place by which it is assimilated and re-shaped to an individual's own needs and perceptions. It is this process of interiorisation which makes someone a Londoner or a Mancunian, as opposed to merely an inhabitant of London or Manchester. Interiorisation is a process not unlike the act of reading, especially the act of 'concretisation' which the reader-response critics identify. Concretisation is the process whereby in the act of reading much of a 'text' is mentally discarded by the reader, and a radical thematisation is imposed on the mental residue, with a few key episodes or sentences being linked up into a constellation of focused meaning, so that the eight-hundred-page physical fact of (say) *Middlemarch* becomes the *Middlemarch* which a reader may still carry in the head twenty years after the reading took place. This *Middlemarch* comprises, perhaps, a few verbatim phrases, some scenes still retrievable in semi-pictorial form, some quasi-abstract thematic formulations, and, suffusing all, a certain aura or atmosphere which is difficult to define, but seems to include a certain paced, reflective way of thinking. This unique, highly personal *Middlemarch* is like the 'inner' city, of 'London' or 'Manchester', in which each of us lives. Like the inner *Middlemarch*, the inner city is a radical slimming down of the 'full-text' city. It too is highly 'thematised' (by factors to do with age, gender, profession and leisure interests), its plenitude radically narrowed to a series of frequently used tracks, both physical and mental, which are like the heavily underlined passages in a read text. The 'inner' city is always a fragment of the notional whole, but it is a fragment which coheres. It is, not system, but event, a series of well-tried actual 'moves', as in a chess game, or actually occurring utterances in a language, rather than the game or language itself seen as a totality. This city-as-read is always, paradoxically, more real than the complete text – than whatever is represented by those crowded pages in an *A to Z* which can mean nothing at all until the process of interiorisation begins.

But of course, the notion of the 'inner city' is also a term used by relevant professionals (vicars, teachers, social workers, probation officers) to designate the decaying centres of post-industrial cities, where the disadvantaged, the old and the unemployed are stranded in inner exile, condemned by their postcodes-from-hell to social exclusion, to lives without bank accounts, post offices or life insurance. The process of de-industrialisation, demolition and 'renewal' in the 1960s and 70s resulted in the production of these urban dystopias: the city then was an expanding universe, with centrifugal forces driving it outwards, to 'overspill' estates on distant peripheries and to 'out-of-town' shopping centres. The works discussed in this chapter all focus on the 'inner city' in this accepted social sense of the term, for there is an evident drive in these works to represent the social reality and register the brutal consequences of social policy as they impact on the city. Here, then, our concern is with a powerful tradition of contemporary urban dystopian poetry. These poets resist the 'Eliot' effect, the superimposition of a preferred psychic-geography upon the physical geography of the present. Formally, all these poets abandon the free-standing, single-topic, short lyric poem (which it is sometimes tempting to see as the most conservative of poetic forms in the present age) and instead adopt a longer composite, sequential form.

Ken Edwards, 'Drumming'

Ken Edwards is a poet and publisher associated with the British avant-garde since the 1970s. His sequence 'Drumming' appeared in a small-press booklet called *Drumming & Poems* which was published in 1982 by Peter Hodgkiss's Galloping Dog Press of Newcastle upon Tyne. The booklet is a fifty-page, mimeographed, A4-sized publication with pages set photographically from typed sheets. It is the product of a distinctive urban poetic sub-culture which flourished in the 1970s and 80s, and which I will briefly characterise here. Galloping Dog was a member of the Association of Little Presses, an umbrella organisation then at its height and run by sound-poets Bob Cobbing and Chris

Cheek, and linked with the Poetry Society and *Poetry Review*, in their
dissident period under Eric Mottram in the mid-1970s.[1] It is the
product, then, of a vigorous urban sub-culture, one, indeed, which
was apt to polarise and stereotype the country/city dichotomy.[2] ALP
member presses were based in urban centres round the country, sold
their books by mail order, or at a range of specialist poetry bookshops,
like Compendium in Camden Town, London, Bernard Stone's Turret
bookshop in Church Walk, Kensington, and the Oriel bookshop in
Cardiff, run by Peter Finch. One feature which distinguished this
world from its 'large press' counterpart was that those who owned
and ran the presses were usually practising poets themselves. Their
books were also sold at poetry readings at urban venues (like the
White Swan in London), and listed and reviewed in publications like
Hodgkiss's *Poetry Information*, which ran throughout the 1970s and
into the early 1980s. Those involved in this activity were mainly
young (in their twenties and thirties), a mixture of graduates, autodi-
dacts and drop-outs (and some who were all three). They were mainly
left-wing in political conviction and committed to various forms of
neo-modernist, avant-garde practice in poetry. There was widespread
interest in both new technologies and cultic mysticism: one of the
symptoms of the urbanism was a certain kind of pastoral mysticism
(an interest in ley-lines, body culture and ecology). The booklets were
produced mainly in editions of two to three hundred copies.[3]

That, briefly, is the poetry 'scene' from which 'Drumming'
emerged. It takes up ten pages (pp. 35–45) of the booklet, and is the
culmination of the series of urban pieces which make up the rest of
the collection ('Waterloo Bridge, towards Westminster', 'Near the
Elephant & Castle', 'Old Man, Camberwell', 'Poster, Walworth Rd,
Winter '80', 'Geraniums, South London', 'Portobello Road', 'Short-
life Property, Bayswater, mid-70s', 'Southall', and so on). Like much
of Edwards's work around this time, 'Drumming' is linked in a head-
note to a piece of music, in this case the piece of the same name by the
American 'minimalist' composer Steve Reich.[4] A reviewer of a 1996
performance of Reich's piece described how in this work 'subtle voices
and percussion weave in and out of one another creating an almost
static field', and Edwards aims for a cognate 'interweave' effect
whereby the 'cut-up or 'fold-in' technique is used, working in phrases
or sentences from newspaper reports which are repeated in varying
permutations. The effect is incantatory, suggestive of shock or trauma,
appropriate for a piece which has the grim subject matter of the racial

tensions in urban Britain in the late 1970s and early 80s, against the
backdrop of National Front agitation and the passage through Parlia-
ment of a Nationality Bill in 1980–81, which had the intention of
stemming immigration by re-defining Britishness. The note on the
poem makes a specific link with the New Zealand teacher Blair Peach
who was 'beaten to death by an unidentified officer of the Special
Patrol Group on 23rd April 1979, while demonstrating against a
National Front meeting in Southall'.

The opening section, which takes up the first three pages, permu-
tates snatches of newspaper report and a kind of traumatic proleptic
reminiscence:

> Stranger in a strange land,
> men controlling entry,
> hold the pitiful shoes.

Here the elements seem to be, first a conventionalised description of
the helpless immigrant on arrival ('Stranger in a strange land'), then
the immigration officials, and finally an image of the terrible end-point
of racist attitudes – the piles of shoes taken from Holocaust victims.
The poem goes on to evoke the thuggish street violence of racist gangs
('Terrorise the subways,/ it's us or them they say, /ecology of the
street'), with allusions to the White Paper's proposal of three classes of
nationality, to the virginity tests carried out for a time on Asian
women entering Britain, and to the death of Blair Peach:

> Who inspected vaginas,
> british movement skinheads,
> even those who had yet
> by commerce & crossfire
> to look outside or to
> anything 'we' elect.

> They murdered a white man
> and the fists in the air
> and he was a teacher
> underneath 'our' culture;
> the swastika hidden,
> easily interrupted.

These phrases from newspapers and other commentaries are recurrent and fragmentary: there is a strong sense of the intimate invasion of racist attitudes into 'Home, school, shop or office' and of personal violation ('Men controlling entry/ in my lungs') and seepage, against which there seems to be no defence, as with the pollen in the English spring, as with the aerosoled swastikas which appear on buildings ('To bloom on a dry day/ in the english springtime/ to redirect the flow.// Life we could be living. /Fuzzed writing on concrete, /the swastika hidden,/ aerosoled swastika'). Each time the phrases recur the 'drumming' interweave mimes the static fixity of obsession, creating a claustrophobic build-up of tension (very apparent in Edwards's memorable performances of this piece in the 1980s):

January '81,
And the british people
were divided in 3,
the swastika hidden
underneath 'our' culture,
TV's frozen music.

Hold the pitiful shoes.

As already indicated, the poem is part of a small-press, oppositional cultural movement, and the intertextuality at its core takes in other material from the same ambience. The 'community publishing' movement of the period, then enjoying pockets of Local Authority support, was encouraging working class people to write about their experiences for booklet publication. One such was a pamphlet called *Going Where the Work Is* by Jamaican immigrant Isaac Gordon (published by the Hackney Reading Centre), which Edwards uses, within the 'intercutting' method, in sections 2 and 3. Gordon had been the victim of an accident which had cost him several fingers while operating badly maintained machinery for the cutting up of scrap metal. Edwards uses the text partly 'treated' (that is, with re-editing and re-lineation, and some re-ordering), inducing the same 'throbbing' or 'drumming' tone as the rest:

... cutting
up metal, I have to
take up the metal with

a knife, just pulled my hands
straight into the knife.

This section opens and closes with the phrase 'They break up the motion', which, in the sources from which it is lifted, refers to the strategies used to secure the passage of the Nationality Bill through the House, but which, of course, begins to pick up other resonances each time it is re-used in the poem, as it is to open Section 3, which is the longest section – five-and-a-half pages – all written in couplets re-permutating phrases from the earlier sections, and again increasing the sense of drumming threat and tension:

They break up the motion
just to stop from being bored.

When i come to this country
and boil it for pigs.

they break up the motion
by commerce & crossfire.

They break up the motion
straight into the knife.

The strategy of the poem is to link together as vividly as possible the racism of the streets, the callousness of the unscrupulous employer of unprotected immigrant labour, and the manipulative politics which secures the imposition of restrictive immigration practices. The phrase 'straight into the knife' becomes the repeated refrain, embodying this idea, and encapsulating the notion of the immigrant's vulnerability, and seeing it as the stimulus to the presence of Blair Peach on the fatal march. The brief final section (quoted here in full) makes a last inter-weaving juxtaposition, a forensic account of Peach's injuries with part of the one of the clauses of the Act:

The blow had split his skull
from its base to his right ear.
People holding the new citizenships would be
eligible to have
passports describing them,

splintering the bone &
bruising the brain to
a depth of an inch.
It will be necessary
to restrict the right of
entry to each of them.

I have chosen to comment on 'Drumming' for a number of reasons: first, it's a document which vividly encapsulates the social tensions of the period at the end of Labour rule (for nearly two decades) and the start of Thatcherism. What is intriguing is the way poetry can be the witness here, and how powerfully its avant-garde techniques can work to convey anger, atmosphere and a certain feeling of helplessness. It is poetry which seems to care very little about achieving a purely aesthetic effect, and is primarily interested in using its artistic resources to make a polemical impact. It has much in common with Robert Hampson's *Seaport*, discussed in another chapter, as is to be expected, given the long working partnership between the two in various poetic enterprises since the 1970s. The affinity can be summed up as comprising, first, content affinities – Hampson's use of the 1981 Toxteth riots has evident similarities with the way Edwards deals with London tensions in the same period, second, methodological affinities – the use of 'treated-text' and 'cut-up' techniques, and finally attitudinal affinities – the 'anti-aesthetic stance' and the abnegation of the personal 'lyric' voice in favour of a textual interweave.

Barry MacSweeney, *Hellhound Memos*

By contrast, the work of Edwards's contemporary Barry MacSweeney, who died in May 2000, inverts the landscape and technique of 'Drumming'. Where Edwards maintains a cool detachment and remains resolutely outside the material, MacSweeney projects his inner city through the personal hell of alcoholism and the fight against it, building an atmosphere of baroque, hallucinatory excess, a kind of hyped-up paranoia of victimhood. There is no measured, middle-class empathy with the underdog here, first, because this *is* the underdog speaking, pursued by his personal manic-depressive hellhound, and second because he isn't middle-class. Born in 1948, MacSweeney came to prominence in 1968 as a nineteen-year-old *wunderkind*, unusual in the small-press scene in having his first book published by a 'real'

press, *The Boy from the Green Cabaret Tells of his Mother*, which was
published by Hutchinson in 1968. Books from the 'posh' end of the
small-press publishing scene followed throughout the 1970s (from
Fulcrum, Turret, and Trigram in 1971, 1972 and 1978 respectively),
and then a gap before a re-start in the 1980s, with *Ranter*, from Slow
Dance Press in 1985, followed by *Hellhound Memos* from the Many
Press in 1993, and *Pearl* from Equipage in 1995. This sequence of
three books seemed to have returned him decisively to the small-press
ambience. Then his career again seemed to move into a different
dimension. The Royal Literary Fund and the Society of Authors
supplied 'substantial financial support which enabled him to attend
Farm Place addiction clinic for two months, and to receive aftercare
treatment' (see the 'Acknowledgements' to *The Book of Demons*) and
the result was *The Book of Demons*, published by Bloodaxe in 1997,
which was a Poetry Book Society Recommendation. MacSweeney had
also featured in the 1990s in the third 'Re/Active Anthology',
published by Paladin Poetry under the title *The Tempers of Hazard* in
1993, the other two poets in the collection being Thomas A. Clark and
Chris Torrance. In addition, *Hellhound Memos* was reprinted in full
in the Picador anthology *Conductors of Chaos* (the edition to which
the page numbers given here correspond), edited by Iain Sinclair (who
was also the Re/Active series editor) in 1996. At the time of writing,
this and *The Book of Demons* (which reprints the 1995 *Pearl* in full)
are the most readily available in-print examples of his work.

'Hellhound Memos' is a sequence of nineteen lyrics, printed one to
a page in the *Conductors of Chaos* reprint, and I will refer to them in
this discussion by their number in the sequence and the number of the
relevant page. Some of them have individual titles and some don't, but
whether titled or not, they may have a brief quotation as epigraph,
and/or a dedication. These variations in paratextual features (that is
in 'boundary markers' like titles, epigraphs, etc.) create a notional
repertoire for the sequence which runs from an old-fashioned 'triple-
headed' style (a piece that opens with the 'full monty' of title,
epigraph, and dedication) to a 'zero-headed' style (pieces which have
none of these paratextual elements at all and are simply separated
off from the previous piece with a bulleted space-marker). In fact,
only the sequence overall has the full triple-headed treatment, and the
effect of these variations is to raise questions about what the integral
units of the artefact are: the separate titling, for instance, implies free-
standing units with a degree of relative artistic autonomy, but in fact

a series of running motifs and an overall homogeneity of tone give the piece a strong integral identity. Likewise, the word 'Memos' in the title seems to promise a series of informal, off-the-cuff out-takes from the flux of a life in crisis, but the use of formal paratextual features like internal titles, and the rest, cuts across this, making some of the pieces assume the look almost of lapidary inscriptions on a monument.

Overall, the effect is like that achieved by any deliberate refusal to stick within an utterance to a single and consistent verbal register (an 'utterance' in this sense means any self-contained, demarcated 'discourse situation', which might be a brief exchange with an acquaintance, at one extreme, or a chapter in a book at another). The effect of such code switching is always to assert superiority in exchanges where there is a power imbalance (it is the MD or the VC who decides when we shift from a formal, business-like register to matey slang, and back again) or else to challenge the defining parameters of the whole discourse situation. MacSweeney, in a sense, does both here.

The title of the sequence, and the long opening epigraph (ten lines) are from the track 'Hellhound on My Trail' by Mississippi Blues singer Robert Johnson, who died mysteriously in 1938 at the age of twenty-seven. Johnson is used as a motif throughout the piece and within its image-economy he connotes art pursued self-destructively – he was rumoured to have sold his soul to the devil during a six-month disappearance, in return for the gift of being able to play anything. He died mysteriously, possibly poisoned by whiskey proffered by a jealous husband. The speaker in the sequence materialises at the start of the third piece (p. 257) as a kind of transgenerational urban Lord of Misrule – 'Me the multiplex moron, multigenerational/ multiplicity, many-fingered man with a violet/ shell-suit, stolen BMW and a rack of E. I'm here!' He is defiantly ubiquitous ('I used to be nowhere, now I'm all over the place'), polymorphously perverse ('I've been to bed with the black-pudding. Keep it.'), an embodiment of the anarchic gang spirit of the overspill estates, prince of the ram-raiders ('estate joy-rider/ extraordinaire'), terrorising neighbourhoods in the long weeks of summer when the police are thin on the ground ('when the boys in blue are in Marbella on the piss'). He revs in like a Hell's Angel, dealing stolen property, scorching a trail through other people's lives ('I can scorch a line, a beautiful/ blue and true line through the hull of your lives'). He is scandalising, reckless and electrifying, like Robert Johnson, claiming a privilege for his destructive/deconstructive art ('Cut, cut, cut. It's my dark, dark memo,/ almost a badge'), and descending on his helpless urban environment like a force of nature ('I come down like slate-grey rain. That's all. No God available.') The lines have a stark energy, and the rhythmic control is brilliant and arresting. The force often comes from the placing of broken-off sentences or fragments at the end of lines (like 'Keep it', 'That's all' and 'No God available' in the lines quoted above), giving an edgy, threatening tone, with the characteristic, plangent down-note at the end which is typical of masculine utterances in aggressive mode. The locutionary effect is to construct the reader as an intimidated bystander (for instance, when football fans go on the rampage in a shopping mall, as later in the sequence) and the 'multiplex moron' in a shell-suit, in a world with 'No God available', might be taken as an embodiment of the malign urban influence, not 'safely' confined to cities, which is feared by John Barnie, for the sequence conjures up not just the lost lands of the inner city, but a despoiled rural dystopia as well.

Robert Johnson is one of a string of died-young artist figures who feature in the sequence. Another is 'PBS', Percy Bysshe Shelley, with whom affinity is claimed in a day-early birthday ode (poem 4, p. 228) – 'Happy birthday, wake up, let's drown together'. A couple of poems later Anne Sexton is added to the list ('Anne Sexton, Robert Johnson, Barry MacSweeney at the crossroads/ Swapping riffs on an Olympia portable'). The urban/rural conflict is strongly felt in the sequence, but it is the intensively exploited countryside which appears (not the nostalgic vision), the yellow rapefields interrupting the colour harmony of the scene with a GBH of the retina ('Hellhounds horning in the rapefields') that seems to connote more general kinds of violence. The Edward Thomas vision of the English countryside, indeed, seems mocked and taunted, his loving roll-call of English wild-flowers viciously satirised ('I fear for my cusloppe, my betany, my bane, my cranesbill, my cuckoo/ pinting gob of wayside spit.// The soapwort will best us all'). The haunting hellhound stalks and meta-morphoses ('Devil in a pink shell-suit'), pursuing the helpless poet, sniffing out his trail, the speaker seeing himself as a latter-day Roman-tic poet, avatar of Chatterton and Shelley (a recurrent motif in MacSweeney's work). The speaker identifies with the poet-figure pursued to his doom by fate, affecting a callous indifference as the fiends rake through the embers of the drowned and cremated Shelley ('Me, I kick his sizzling heart around just as I like').

The economy of the sequence constantly juxtaposes images of run-away urban materialism with his group of artist-victims who seek rural escape, or challenge this ambience with defiant and self-destructive hedonism. The poem has been taken as an anti-Thatcherite protest, though seeing it this way attributes to it a disciplined thematic unity which it really doesn't possess and wouldn't aspire to. The anti-Thatcherite element, in so far as it is in the poem, may be seen in the recurrent 'B&Q' motif, B&Q being a British chain of DIY 'superstores', founded in Southampton in the late 1960s, and expanding rapidly throughout the 1980s (from 26 to 280 stores by the end of the decade), riding on the back of the house-price boom of the period and the Thatcherite crusade to produce a nation of 'owner-occupiers'. MacSweeney makes a Bakhtinian *melange* of registers, mixing those of advertising, moralising vicars, and bar-bigots ('Hanging's too good for them') bringing in the B&Q motif at the start of the Shelley poem (poem 4, p. 228):

> The very low odour tough acrylic formula
> of B&Q Safe Paint with satin gloss finish
> is venal. Civilisation too good a word for it.
> Percy, why won't anyone leave us alone? Pass
> the 10-litre can of Professional Obliterating Paint,
> please. Pass the zinc-plated wing nuts, the spur
> budget gold effect bracket and inspiration shelf.
> Not to mention the Zamba Wall Shelving with Tool Rack.
> Hardbeam I am for both of us against the intrusions.

The satire is humorous but high-minded, the stance lofty and disdainful. The speaker seems to protest at the privatisation and selling-off of national utilities ('The very floodlit light of heaven has already been/ sold, as you predicted'), invoking a kind of instinctive communism which at the same time seems pretty elitist too, and much imbued with that familiar product of surveying the urban scene from a great height (Eliot in *The Waste Land*, or Christ weeping for Jerusalem when he goes up the mountain to pray), namely an overwhelming sense of its emptiness and superficiality ('The rest is trash./ Babble, babble, babble. Slick, stink, stink'). In poem 6 (p. 230) the B&Q motif is again given free rein, literally, almost, as the hellhound is unleashed on a shopping spree:

> Hellhound, thee with vast purchase, off, off!
> my siren, my knocker, my foghorn, my bell.
> Off my loose nails, my gate furniture, my slide
> action latch, my epoxy-coated wire hasp, my B&Q
> gate bolt, my free-delivered catalogue.

In the sequence, shopping at B&Q is mocked as virtually a substitute for both sex and religion; in the section just quoted, the language has an almost prurient air of sensual, close-up detail ('my slide action latch' etc.), and the piled on clauses work up to a climax of onanistic, yet polymorphously perverse shopping, stimulated by the images in 'my free-delivered catalogue'. In poem 11 (p. 235) being in B&Q is like a premonition of heavenly peace, a momentary and savoured lulling of the tumult in the heart (this poem has as epigraph the line 'The wild confusion dwells in me'): the poem begins:

> So quiet tonight I can barely hear the brushing
> of an angel's wings.
> So quiet and pleasant it is as if I am in B&Q.

It then slides in to another familiar trope, juxtaposing this materialist heaven, able to satisfy the heart's innermost yearnings, with images of erotic fulfilment in a pastoral landscape:

> we fled into the dales and yards, the yearns,
> the raw grass which greened our thighs and knees.
> the sun was like a bucketful of gold!
> The argent streams bubbled through our fingers and we
>   hoorayed
> with monumental whoops of elemental joy.

Generally, the sequence relentlessly lampoons the environmental degradation which is the result of unrestricted materialism ('the acid rain/ comes down relentless, Bladerunner-style', poem 14, p. 238). The culture's high ideals of the city as the 'New Jerusalem' have been (literally) sold out, and the countryside has been sacrificed to mono-crop exploitation. Indeed, both the city and the country are reduced to commercialised simulacra – 'Chelsea' is a brand name for styles of furniture, and the Lake District merely a source of Beatrice Potter images on cheap bric-a-brac (poem 15, p. 239):

Jerusalem has been sold and is a mall
with cross-Channel counter-culture accountants
selling rapefield hectares.   Instant zero-degree credit for the
    Chelsea sofa
and the hand-painted Lake District bookends.

The speaker passionately identifies with social and religious revolu-
tionaries, with anyone who might tear down this hated commercial
fabric, such as the 'Levellers and prince-fingerers' of poem 12 (p.
236), which has the title 'Shaking Minds with Robespierre', and 'Jesus
Christ Almighty in white lawn/ turning the tables and phlegming
the fools (poem 13, p. 237), where the heroic image of Christ in a
toga, overturning the tables of the money-lenders provides relief at
a low point, when the speaker has been badly mauled by the manic-
depressive hellhound. The poem is untitled but has the dedication 'for
Rachel Brierley' and begins:

Rachel, darkness broods upon the temple tonight
and the account is almost to the bone.
The mallet's blow has once more hurled me down
and there are pawprints all over from ankle to craw.

These 'victim' poems contrast with a few 'avenger' poems, in which an
urban vengeance seems to be envisioned and savoured, and the
dangerous fantasy is entertained of having the power to sweep away
the whole of the hated fabric in a great apocalpytic, orgiastic clean-
out. Here the terrible precedents are the Stalinist Purges, the Nazi
Holocaust, the Chinese Cultural Revolution, and Pol Pot's Killing
Fields, the latter explicitly evoked ('Dirt Pot at 23.59, sixty seconds
before Year Zero, beck/ running redundant lead ore waste and human
blood', poem 14, p. 238). The next ten lines envisage a rampaging
gang working its way through a shopping mall, and MacSweeney
presents it with some apparent relish as an anarchic force of
irresistible urban energy, defying petty authority figures, such as bus
inspectors, and gleefully massing on the page a whole flurry of
signifiers of aggressive working-class masculinity (Rotweilers, strong
cider, shell-suits, shoplifting, tattoos and public-order offences):

Swapping Staffordshire pit bull and Rotweiler win
tokens, they swank delirious with gallons of snakebite

on what common ground's left, urine-stained madder and
harvest-gold shell suits, almost ready for an unwaged
basketball booted shoplifting forage into the mall, where
they'll meet popped tattooed dad, flung pissed out into
Gallowgate, who slurs; Stuck my finger right up the bus
inspector's nose, forecasting his immediate mortality

unless once more his inner breast pocket received that
leather-covered report book.

Again, here, the mix of voices is remarkable, blending in the names of
cheap brands of strong cider ('snakebite', 'harvest gold'), parodying
the euphemistic evasions of the middle-class authorities (the spree is
carried out by the 'unwaged', not the 'unemployed'), mocking the
abstract, gutless language of officialese ('forecasting his immediate
mortality' reports a remark which verbatim would have been some-
thing like 'Put that book away, or you're dead, mate'), and parodying
the hyped-up language of commercial descriptions of objects for sale
(the 'leather-covered report book'). Further, the phrase 'on what
common ground's left' manages to associate this act of re-claiming
public spaces with historical protests against the enclosure of public
land, such as the famous occupation of St George's Hill in Surrey in
spring 1649 by Winstanley and the Diggers to plough the earth and
plant vegetables, aiming to restore the Creation to its former condi-
tion. Thus, MacSweeney's shoplifters become the latest in line which
expresses an endemic English libertarian, egalitarian spirit.

The last poem in the sequence (poem 18, p. 242) ends with a note
of blighted spiritual yearning. The epigraph ('The darkness fell, and all
the glory vanished') is from Augusta Drane, biographer of Catherine
of Sienna, recording the fading of one of her subject's inspirational,
heavenly visions. The opening shows the city at dusk, viewed this time
with a kind of panoramic compassion:

Vapour rises from the ducts and flues, ashen and feathered
against the Batman cape sky like smoked bone, ascending
wounded inside the theoretical bruising, burdened
with the small matter of mankind and the grit
in its windows and eyes, which are silver and aquamarine
here in the Fauvist metropolis.

This last poem in the sequence switches in these opening lines into an Expressionist mode of urban descriptive writing familiar since Baudelaire and Rimbaud. The mode is also strongly pictorialist and moralistic, a Jansenist, Gotham City version of reality in which helpless masses are at the terrorising mercy of villainous forces which rise with those vapours from the city's dark underworld. It is then dependent for rescue and re-alignment on a saviour figure (a Batman, or a Jesus Christ) who will, for mysteriously altruistic motives, be moved to redeem them. The job done, it will revert to metropolitan type, stoning its own prophets, refusing, like Jerusalem, to be gathered safely under the saviour's wing (a motif MacSweeney employs directly in the poem). The stoned prophets include the cast of 'Holy Rollers' who are in fact roll-called several times in the poem – Anne Sexton, Bessie Smith, Robert Johnson, Barry MacSweeney. Johnson is the matrix of this group, seen in this final poem as:

> Chapped fingers play the bottleneck
> at Gallowgaste crossroads
> where we have lost Robert Johnson to some deep connection
> down the hellhound trail
> passing Anne Sexton details of the Christmas late chemist rota.

The Christmas epitome of materialism and spending is a fitting culmination of the poem; it ends with shopping, that defining and self-defining act in a consumer society: as in Larkin's poem, the shoppers push through the plate-glass doors towards their desires, entering the simulacrum (the 'falsedom', as the moralistic speaker calls it here): like Prospero's island, the poem is 'full of voices', and here the echo of the opening of Milton's 'Lycidas' ('Yet once more, O ye laurels') links neatly with some of the poem's major emblems and concerns (another drowned Shelleyan victim, more material corruption – Milton's descriptive sub-title 'foretells the ruin of our corrupted clergy'):

> Yet once more we enter the falsedom in scarlet and gold,
> attracted by automatic defrost function
> and full range of hostess trolleys available.

These synthetic desires, as MacSweeney (like Larkin) implies, are concocted by the atrophying of the capacity to desire anything more worthwhile. The fastidious eye moves away, back to the evening sky,

through which snow falls, this time echoing the tone of fellow
Newcastle poet Basil Bunting (who, as John Wilkinson reminds us in
a useful general account of MacSweeney's career, had praised
MacSweeney's early work as being 'for unabashed boys and girls', a
horrible phrase, as Wilkinson rightly calls it):[5]

> Snow blurs the moon
> and the sky is whipped by the blizzard's tail.
> It is all like smoke
> in the swiftly changing hands of the trees.

Bunting, near the end of *Brigglatts*, looks skyward with similar senti-
ments, disdaining 'the falsedom' and claiming a lofty affinity with the
self-sufficient stars ('Furthest, fairest things, stars, free of our
humbug,/ each his own, the longer known the more alone'). At the end
of the sequence MacSweeney proclaims the ultimate, vapoury base-
lessness of the urban fabric, not without that touch of relish with
which such observations are usually made.

Edwards and MacSweeney, then, represent two urban-presenta-
tional extremes, the former a determinedly cool and *heterodiegetic*
mediator (that is, one who doesn't figure in his own narrative), a
medium undramatised into an identifiable 'speaker', while Mac-
Sweeney is *homodiegetic* (the content and the hero of the narrative as
well as its medium), a dramatised figure named and centred in the
narrative, in many ways the familiar suffering 'I' figure of Romantic
and post-Romantic verse. And where Edwards imposes a rigid
economy of language (by re-cycling and re-permutating a small reper-
toire of phrases, for instance), MacSweeney manifests a constant
verbal exuberance and conspicuous, register-blending, excess.

Yet both Edwards and MacSweeney, while portraying a fundamen-
tally grim urban world, still manage to convey a sense that the city
both could, and ought to be, better than this. While recording and
exploring its squalor there is still a sense that these cities are a falling
off from an ideal – that cities ought to be otherwise. A similar kind of
inverse (or implicit) Utopianism is pervasive in the great American
turn-of-the-century exposés of urban corruption and exploitation, like
Jacob Riis's *How the Other Half Lives* (1890), which showed the
living conditions of immigrant groups in the New York's slums, or *The
Shame of the Cities* (1904), by the 'Muck-Raker' journalist Lincoln
Steffens, which exposed municipal 'graft' and corruption in major

American cities, or Upton Sinclair's novel *The Jungle* (1906), which
revealed the squalor and misery endemic to the Chicago meat-packing
industry. In a sense, it could be said that *The Waste Land* is part of this
same American tradition (Eliot's home town of St Louis was one of
Steffens's case studies in *The Shame of the Cities*), where the whole
point is to make the implicit Utopianism explicit, juxtaposing an
idealised London past with its sordid present. The same essential trope
also forms the basis of Joyce's *Ulysses*, coming to the fore, for
instance, in the National Library scene, where there is a vivid recre-
ation of a day in Elizabethan London when *Hamlet* is about to be
performed and people from all sections of society – from 'canvas
climbers who sailed with Drake' to the nobility – are flocking to the
theatre. All this energetic activity is contrasted with the state of torpid
and moribund contemporary Dublin.

John Barnie, *The City*

Yet this literary tradition of an implicit urban utopianism lying
beneath a powerfully dystopic surface contrasts vividly with a book
like John Barnie's *The City* (Gomer, 1993), where the city is shown in
all its misery and squalor, but with no sense at all (either stated or
implied) that cities might ever be different from this. The book has
two major sections, both untitled, and indicated simply with roman
numerals 'I' and 'II' respectively. The first section is by far the largest,
taking up seventy-two pages of a book which has eighty-nine pages in
all. The seventy-two pages of Section I comprise sixty untitled pieces,
which are numbered, again in Roman numerals, from 'I' to 'XL'.
The pieces vary in length from a little over a page to just a couple of
lines. All are written margin-to-margin and have the appearance of
prose. The second major division of the book contains fifteen short
lyric poems, mostly of about eight or ten lines. They have slightly
terse, but on the whole fairly conventional, titles, and are not
numbered. The effect of the Roman numerals for the sections in the
first major division of the book is to make a large claim, proclaiming
the public nature of the utterance: Roman numerals are seen on public
monuments and inscriptions, and this is the milieu evoked, which is
always one in which a privileged minority abrogates the right of
voicing the feelings of a silent minority (a city, or a nation, for
instance). As a paratextual device Roman numeration usually signifies
the occupation of the public sphere to voice triumph or tragedy, elegy

or commemoration. In Barnie's sequence, by contrast, each of the
enumerated sections is a brief cameo, often novelistic in technique
(though there is no narrative continuity between one section and
the next), and usually showing something threatening, horrific, or
vapid about the contemporary city. I will quote one of the briefer
pieces in full to try to convey something of the overall atmosphere of
The City:

XIX

– Yer. Think you're clever. bastard. three times round the world,
that's me. Three times round the world. And I wouldn't give
you tuppence. Yer. Keep your travel. Keep your Costa del Sol.
Yer. Keep your charter flights and cruises. Fat bastards going
out all pink. Yer. Coming back brown from a bottle. Yer. Mister
Clever. "Think I'll check the time on my twenty-four hour Rolex
watch." Yer. What's the time in Hong Kong, then. San Fran-
cisco. Yer. Look down your nose at me. Think I'm shite. Yer.
Shite comes from somebody's ass. Yer. What's that make you.

This, obviously, is a verbatim impression of one of those encounters
which take place on buses, tubes and pavements in cities everywhere.
The narrative viewpoint here constructs the reader as the addressee,
studiously avoiding saying anything at all, avoiding eye contact,
concentrating simply on remaining alert to anticipate any sudden
potentially dangerous change of gear in the relentless dialogue-for-
one. Though the word 'narrative' is used here, the piece isn't actually
part of a story. But, at the same time, it isn't simply an extended
metaphor, in the sense in which this term used to be applied (for
instance) to the work of Milton, for the Miltonic extended metaphor
or image is essentially descriptive. The nature of the pieces is best
conveyed by coining a term like 'narrative image' for it, for although
the accosting figure here becomes an image of the dangerous vacuum
which Barnie sees as existing beneath the surface of the city, it is all the
same a *moving image* – a *story-like* progression of events is being
related (through dialogue), even though no story is actually being told.
'Narrative image' therefore seems a useful term to delineate the tech-
nique. Many of the pieces are, in fact, more overtly narratorial than
this one, but all are motivated by a primarily imagistic or metonymic
intent. The same kind of narrative imagery is seen in XX, describing
the demolition of a redundant factory ('The face of the building

ripples with cracks, holds for a moment before the collapse. *Voon*. A sun-flash on glass shatters. Bricks clatter and tinkle'). Disturbed by the crash, rats emerge from the sewers. Again, this is an image with obvious emblematic overtones. The narrativised incident of the demolition flushes out the rats in the sewers, which stand for the 'reality' of the city. When viewed from on high (from a revolving restaurant at the top of the city's highest building) the effect is not a sense of euphoria or excitement, but of moral revulsion (as in the Ferris Wheel scene in Orson Welles's film *Citizen Kane*). Viewed from this height (in XII):

> The city extends to the curve of the horizon. It ends in grey heat and exhaust haze in all directions. It is so vast, one mind cannot comprehend it. It spreads everywhere, lazily. Yet it is turned in on itself as on a complex thought, meditating a problem which, if solved, would have no application.

Here the culmination of the narrative image is a notion of the city as an embodiment of directionless moral torpor – it spreads aimlessly in all directions till it exhausts itself, and teases the mind out of thought. Barnie, too, then, seems to be in agreement with Heaney, Montague and R.S. Thomas that thoughts cannot grow in cities, for the thought here is 'turned in on itself', unable to flower into anything which is of any use.

The overall structure of *The City* consists of a series of cameos or scenes or vignettes, most of which are arranged as a monologue or a mini-narrative. Each presented scene, because of the generic comprehensiveness of the title – the work is called *The City*, not *Berlin*, say, or *Toronto* – demands to be read as an emblem, as a kind of Joycean urban epiphany, nearly all of which reveal some kind of vacuity at the heart of the modern city. VIII, for example, shows passengers boarding a plane and awaiting take-off. Vivaldi is being played over the intercom to soothe the tense atmosphere: this focuses the familiar trope of past/present juxtapositions: the music signifies a more gracious past, whereas the music of our time is the roar of the plane's engines, one of many mechanical noises and inarticulate human sounds which reverberate through the piece. The section ends:

> We bank, so the city slides into my window and the sky glides down into the one across the gangway. We swing round into our course, still climbing. There's no more Vivaldi Music of the

museum. Only the roar of the engines, our own merciless music
out of which we must make our peace.

Many of the pieces trace the build-up of confined, negative tensions
within the city, for instance, XIV, where the hospital patient watches
the build-up of a storm, registering an air of threat and menace ('The
air grows less oppressive but the sky is still dangerous like steel lit
from within') which is frequently replicated in the street scenes which
feature elsewhere in the sequence. Briefly cataloguing such scenes: they
include an encounter with a down-and-out showing the passer-by a
repulsive sore on his hand (IV); a racist monologue in another
encounter (V); an anonymous, nuisance phone-call (XI); petty bully-
ing in a workplace (XVI); another encounter with an abusive stranger
(XIX); an encounter with a wino (XXVI); a monologue from the
perpetrator of a domestic murder (XXVII); and a fundamentalist reli-
gious rant (XXIX). This is not a comprehensive list, and it goes only
halfway through the sequence, but it makes it clear how grim a place
Barnie's generic city is. Indeed, the atmosphere is Zola-esque, and the
implicit philosophy is a variant of Naturalism, defined by J.A. Cuddon
as concerned with 'depicting the social environment [It] dwelt partic-
ularly on its deficiencies and on the shortcomings of human beings'.
For Zola 'lives and actions were determined by environment and
heredity and it was the business of the novelist, as he saw it, to dissect,
to perform an autopsy on life' (A Dictionary of Literary Terms and
Literary Theory, 3rd edn, Blackwell, 1991, p.575). Barnie's rites of
urban autopsy very much fit this pattern, and he seems to see himself
as exposing the inevitable vortex of moral and spiritual degradation
which city conditions produce.

As well as the narrative-image sections, the poem contains some
'discursive' passages in which aspects of the city are discussed in a
register which sometimes suggests the tone of notes made from a soci-
ology textbook, sometimes evokes the elegiac atmosphere of
'Ozymandias', and sometimes strikes a more generalised apocalyptic
note, as in XXV, which begins:

New names for the city. Not urbs or polis, or metro-polis. The
ancient cities flourished vividly as dreams cast against a glare.
Stone lions and winged victories and temple columns. To be
trowelled out of the desert, brushed, picked clean, labelled,
numbered, described, drawn. The ancient cities.

> As for the city now, it has no adequate name. We can hardly start because we do not know where to begin. Many names. That which subsumes us. Within limits, no limits.

These discursive dialogic sections contrast with several which are relentlessly monologic, like the religious ranter of XXIX, the voice on the phone in XXXVIII making a long series of phatic noises ('Mmm. Mm. MmmmYe', etc.), or the eco-conscious urbanite in LVI explaining why his family needs two cars. All these in their different ways seem to suggest minds in tethers. Yet another sub-group is a series of sections in which a voice talks back to the writer, challenging his bleak view of the city. Some of these 'talk-back' sections directly challenge the propositions of the section immediately before, like XXXI, which takes issue with XXX, which had presented a bleak picture of closed city churches with wire mesh over the windows, while (bereft of spiritual enlightenment, presumably) the 'city rushes on, obsessed with its motion', its citizens fatally confined within egocentric, short-term views (*'What about ME'*). In XXXI robust issue is taken with all this:

> I don't think it's daft to ask 'What about me?' He's saying we've abandoned identity in the city. That it all doesn't count. And I didn't like the implication about churches: if they're empty or abandoned it's because in some sense we're free ... And who says the churches are empty? I read that religion's coming back. Not necessarily just Christianity. There's all kinds of approaches to God.

The same robust, talk-back voice features in XXXV, expressing the view that someone with an education ought to be able to say something positive (here the opening and the closing of this section are quoted):

> Your're a canny beggar, aren't you. Trying to confuse people over their faith, undermine their identity. And blame it all on the city. ... The city's not half as bad as you say it is. I've lived here all my life and I don't feel a nonentity. I've never had difficulty believing in me. I think it's a shame that someone with education can't set an example. Your trouble is that you think too much. It'd be far better for you if you got out there and did some good.

The 'talk-back' technique is also used in XVIV and LX, but the problems with it are those which occur whenever a dissenting voice is incorporated into a dialogic structure (such as in Tony Harrison's *V*). A major one is that the dissenting voice is not allowed any moments of hesitation or self-doubt, like those which confirm the intimate subjectivity of the main speaker. 'I've never had any difficulty believing in me', says the talk-back voice, immediately making it impossible for us to believe in (or believe) him/her. The desire to set a decent limit to the ramifications of subjectivity ('Your trouble is you think too much') and to curtail it with action ('It'd be far better for you if you got out there and did some good') necessarily contain it within a skein of novelisation in which it merely exposes its own limitations.

Another group of sections delineate emblematic locales within the city, like VI, which shows a worker descending an iron ladder which leads down into the sewers: the description is graphic: 'The effluent swells here, ripples a supple brown in the light of his torch. A slight steam rises from it, almost as if it were the visible stench, clouding the further recesses of the endless tunnel.' We are then told that 'This man knows more about the city than most. How it lives and breathes on its own. He knows he is its servant, fuelling it, fulfilling its needs. We are not, as we think, its purpose.' Another of these summative urban emblems is XLVI depicting the rubbish tips, with their 'rain-filled ruts and potholes', where 'piles of waste spill out like viscera'. Again there is a sense of some vaguely malign force with a life of its own. The section ends by depicting the waste tip at night:

> The red flicker of a glow from spontaneous combustion deep in the tip. And nosing in plastic yoghurt cups, bean tins, frozen dinner trays, the nimble, furred faces of the rats, with sensitive nostrils, insatiable eyes.

Here again there is an uncomfortable sense of an organism which has a life of its own, a life which is properly embodied, not in human form, but in the form of the constantly foraging rats. The final section, LX, seems to be spoken by one of the talk-back personae, briskly asserting the need to face the future whatever it may bring, and adopting quasi-heroic explorational imagery, suggesting a ship on a voyage into the unknown, or a space probe blasting its way through the atmosphere and into outer space (again, the beginning and the end of the section are quoted here):

Alright. If we're on a journey, let's get going. No use being blind.
Up and go. Cut the weepy eyes and the wishing we'd never left
the quay. The past is dead. Only us-now and the future. ... Stay
on the bridge. Crowd to the bows. Look ahead. Put on the
mask. See through the slit. Dawn's rising. We'll meet it coming
over the treadmill of the Earth.

Since the previous section was a vivid depiction of a shipwreck, this
cheery voice with its sawn-off phrases doesn't carry a great deal of
conviction, especially as it is casually able to accept in an aside that we
are 'Finished as a species. So what.' Hence a reading of this final
section would be that it is criminal not to read the signs, idiotic to turn
away from the writing on the wall which warns of approaching
Armageddon.

Barnie's *The City*, then, is bleak and powerful, and almost
completely despairing. It gains its force partly from what might be
called its counter-subjectivity, that is, from the fact that the voices
which speak in it are not dramatised into personae but resonate eerily
in an urban echo-chamber, a stark metropolitan landscape which we
have seen in film (Chaplin's *Modern Times*, the Vienna sewers in *The
Third Man*, the *Bladerunner* scenario), and indeed in prose literature
(Orwell's *1984*, and Doris Lessing's dysfunctional urban spaces, for
instance) but which poetry has seldom entered. It is difficult to
conceive of a poetic depiction of the city more pessimistic and sombre
than this.

Peter Reading, *Perduta Gente*

And yet, that may be just what we get in Peter Reading's *Perduta
Gente*. In his chapter on Reading in *Deregulated Muse* Sean O'Brien
quotes Dennis O'Driscoll's apt placing of Reading as being starkly
outside the 'evasive miniaturism' of much contemporary verse with its
'Elegies, childhood reminiscences, ironic anecdotes and holiday-
cottage nature poems' (p. 123). O'Brien is not entirely approving here,
insisting, in effect, that poetry does not become important just by
tacking important issues, nor trivial just because it restricts itself to
apparently trivial ones (like childhood reminiscences, for instance).
But his judgement on Reading is that 'It is not that his gloom and
despair are objectionable ... but that his imaginative power seems
whether coincidentally or consequently, limited by his attitudes'

(p. 125). The same judgement should, of course, be considered in the case of Barnie too, but in Reading's case O'Brien's assent to it seems to me pretty well unhesitating, for he writes that 'his immense ingenuity disguises a hollowness at the core, an absence of verbal life, for which no amount of patterning or interior allusion or incorporation of found, borrowed or adapted materials can compensate' (p. 126). This is the proposition I want to test against *Perduta Gente*, but let me raise first the hypothetical case of a poet who, confronted by an appalling reality (the Holocaust, for example), *deliberately* turns off that faculty of 'imaginative power' which is usually the driving force in poetry, and feels that this 'anti-poetic' stance is the only response which does not trivialise or in some way belittle that reality. This is the strategy, for instance, of the Vietnam Memorial in Washington, DC, which abnegates any attempt at graphic pictorial representation, any attempt to provide an emotional or spiritual correlative, and instead consists simply of a deep open tunnel the sides of which are lined with the names of all the American dead. Paradoxically, of course, the effect is deeply moving, which may be considered the result of an artistic effect, but it is so partly because it substitutes the ascetic for the aesthetic. The case of *Perduta Gente* is similar. Confronted with the effects of Thatcherism in British inner cities in the 1980s the poet seems to put the imagination deliberately aside. What he sees is too appalling for poetry, and he takes a total risk with his own poetic reputation by presenting *as* a book of poetry a series of scraps and jottings and strings of verbal obscenities.

Perduta Gente appeared in 1989 at a time when the Conservative government under Margaret Thatcher had been in power for ten years and had won three consecutive general elections. Picked out from the shelves of a bookshop, it seemed the archetypal slim volume of verse in a chastely elegant, mainly white cover, with the title and the author's name in the same typeface and point size, and the publisher's name, Secker & Warburg, in a smaller, italicised face a little above the lower edge. I can still recall the sense of shock I felt on glancing through the contents of the volume (which has no list of contents and no pagination) and realising that a major 'establishment' press had published something far more politically uncompromising than most of the small-press material I had long been familiar with. As intended, lack of pagination makes critical discussion of the writing difficult. In fact, the page is the integral unit – a trend in recent contemporary poetry – which is to say that each page contains a complete item. This

is the first, which depicts a moment emblematic of the period to count-
less thousands of Londoners attending concerts, films or exhibitions at
the South Bank arts centre, of leaving the concert hall or the cinema
in a pleasantly uplifted frame of mind and then being confronted, in
the underpass leading to Waterloo Station, with the first of the 'card-
board cities', where the homeless and the unemployed had set up
primitive living quarters in cardboard boxes:

> South Bank: Sibelius 5's
> incontrovertible end –
> five exhalations, bray of expiry,
>   absolute silence ...

> *Under* the Festival Hall is a foetid
>   tenebrous concert
> strobed by blue ambulance light.
> PVC/newspapers/rags
> insulate ranks of expendables, eyesores,
>   winos, unworthies,
> one of which (stiff in its cardboard Electrolux
>   box stencilled **FRAGILE,**
> **STOW THIS WAY UP, USE NO HOOKS)**
> officers lug to the tumbril,
>   exhaling, like ostlers, its scents:

>   squit,

>   honk,

>   piss,

>   meths,

>   distress.

The force of the juxtaposition is evident: again, two cities are
contrasted, an ideal and an actual, but instead of mapping them on to
the dichotomy of past and present, both concerts are here and now,
the musical masterpiece with its Romantic transcendence, and the
subterranean nightmare in which people are treated with less care than

material goods, like animals at best. Strangely, though, art and
aesthetics are less abjured than at first seems the case; the 'high' verbal
register used ('incontrovertible', 'exhalations', etc.) is consonant with
the subject matter in the first four lines – bluntly, using words like
these is an indication that your birth or your education will probably
protect you from ever sharing the fate of those depicted in the rest
of the poem. But in the remainder the use of this register (as when
reference is made to a 'tenebrous concert', or a literary, 'interrupting',
form of syntax is used, as in 'exhaling, like ostlers, its scents') is
strangely at odds with the content, so that the *language* seems to lack
sympathy with the subject matter. It is puzzling, too, that the language
retains its formalities, being punctiliously punctuated (those commas
after 'squit', 'honk' and so on, for instance), so that the very 'correct-
ness' of the usage seems to draw attention to the sheer pointlessness
of these punctuation points. Likewise, there is an over-arching poetic
shape to the piece, which gives us two concerts, two exhalations, and
so on.

Yet it is not the fact of the persistence of the 'shaping' impulse in
the face of such material which is surprising, but rather the puzzling
way in which these features are sometimes used. The material includes
found-text 'realia' (such as snippets from newspapers and advertise-
ments presented in facsimile, holograph pages torn out of a notebook
depicting a kind of *Down and Out in Paris and London* among termi-
nal winos and drop-outs, and typed pages ripped from secret govern-
ment reports on the effects of radiation). The people shown are social
and economic victims, but also the victims of viciously self-destructive
addictions (to rough cider, meths, surgical spirit, bottle-bank cocktails,
melted down boot polish, Brasso). But the voice also emphasises that
the state of victimhood is potentially classless in a society without
safety-nets, in which the economic and industrial base of society had
been transformed in less than a generation (a quarter of a million
mining jobs disappeared in the twenty years from 1979 to 1999, for
instance):

> [And don't think it couldn't be *you*:
> grievously wounded veteran of the
>   Battle of Bottle,
>   jobless, bereft of home, skint,
>   down in the cold uriniferous subway
>   spattered with drooled spawl,

lying in layers of newspaper ironies –
        Property Prices,
smug To the Editor platitudes on The
        Vagrancy Issue,
    ads for Gonzalez Byass;
dosser with Top Man carrier-bag, en-
        swathed in an *FT*;
Gizzera quiddora fiftyfer fuggsay,
        bankrupted, I been,
    fugginwell bankrupted, me;
    dolent, the wail from the Tube;
and don't think it couldn't be *you*.]

This kind of 'in-your-face' *verité* material, however, is 'crossed' with
literary echoes which try to convey the pathos of destroyed lives. At
one point an image of dossers and winos huddled round a fire draws
visual imagery from films like Tarkovsky's, with accompanying sound-
track, and from the lament for a vanished past which is found in Old-
English poems like 'The Wanderer' and 'The Seafarer':

Distant, a plangently-played balalaika ac-
        companies wailing
    vocals whose burden is loss –
Gone are the youthfully beautiful whom I
        loved in my nonage;
    strength and vitality gone
    roof-tree and cooking-hearth, gone.

Thus, the poet's determination to enter the Lower Depths of the city is
tempered with these strains of antique pastoral deprivation, in which
solitaries and outcasts lament their lot. The tone of biblical lamenta-
tion for the sacked city mercifully takes the edge off the documentary
tour of the underworld with Reading as our Virgil ('How doeth the
citie sit solitarie that/ *was* full of people? She that was great among
nations hath no/ comforter'). When Virgil motions to us to descend
further into the horrors, we can try to believe that it is, like Dante's,
only a dream ('Sometimes it seems like a terrible dream from/ which
we'll awaken; but mostly it seems that we won't'). So we are
summoned to continue ('Let us descend, though, through urinous
subways to/ miseries greater'), and they are greater because they are

the sufferings of 'the newly tormented', that is, of those who have only
recently slipped down into this world (when the Bailiffs arrive at three
in the morning to evict them from the squats they had been living in
since losing a job, as in one of the pieces). We might have assumed that
anyone who can insert commas in the correct places in a text is
unlikely ever to be in this down-and-out position, except in the kind
of journalistic witness role that Reading plays here, just as anyone
who has learned the skills needed to analyse *King Lear* will always
have an escape route (or root, perhaps) from the working-class
seaward terraces (see Matt Simpson in the Liverpool chapter) or the
soon-to-be demolished tenements (see Edwin Morgan in the final
chapter). But Reading insists that new post-industrial employment
patterns have meant a radical extension of socially coercive anxiety.
The dispossessed 'other' could, after all, easily become none other
than ourselves.

Ken Smith, *Fox Running* and 'The London Poems'

Ken Smith's earliest major incursion into urban territory was the
sequence *Fox Running*, first published in 1980, and included in
revised and extended form in *The Poet Reclining: Selected Poems
1962–1980* (Bloodaxe, 1982). The poem is often highly praised; Neil
Corcoran, for instance, calls it 'outstanding' in *English Poetry Since
1940* (Longman, 1993, p. 153), but only mentions it in passing, as a
prelude to a discussion of Dunn and Harrison. The fox in the poem
is itself a textual palimpsest, partly a version of the dispossessed
protagonists of the Anglo-Saxon poems 'The Wanderer' and 'The
Seafarer' again, (first encountered by Ken Smith as an English student
at the University of Leeds), but partly, also, a Hughesian fox. The
Hughesian tone which is very marked throughout this piece is indi-
cated in the title: the animal persona (the urban fox) which is the
writer's *doppelganger* in the poem is related to Hughes's 'Thought
Fox', a poem for which Smith has expressed great admiration.[6]
Indeed, and to his chagrin, Anthony Thwaite's *Twentieth-century
English Poetry: An Introduction* (Heinemann Educational, 1978)
lumped him in with 'the Tribe of Ted', but that bad moment was
beneficial in helping Smith to identify the anomaly of the long-term
city-dweller poet whose work lends itself to unproblematic incorpora-
tion under the 'nature' slot:

I was annoyed to be classified and pigeon-holed as a minor partic-
ipant, but that was also a warning to get out of this 'nature' slot ...
it also alerted me to fight this tendency even more. I realised at the
time that I had been writing a pastoral nostalgic lament for the
country, whereas in fact I was a townsman. I remember realising
this and deliberately forcing myself to look at the place I lived in,
to look at the city around me, and to work from that rather than
reflective old memory. (Interview, p. 10)

The Hughesian residue of *Fox Running* is, all the same, substantial
and quite frequently detrimental. Raw mentions a 'sense of driving,
vehement plain-chant, of nominal and participle phrases being
jammed together shorn of elaboration and connectives by narrative
urgency and commitment' (p. 11). But the idiom disconcertingly
imports the linguistic quirks of Hughes's ultimately monotonous
animal-inner-monologue register (dropping the definite or indefinite
article, for instance, and using lots of very short sentences beginning
with 'And'). Smith in the interview claims a quasi-romantic bedrock
for his chosen linguistic register, suggesting that it is 'a sort of English
ur speech, most of it spoken, much of it non-educated ... going all the
way back to the Germanic'), but one could argue (rather unkindly)
that this is really an educated writer's notion of how such a speech
might sound; how it sounds, in fact, is *writerly*, which is to say, not
spoken at all but written, and, to be specific, written by Ted Hughes.
An example from almost anywhere in the sequence will serve:

> And I've thrown my keys
> on the railroad tracks.
>
> And I'm gone.
>
> And I'm Fox, running out.
> *Into holes under leaves across water.*
>
> So far on the hill
> and no running back to the treeline,
> on in the open.
>
> Fox: hidden in landscape,
> visible on it. I run
> and my sleep is a dream of running.

Between that and waking
I've glimpsed between fern
and heron's wing the old life. (p.150)

This idiom is too much focused on 'the old life', and at moments the voice, as if inadvertently, becomes that of Hughes's crow: 'today I'm crow/ adrift/ wingbeat on wingbeat/ split vision/ across wet slates/ lopped plane trees/ hated somehow// the rainbird of Finsbury' (p.155). The key question, I think, is whether the animal persona actually helps at all in this enterprise of registering and exploring urban experience. The problem is, perhaps, that the very driving, vehement plainsong which the animal persona seems to validate drives too fast and fluently when the need is for some expression of hesitation, confusion, and uncertainty. The homogenous identity of the wily-scavenger-outsider is too comprehensive an alibi: the poem is at its best, therefore, when the plain chant falters, the animal-personaic mask slips, and the voice is at a loss and says so, unable to solve the ever-present register problem – 'Word// I want a word/ a beginning word forming in its water bead' (p. 161). Even here, the temptation to lapse back into animal imagery is always close, and to do so can impart a false sense of take-off into the driving lilt, 'I want a word with a gull's lift/ and easy shadow/ I want a word with a bat's inaudible sound/ I want a word like a snail/ round and round the rim of a glass/ I want a word for these days these miles/ these trains this distance/ the wanderer covers aloof/ on the star-glinting rails'.

Where the voice slips out of this idiom, it often does so through naming London districts, shifting from urban 'setting' to urban 'geography', from urban-generic to urban-specific, so that the urban fox's alter-ego, an outlawed figure riding the Tube for warmth, for activity, is envisaged as trapped on a Circle Line which is seen as one of the circles of Dante's Hell. (It is, says Sean O'Brien, 'a contemporary version of Hell, with the Tube map as Virgil and no overarching theology to redeem the plight' (*Dergulated Muse*, p. 83). The bleak registering of the cityscape seen from the tube, the railway embankments intermittently lit by short-circuiting sparks from the wheels of the electric trains, is a scenario of absence and traces:

Surbiton Norbiton Sanderstead
blue scatter of sparks
smokey embankment flowers

ownerless back lots of flats
Langham Court Riverdale
in Sledhurst and Streatham
and Gypsy Hill sniffing
amongst the paper plates
the Wonderloaf wrapper detritus
in Hammersmith sniffing the amyl
where I lost sight
lost my name lost my number
my ticket (p.162)

Here, the London postal districts, which Larkin in 'The Whitsun Weddings' curiously saw in rural terms as stacked sheaves of corn, are irredeemably re-urbanised, even if they are still metaphorical too (the journey on the Circle Line is also the individual's lifecycle, from the red form of the birth certificate to the black form of the death certificate – 'his last account cleared/ his black form/ filed with his red form', p. 160), yet the poem is at this point notably hybrid, quite literally, in that it's a fox which is sniffing amongst the Wonderloaf wrappers, but a man who has lost his ticket. The problem with the fox motif is the need to keep making this transition between the tenor and the vehicle of the metaphor. At this point the join is assured and effective, but what use is the fox motif when the seeing eye moves into close-up on one of these districts and expresses a *social* concern, quite out of key with the romanticised 'outlaw-fox' viewpoint, and attempting to delimit, from an anti-racist, anti-Thatcherite viewpoint, a specific late 1970s, early 1980s London scene:

stepping out in the cool skinhead wind
into NF occupied country
to Lambeth evicted boarded-up

through Pakkibashers' Court
through Martin Webster Gardens
to Brick Lane to Bethnal Green

dreaming London Fields and Hackney Downs
spaces between other spaces
states or conditions of mind
a man in a yard bouncing a ball
way down Thatcherland

past the closed-down clinic
and the short-staffed school
such a vision of the street (p. 163)

The Hughesian fox persona, quite obviously, could never with any
plausibility notice such things as closed-down clinics and under-staffed
schools, and what could its super-charged Darwinian perspective
possibly have to say about racist attacks, 'NF occupied country' or
evictions in Lambeth? Hence, what we see in the poem is a consider-
able strain imposed on the central 'fox running' motif. I don't think
that this kind of strain is really a surprise: after all, other city poems
have set themselves a similarly neat metaphorical and imagistic agenda
for depicting their city and then found it impossible to keep to: in *The
Waste Land*, for instance, there is ostensibly a similar kind of all-
containing motif, that of the blind-seer Tiresias whose vision suppos-
edly encompasses the whole poem, as Eliot's note claims, though in
practice this is clearly not true to most readers' notion of the poem.
Smith has Eliot's example in mind in his search for an urban register
('such a vision of the street' quotes Eliot's 'Preludes', of course, and
this line is used elsewhere in the poem), and one sign of the registerial
uncertainty of the sequence is the number of such echoes it contains;
a non-comprehensive round-up would include a touch of the DTs
(Dylan Thomas) in 'the rattling milk bottle dawn' (p. 131); Peter
Porter in 'Your attention please' (p. 133); Simon and Garfunkle in
'turning up his coat in rain' (p. 139). But the dominant echoes are
those of Hughes and Eliot; Sean O'Brien strangely discounts the latter,
remarking in an introductory list of influences on Smith that 'the
usually central figures of Eliot and Auden simply don't apply' (p. 81).
However, the Eliot who figures is often the post-*Waste Land* Eliot,
where a certain radical simplification of vocabulary combined with
patterns of repetition give a kind of liturgical solemnity, as in:

Between the image and the image
and the next motion of the image
Between the seer and the seen

Between the moment and the moment
Between the next and the next
Between denial and the fact

Between the running and the running
Comes the memory the space
Comes the man with the ball
Comes the one still space
for a brief time
in the city (pp. 141–2)

Here the fox has run without stopping out of a Ted Hughes poem and headlong into *Four Quartets*. Between these extremes it tries out other voices, sometimes very self-consciously as in this passage (of a section prefaced '*Fox writes:*'): 'Midnight. Clocks shedding/ at variable distance the several sounds/ of another night halving the planet/ is one fancy English way to say it' (p. 142). This distancing and ironising is mainly interesting in the way it implies the integrity and authenticity of everything in the poem which isn't overtly put down in this way. For instance, the 'rattling milk bottle dawn' cited earlier is not explicitly ironised as 'one fancy Welsh way to say it', so are we to presume the author unaware of the echo and, as it were, pleased with the effect of this line? Elsewhere, there is a running image of the tube lines as the 'underground veins of the city' through which the trains shift stale winds. This works well at a mimetic level, evoking the distant whoosh of forward compression which presages the imminent arrival of the underground train; but also at a metaphorical level, imaging enclosure and suggesting an eco-system which is approaching stagnation by having to ingest its own waste products (the two words in 'stale winds' collocate with deliberate incongruity). Also, the word 'veins' animates the city in a notion of a vast subterranean giant. But these lines are also undeniably 'fancy', overtly 'poetic' in a register which some poets might hesitate to use without the kind of ironic disclaimer about fancifulness which Smith uses elsewhere. The question of linguistic authenticity, once raised by a poet, as Smith raises it when he condemns some of his lines as 'fanciful', can never be localised and contained but will spread silently to everything in the poem, for the implication is that there is a poetic language which is plain, straight, authentic, natural and true, and the inevitable question of any line will be 'Is this it?'.

My own sense is that it would be much better not to raise the matter explicitly at all, for there is plenty in the powerful opening of the poem to open up several layers of suggestiveness, as the Hughesian

fox-on-the-run runs into the pre-dawn city from its rural habitat,
following the constantly re-used lines of communication:

> Fox
> running
> loose in his sleek skin
> loose in his slick fur
>
> Fox
> between lamp dark and daylight
> loping through the suburbs
> miles bridges canals rails
>
> Through the town littorals
> chicken runs long bricked over
> wild places put to the plough
>
> Streets keeping their tilt
> and curve of old lanes
> over Crouch Hill into Seven Sisters (p. 130)

Here the view is chronologically 'panoramic', envisaging a process of
constant change and re-use: first the wild land becomes ploughed land
('wild places put to the plough'), then the ploughed land disappears
under the newly built streets of the city, but not completely, since
the shapes keep the 'tilt/ and curve of old lanes' (as Blake says, 'the
fields beneath lie sleeping'). It goes on to register shifts in the cityscape
as the journey moves on inward, and in districts like Hampstead
and Paddington it is not rows of cheap red-brick houses which
predominate, but well-to-do villas in expensive 'galt' brick (the 'grey
yellow bricks' mentioned here, p. 130). The houses are the flat-fronted
Georgian 'desirable period residences' (p. 131) of Nash's Regent's
Park, the gardens having boat slips on to the Regent's Canal, rather
than commonplace Victorian bay-windowed terraces. All this has a
precision of observation – the architectural details will check out
against standard works like Stefan Muthesius's *The English Terraced
House* (Yale University Press, 1982) – and any temptation towards
fancifulness (which of course includes the question of whether or not
its language is fanciful) is screened out. In a word, the language
achieves in the end a memorable poise and confidence, the steady
nerve and sustained linguistic discipline which the long poem requires.

Ken Smith's other major urban piece is the sequence 'The London Poems', a group of thirty short poems which are part of his 1986 collection *Terra*, published by Bloodaxe. The poems are formally very tight, all being twelve-line 'curtal sonnets' (as Hopkins might have called them), each consisting of three quatrains, and there is a sense that this rigid textual architecture is a negative counterpart of the Isle of Dogs, with its inner-city decay of the run-down Docklands near which the poet was living at the time they were composed. The poems are prefaced with two stark black-and-white photographs of the decayed, partly demolished dock estate, and the sequence registers the moral panic of the time formented by the 'inner city' riots which were the product of the 'no turning back' hard-line Thatcherite economic policy that allowed the rapid industrial decline which Ken Smith's poems confront. The first poem, 'After Mr Mayhew's visit' conflates the visits to the East End of the Victorian reformer Henry Mayhew (author of *London Labour and the London Poor*, 1864) with the well-publicised 'fact-finding' visits by cabinet ministers to suffering districts (Michael Heseltine's to Liverpool was the most skilfully handled) which inevitably evoked echoes of the past, like the helpless 'Something must be done' reaction of the hapless Prince of Wales on seeing the effect of unemployment in the 1930s. 'So now the Victorians are all in heaven', the poem begins, evoking the 1980s Tories' 'Victorian values' propaganda with ironic intent in the setting of the decayed Victorian industrial heartland. The tone of the visit is paternalistic, like (to take yet another retro-parallel) the King and Queen touring the blitzed East End during the Second World War; the vicar and 'the young conservatives' are 'visiting again/ the home for incurables who never die' (p. 53). The despair is pretty well total: 'The old damp soaks through the wallpaper ... Only this time it never ends: ... the brandy flask stands empty, and the poor/ are pushing to the windows like the fog' (p. 53). The air of listless inactivity is pervasive: in poem four, 'Movies after midnight', 'From Canning Town to Woolwich/ the tall cranes rust. The pub's shut/ and the lift's out in the towerblock,/ everything you see is up for sale' (p. 54). The economic mechanisms which produce the new waste land are strangely absent from the poem: the land is blighted as if by an ailing Fisher King or an inadvertently sinning Oedipus, and what you get is simply what you get. As Arthur Miller said of 1929, representing the victims' sense of utter helplessness in the face of 'Depression', or what was called in the jargon of the 1980s an 'economic down-turn', 'It was our Greek year – the gods had spoken'. The very ability to reason, to calculate, to *compose*, in the widest sense of the word, is beggared at the sight of this plague – 'Even the prime numbers are giving up,/ all the best words have moved to Surrey/ and we have just a few at discount now/ to make farewells that vanish with us' (p. 54). A silent force appropriates not just the means of communication, but its content; the 'government is known as *sh*,/ they own the miles of wire, the acids/ that devour forests and white words out,/ and they are listening in the telephone' (poem five, 'In Silvertown, chasing the dragon', p. 55). The sense of disempowerment is carried through to its logical conclusion as the very sense of self disappears: in 'Movies after midnight' there are 'farewells than vanish with us', and in 'In Silvertown', 'we are all going away now/ into some other dimension'. The self's interpellation is cancelled, and subjectivity held in abeyance. What is happening is that 'our' territory has been annexed, and is being re-mapped according to plans which are not revealed to us: on what had been familiar home territory we are no longer at home. In 'Beyond hope and the Lea River' (poem six): 'My friend Napoleon visits Farina's Cafe. /There is no message. He meets no one./ It is mysterious because there is no mystery/ but Napoleon is now in the house of numbers' (p.55). What they have in store for us we can't know, but soon we won't even recognise the streets we used to live in:

> We are entering the capital of a lesser empire
> where the plans of our masters surface betimes –
> pins on a map at the Ministry of Natural Calamities,
> and the statistics like crisp new folding money. (p. 55)

These two quatrains from 'Beyond Hope and the Lea River' illustrate both the technique and perhaps a problem with it. Each quatrain in each poem delineates a separate element in a kaleidoscope, usually with a formal syntactic integrity, so that each begins with a capital letter and ends with a full stop. The picture of the 'slow workless docklands going cheap' ('Clipper Service') is stalled and static; appropriately, the observer of this waste land (like Eliot's) 'can connect nothing with nothing', and is just an observer, living perhaps 'too much by the eye', like Roy Fisher's persona in his *City*, and needing to be told the most basic facts about the place. He listens like a curiously mature grown-up boy from the Victorian genre painting 'Raleigh's Boyhood' as the old men tell him about the ships that used to dock here and the bustle there used to be in these streets – 'Ships there were son,/ and lascars, then as now the afternoon/ brought sulphur on the wind and no comfort' (p. 56). Here (in 'Clipper Service') the register shifts curiously from one representing the yarning, informing old man ('Ships there were son,/ and lascars'), to an omniscient-persona voice which uses the sad, slightly 'droopy' (Hardyesque 'Coppice Gate') tone of the pained-but-resigned observer who is omnipresent in English poetry at least since Gray's 'Elegy', and whose voice is a kind of fused composite of Hardy, Eliot and Larkin: the lines 'then as now the afternoon/ brought sulphur on the wind and no comfort' are clearly in this composite register. In the final stanza this voice takes over and seems always already to know everything: 'Now the natives are proud and scattered/ and lonely in the high rises, living/ as they always lived: thieving or work/ when there's work. There's none now' (p. 56). Yet the poet's right to appropriate even this earnest middle-class voice (eager to alleviate suffering without transforming the conditions which produce it, like Henry Mayhew, like the Jacob Riis of *How the Other Half Lives*) is perhaps questionable, and the next poem seems to dwell on this matter of uncertainty of register, playing with the widespread unease about how to compose an answerphone message (brisk? jokey? ironic?). The poem begins 'Your protagonist is not at home just now./ He's out, a one way window in his head'. The one way window suggests the tinted mirror glass windows of the postmodern buildings which are going up throughout Docklands, and there is an edgy atmosphere of anticipated confrontation (an alarm bell left ringing, a signboard banging in the night, and so on). But this protagonist's engagement seems somewhat thin, a rapid trying on of various roles, first (in 'Unfinished Portrait') a tramp ('Today I'm Red Rover, late the Queen's/ Own Leicester Square Irregulars, DSO/ and several bars', p. 57), but one envisaged as a kind of licensed fool, mocking and miming the codes and linguistic registers of the 'straight' world ('Henceforth I shall speak basic and fortran') and ribbing tube officials by responding to the notice 'Dogs must be carried' at the foot of escalators with 'excuse me sir I don't have a dog to walk'. The end of the poem metamorphoses this character into something more sinister – 'I'm primed, armed, fused, and now I'll tick/ till I go off. Think of me as a deterrent' (p. 57), but this, I think, is to glamorise exclusion and misrepresent it as dissent. In other poems the delineated experience is that of a poet-persona whose life is lived less close to the edge than this, annotating a quarrel between two lovers in 'Leaving the

Angel' (the Angel is a tube station) and overhearing women's conver-
sation in 'At the Barbican' and joining in with a wryly self-regarding
run-down of male braggadocio. In 'The talk at the big house' the focus
shifts back to a kind of 'X-Files' scenario in which 'they' continue their
sinister covert operations to take over 'our' territory ('By nightfall
when they hope no-one's looking/ the paramilitaries are out shifting
fences/ dressed in each other's uniforms', p. 59). The scenario is
powerful, and the prettifying surrealist veil isn't allowed to conceal
completely the underlying brutality ('The dissidents are hosed down
hour on hour,/ the guitar player's fingers smashed by rifle butts',
p. 59).

All the same, what remains puzzling is the attitude embodied here
towards what existed before the 'paramilitaries' moved in and began
shifting the fences. Indeed, the same question arises in the case of Iain
Sinclair's dealings with the same territories (the territory, to be precise
of his *Lights Out for the Territory*). Is the ground before its commer-
cial despoiliation viewed as an industrial 'organic community', an East
End 'manor' where 'diamond geezers' weave and dodge to turn an
honest penny, and villains like the Krays and the likes of 'Mad'
Frankie Frazer provide the local colour? But the Isle of Dogs before it
became 'Docklands' should not be viewed, in 'dark-pastoral' mode, as
a kind of working-class heritage site. It was from here, for instance,
that the London dockers set off to march to Westminster in support of
Enoch Powell's racist 'rivers of blood' speech in 1968. In Smith's
'Clipper Service', discussed earlier, the older voice who remembers the
ships and the lascars may well be one of these, content that the
'lascars' should crew the ships of the British-India Line and the P&O
(below officer-level only, and in segregated shipboard living space),
but drawing the line at having them permanently 'here' (like Powell's
Wolverhampton constituent whose views on how the 'black man'
would soon hold the whip over the white were quoted by Powell in
his speeches). If crime and bigotry are largely the result of social depri-
vation, then middle-class and educated nostalgia for this landscape
would be problematical, and we could legitimately expect this tension
to be registered in urban poetry. It may be that the already-noted
unease over matters of register is the surface turbulence which
indicates the spot where such matters have been buried. At any rate,
this issue of register confronts the urban poet everywhere; poem
fourteen, 'Dosser', for instance, might have been called (say) 'Tramp',
but that word suggests a predominantly rural and benign figure (as a

child I read *William and the Tramp* with pleasure, but a children's book called *William and the Dosser* is inconceivable). The dosser is ineluctably urban and undeniably menacing, though the poem quickly reduces him to a semi-comical figure who presents himself in mock serious social-worker jargon ('I *am* says he *an exploited human being*', p. 59): here even the inverted speech-tag ('says he' instead of 'he says') is a subtle put-down by the narrating voice, for this is the way utterances are tagged in a comic anecdote or recitation. Likewise, the men at Charing Cross in 'cardboard apartments' rather than 'cardboard boxes' are oddly ironised by this tone – if one of them had nothing but a bucket this register would call it an en-suite bathroom. But then, they are being ironised from a wider 'over-arching' viewpoint available to the middle-class speaker, who points out that 'every man jack of them/ upholds the free flow of market forces,/ weary with his tale of dull misfortune' (p. 59). Curiously, that phrase 'every man jack of them' (which seems to require a disdainful snort for its adequate performance) would be unavailable if they were estate agents, or Lecturers in English – 'man jacks' only occur in stations of life lower than one's own. Of course, I am not here accusing Ken Smith of *feeling* such disdain: what I am pointing to is the enormous difficulty of finding a 'true' register for the job of urban delineation which this poetry is trying to do. The dosser's final bequest of his plastic bags 'in lieu of taxes to the nation that bore me' is more obviously *dialogic*, in that it clearly isn't trying to represent what such a person would actually say, but is rather a mixture of a 'seeing' voice and a 'saying' voice, speaking in double register, enabling the use of the word 'nation', linked with the image of a mother, and hence drawing bitter attention to the social 'orphanhood' in which this person has lived.

The sequence continues with an attempt at some comprehensiveness of social picture: in 'Slow dancer's epitaph' a 'Black boy', out of work and enlisted, is killed in a heat-seeking missile attack on a ship: in 'The house of the androgynes' a presumably straight 'we' are invited to an exotic-seeming flat where 'they' ('which [is] wife,/ which husband, that we never figure out', p. 60) intrigue and apparently baffle an 'us', which it is taken for granted will include the reader. Several of the poems depict encounters on late-night tube trains: in 'Tube talk', 'She tells him her dream, she arrives/ with a suitcase full of her poems/ she's not written yet, her initials/ in cursive tooled in the leather' (p, 61). The aspirant poet – a distinct metropolitan type – is a counterpart of 'Your friend the drifter' (the title of another of the poems), all with their inner scenario which they have merely to translate now into actual words on a page or rolls of movie film – 'Some work up cures for new diseases,/ ... Others are mapping the new dictatorships, others the movies they will make of them' (p. 62). The speaker dreams of materialising as the longed-for producer with the film-deal, the dealer with the offer that will change a life 'I have a deal for you. I'm your imaginary friend.' Again, such dreams of personal success and transformation are distinctly metropolitan, as opposed to merely urban, and again there are difficulties of tone here; in what tone of voice, exactly, should the published poet write about the perhaps talentless aspirant poet who has everything but the words? A note of 'there but for the grace of god' will hardly wash; nor can the implied conviction that 'talent will out' be offered in the context of a poem which, among other things, condemns as a sham the Thatcherite meritocracy which consigns the weakest to re-housing (or no housing) elsewhere a long way away from valuable redevelopment sites, where a sense of self quickly begins to fade like an inadequately fixed photographic print. The reaction to such dilemmas is partly to brush them aside, to imagine apocalyptic urban destruction, in which all such distinctions will become irrelevant, as in 'The window of vulnerability', which imagines an *Enola Gay* speeding towards the city to destroy it, and the aftermath of capitulation aboard a *USS Missouri* (where the Japanese surrender was signed on 2 September 1945). The debris after the bombing ('these postal districts/ drifting downwind', p. 63) is envisaged, and the poem ends with one of several images of self-loss which permeate this sequence, as bombers merge in a common loss of identity ('flying home till there's no home to fly to', p. 63). These images may, of course, be open to same objection as Sylvia Plath's use of images of the Holocaust to delineate her personal suffering: the Japanese material seems to continue through to the next poem, where the phrase 'We are perhaps/ the last citizens of an imaginary country' (p. 64) recalls the famous self-description of the Japanese novelist Yasunari Kawabata that he was, after the war, a 'citizen of a lost country'. 'The Soldier's Tale' continues to use the Second World War image, occasioned, presumably, by the frequent suggestion that regions like the Isle of Dogs were 'blitzed' for a second time, by the bulldozers of the 1980s. But the soldier's tale can hardly be adequate to female rather than male experience, and in 'Absolutely no selling' another chance encounter on public transport is recorded, '*I don't work* she says on the top deck/ in machine talk in a little girl voice' (p. 66). The problem of voice, and delineating it, remains, and is encountered again in 'The Botanic Garden Oath', alluding, of course, to Ashbery's *The Tennis Court Oath*, and the problem is shelved as the poet opts for a kind of defensive whimsy ('I've joined the Rupert Bear School of Poetry'). The botanic garden setting seems to betray a pastoral longing, heightened in 'Not talking on the Circle line' – 'maybe I'll just wander off like Lao-tse/ and disappear beyond the western frontier' (p. 67). This poem is addressed 'to Judi', and the last one in the sequence opts for fulfilment in romantic love in a transatlantic elsewhere, to which the speaker is connected by the 'sea cables at the bottom of the heart'. The narrowing of focus in this poem ('Give us peace and to eat') suggests a drastic opt-out which threatens to reduce the whole of this city sequence to a kind of emotional tourism, in which extremes of self-loss and social dislocation are merely sampled, and then turned away from to a much more familiar romantic pastoralism. Of course, this is not to accuse Ken Smith (whose long-term writer-in-residency attachment to Wormwood Scrubbs Prison would make any such accusation ridiculous) of personal dereliction of some social duty. Again, what I am pointing to is the difficulty of solving the poetic problems presented by this urban material. A sequence has to seem to go somewhere, and must shift and modulate as it progresses, hence, it makes a distinct turn into the romantic pastoral which provides the needed sense of closure. But in doing so it merely tacks an unlikely 'happy ending' on to a scenario which seemed to be heading in quite other directions. In the end, the problem might be that the narrator is too *homodiegetic* in this piece, too much part of the story he tells.

Notes

1 For Eric Mottram's own account of this period see 'The British Poetry Revival, 1960–75', pp. 15–50 in Robert Hampson and Peter Barry, eds, *New British Poetries: The Scope of the Possible*, Manchester University Press, 1993.

2 When the Mottram party at the Poetry Society was finally voted out of office by the members, it was seen as a clash between urban and rural cultures. Proxy or postal voting was not permitted, and it was said that those who passed the vote at the crucial meeting had never been seen before at Poetry Society events, but were 'country' members from the

Shires and the Home Counties who had been seen before the meeting emerging from Earls Court tube station with maps and asking directions in the street.

3 Their main availability now is through such places as the Arts Council's Poetry Library at the Royal Festival Hall, London, the Small Press Collection of the Library of University College, London, and the major copyright libraries, such as the British Library, at St Pancras, London, and the National Library of Wales at Aberystwyth.

4 Catalogue details are given as Deutsche-Grammophon DG 2740 106.

5 See *Angel Exhaust, 11*, review of *The Tempers of Hazard*.

6 See 'The Godfather of the new poetry', interview with Ken Smith by Colin Raw, Bloodaxe Books catalogue, 1998–99, pp. 8–11.

Part 2
Local specifics

5 'North of the Word' or 'Why, this is Hull'

The idea of there being a *group* of Hull poets – as distinct from just *the* Hull poet (Philip Larkin) and 'Hull's other poet' (Douglas Dunn) – was a notion first made current nationally with the publication of *A Rumoured City, New Poets from Hull* (ed. Douglas Dunn, Bloodaxe) in 1982.[1] The 'Hull' presence on the national poetry map was further consolidated when two of the nine contributors to *A Rumoured City* brought out individual first collections soon after: Peter Didsbury's *The Butchers of Hull* appeared in 1982 and Sean O'Brien's *The Indoor Park* in 1983, both published by Bloodaxe. Didsbury and O'Brien have remained prominent 'third-generation' Hull poets, but there has never really been a Hull 'school', and their poetic strategies differ crucially and symptomatically.[2] Indeed, the two can be seen as representative of two different kinds of postmodernism, and their work collectively raises the question of whether postmodernism in British poetry grows out of dominant tendencies from the 1970s and early 80s, or whether, on the contrary, it represents a decisive break from what preceded it.[3] One reason for centring this enquiry on Hull is that notions of what constitute crucial trends in recent British poetry were greatly influenced by the anthology *The Penguin Book of Contemporary British Poetry*, edited by Andrew Motion and Blake Morrison, which appeared in 1982, soon after Motion had completed a four-year stint as a lecturer at Hull University, and in the same year as *A Rumoured City*. The latter offered a rather different picture, a kind of regional counterblast to the 'metropolitan' version of contemporary poetry set up by Motion and Morrison. Together, the two books marked out possible directions for British verse, with Hull as their common pivot. If we can come to an adequate understanding of what was at stake poetically in 1982 – the year of the two anthologies, and the year in which notions of British national identity were being starkly polarised and contested in the Falklands War – then we will understand a good deal of what has happened to British poetry since then.

In his introduction to *A Rumoured City* Dunn downplays any suggestion that the work included is regional or provincial in nature ('my contributors detest the prospect of being labelled "provincial"', he tells us, p. 14), but there is an uneasy jocularity about the tone as he continues 'Reader, they are probably less provincial than you are, even if they live, or have lived, in a city which has a fondness for the parochial' (p. 14).[4] The note of simultaneous affirmation and denial is repeated, as Dunn both praises the isolation of the city ('Hull has a marginal, provisional, almost frontier quality', he begins, p. 11) while at the same time denying its provinciality. The effect of the place is not to draw attention to itself, but rather to induce in the poet a certain inwardness and introspection: Hull, he says, 'leads a writer to meditate on the rag and bone shop of the heart' (p. 11), and in Didsbury's work 'the act of imagining appears to be laid bare ... as much as the objects which his imagination serves' (p. 14). Dunn's point amounts to saying that the city does not figure in the work of these poets in a merely documentary way: in the case of O'Brien 'Hull slides into his poems unbidden, as it does in ... Didsbury's: it amounts to an unforced seizure of images which are to hand *and which have been lived through by more than the eye*' (p. 15, my italics). So a sensitivity to accusations of provincialism often seems to rule out the direct depiction of the local. Further, instead of dealing just with 'Hull', the Hull poet's ambition is to engage with 'Englishness'. Indeed, Dunn seems to see Hull as in some way contiguous with the idea of 'Englishness', and as transformed by the poet to an 'England of the mind', for he says of another contributor's work that 'It is close to the kind of Englishness I sense in Didsbury's "The Drainage" where he imagines Hull back into its state of nature ... That is, it is deep, and imaginative'. Hence, taking the 'objects' and transforming them imaginatively is seen as an essentially 'English' trope. It is worth emphasising, though, that it is not always easy to know what Dunn (a Scot who seemed to rediscover his Scottish identity in the 1980s) means by 'English'. His notion of the 'imaginative' is quite a long way from the virtues conventionally ascribed to English verse, which tend to be along the lines of 'enactments' of sense and solidity of setting, rather than imaginative transformations.[5]

Peter Didsbury

The poetry of Hull, then (at least since Dunn's own *Terry Street* of 1969), does not in any real sense 'reflect' the city. Rather, Didsbury often seems to look concertedly away from it. Indeed, we might put together a specific urban poetics of 'looking away', drawn from dicta in various poems in *The Butchers of Hull*. Thus, in 'Upstairs' we are told 'You should learn to look/ elsewhere in cities' (and that word 'elsewhere' belongs to an interesting set of recurrent lexical items in Hull poetry). In 'The Flowers of Finland' the persona ends by:

> Feeling very little really.
> Knowing I was drinking pineapple juice,
> knowing that telling the truth about the world
> mightn't be the best way
> of getting some things down.

Here, the denigration of 'telling the truth about the world' seems to stigmatise and reject a certain kind of literalism, and this gesture is the equivalent of 'looking elsewhere', seeming to involve a marked preference for what Douglas Dunn calls 'the act of imagining' over 'the objects which his [Didsbury's] imagination serves' (*A Rumoured City*, p. 14). This rather limiting dichotomy means that the poet always moves quickly to transform the actual urban environment into something else, and, indeed, has usually already done this with its urban 'material' before the poem begins.[6] This often precludes the use of loco-specific geography and limits the poet to the urban-generic. Certainly, in so far as Hull poets share a tendency, it might be said to be this preference for 'setting' over 'geography'. Whereas a Liverpool poet will refer casually to Dale Street or St George's Hall, Hull poets seem reluctant to do likewise, seeing that kind of explicit local referencing as 'merely' documentary. The implicit aim often seems to be to make the transition to the a-chronotopic ex-temporal hiatus as quickly as possible. In Didsbury's 'The Drainage' we see this transition actually happening. Thus, the poem begins as if intent on registering a mundane reality, 'When he got out of bed ...' but the poet is already making his exit from this world to another before the end of this first line, which reads complete 'When he got out of bed the world had changed.' The world is changed, at the simplest level, by the December frost which imposes the 'making strange' of a freezing fog. Hence, 'he stepped outside. / Not into his street but a flat wet landscape'. Here the opacity produced by the frost and fog obliterates the actual and offers a blank screen on to which the poet's imaginings can be projected, thus facilitating his entry into a world which has no identifiable 'chronotope': what follows this moment necessarily takes place at no particular time and has no particular place as its setting: it is a 'dream' landscape in which 'dream' events take place, governed only by a generative 'act of imagining'. Within this projected space anything at all can happen, but this can be precisely the problem, for whatever *does* happen will quickly strike the reader (I mean, when encountered in book form, after several pages of poems like this) as unremarkable. For instance, outdoors, this is what is found:

It was broad cold day but the sky was black.
Instead of the sun it was Orion there.
Seeming to pulse his meaning down.
He was naked. He had to clothe himself.
The heifers stood like statues in the fields.
They didn't moan when he sliced the hides from them.
He looked at the penknife in his hand.
The needle, the thread, the clammy strips.
Now his face mooned out through a white hole.
The cape dripped. He knew he had
the bounds of a large parish to go.

According to Dunn, as we saw, Didsbury is here 'imagin[ing] Hull back into its state of nature' (p. 16). He has scrolled back, as it were, to a moment when civilisation is still inchoate, when the struggle for food and shelter is still raw and unmediated, so that the pelt which will clothe us has to be stripped from the backs of other animals. This kind of thing, says Dunn, 'looks at first sight as if it is "difficult", but in fact it's not' (p. 14). But these commendatory comments are actually a little intimidatory too, for questioning the technique more closely might seem to put the reader in opposition to the imaginative processes with which the content of the poem is confidently identified. Yet it is surely possible to regret that always very rapid exit from 'here' to 'elsewhere', even (or perhaps especially) in the case of a poet as highly gifted as Didsbury – perhaps just occasionally 'telling the truth about the world' might be one way of 'getting some things down', to revert to the phrases used by Didsbury in 'The Flowers of Finland'.

In the last two lines of 'A White Wine for Max Ernst' an explicit supplement to what I have been calling the poetics of 'elsewhere' or 'looking away' is offered: 'The association of two or more apparently alien elements on a plane alien to both is the most potent ignition of poetry'. Of course, this is not stated as gospel, and presumably it has the kind of textual provisionality which imbues the proclamation about beauty and truth at the end of Keats's 'Ode to a Grecian Urn' (a 'cold pastoral' poem which Didsbury turns into a fascinating 'cold industrial' in 'Building the *Titanic*', which I will discuss in a moment). All the same, the formula does seem to underlie a lot of the work in the book, and it might almost be taken as a manifesto for one kind of postmodernist poetical practice, that in which 'the referent' is disenfranchised from the start.

Yet at times Didsbury 'swerves' violently away from imaginative projections of this kind, and adopts a ruthlessly dumbed-down diction within the drabbest of settings, as if he can only operate at one or the other pole of the material/imagination dichotomy on which he sometimes seems painfully forked. For instance the poem 'A Daft Place', also in *The Butchers of Hull*, begins:

> A daft place this.
> Going south from here to the river
> is to follow a daft line of questioning.
> First the estate with its daft new names,
> then the suburbs with their daft front doors.

Here there seems to be a kind of contempt for the loco-specific, producing a taunting break-down of the poem's diction, as if this kind of inert truth-telling were the only option once the higher verbalism of the imagination (as represented in Didsbury's best-known poems, like 'The Drainage', again, or 'Eikon Basilike' in his second volume, *The Classical Farm*) has been abandoned. In the weaker poems in the genre, the high verbalism, when the carefully counterpointed incongruities are reduced to a single narrative stream, collapses into a lush, theatrical version of the manner known as 'secret narrative', as in 'At North Villa' (in *That Old-Time Religion*), which is perhaps describable as an extract from a quirky Absurdist costume-drama set in an opulent middle-class household in 1902.[7] Didsbury's 'At North Villa' is, all too obviously, I would say, simply going through the Motions of this technique. The mannerisms of both this style (which is at the

'imaginative' end of the spectrum) and of 'A Daft Place' (which is at
the opposite, or 'material', end) impose distinct limitations on what
the poems can achieve. How, then, does this relate to notions of post-
modernism in poetry?

For David Kennedy, in *New Relations: The Refashioning of British
Poetry 1980–1994*, the postmodernist outlook involves 'recognition
of the social construction of "meaning" and "world" and the fore-
grounding of that construction as aesthetic practice underlines a
particular relation between the postmodernist artist and late capitalist
society, one that is neither exclusively oppositional or supportive' (p.
81). Frequently cited key features of postmodernism are accepted by
Kennedy, such as Linda Hutcheon's 'double encoding', in which art
and theory 'both install and subvert prevailing norms – artistic and
ideological' (p. 81), and Lyotard's idea that postmodernism involves
the view that rationality and freedom are regressing, leading to 'a sort
of "bricolage", the multiple quotation of elements taken from earlier
styles or periods' (p. 81). Finally, the use of 'parody and pastiche' in
postmodernism is 'symptomatic of a similarly complex interfusing of
heresy and reverence, irony and deference, distance and involvement'
(p. 81). While it partakes of this *milieu*, however, one of the distinc-
tive features of British poetic postmodernism, says Kennedy, is that it
remains in 'dialogue with realism', and this, he says, is especially char-
acteristic of the work of poets like Didsbury or John Ash. This offers
what we might take as an updated way of discussing the aesthetic of
the prominent Hull poets, providing an alternative to Dunn's recalci-
trant dichotomy between 'material' and 'imagination', for Kennedy
sees in Didsbury what postmodernist theorist Linda Hutcheon calls a
'rethinking of the entire notion of reference': the poems do not
attempt to 'liquidate referentials' (p. 108): this poetic, says Kennedy,
'problematises but does not necessarily deconstruct the real' (p. 111).
In work like Didsbury's:

> the dominant realist surface is being broken down, re-examined,
> reassembled and treated in ways that resist closure: that is, the
> contemplation of an object or the description of an event or situ-
> ation is not used to arrive at a conclusion.

This is useful exposition, certainly helpful to a reader puzzled by the
initial strangeness of Didsbury's writing, but how exactly would *prob-
lematising* the real differ from *deconstructing* it? My contention is that

O'Brien is actually a better example than Didsbury of a poet whose postmodernity remains in dialogue with realism: hence I would see Didsbury as (more usually) 'going the whole hog', and (counter-productively) *deconstructing* the real, whereas it is O'Brien who 'merely' (and more fruitfully) *problematises* it. In terms of the dichotomies introduced earlier in this book, this amounts to saying that Hull poets like to use an 'urban-symbolic' mode, and some degree of 'urban-generic' setting, but they tend not to employ loco-specific, cartographic material. In other words, they tend to go further in the direction of the a-chronotopic than most of the other city poets discussed.

The Didsbury stance involves (effectively) accepting Dunn's dichotomy between imagination and material, whereas O'Brien (as I will try to show) does not do this. My more general point is that it is difficult to see grounds for the assumption (central to Kennedy's book) that there has been, in the British poetry of the 1990s, a 'clean break' with the work and the outlook represented by *Contemporary British Poetry*. That anthology, it will be remembered, was dominated by a newly identified 'mainstream' consisting of those who 'extend the imaginative franchise', showing 'something of the spirit of postmod-ernism' (p. 20), relishing 'the fact of fictionalising' (p. 19) as a performance, and delighting in 'the outrageous simile' and the urge to 'twist and mix language' (p. 18). Kennedy's argument is that the 'resistance to traditional closure' (seen in Didsbury and others) is radi-cally different from all this:

> Paradoxically, this resistance to traditional closure goes hand-in-hand with a highly developed narrative and fiction-making sensibility which is markedly different from the 'secret' or 'new narrative' school of Andrew Motion or James Fenton. Narrative becomes a way of exploring the arbitrariness of the imagination … (p. 18)

Thus, Kennedy sees a clean break between the Motion style of 'new narrative' poetry and Didsbury's. My own view, as already suggested, is that there is actually a strong affinity between Motion and Didsbury, and that the shift (as I will go on to argue) occurs not with Didsbury but with O'Brien (though it isn't one which can plausi-bly be called a 'clean' break).

For Kennedy, one of the components of the difference between the

narrative styles of Didsbury and Motion is the former's 'aestheticisa-
tion of history, and, by extension cultural and political struggle'. This
quality is exemplified by Didsbury's poem 'Building the *Titanic*' (in
The Butchers of Hull). I will spend some time discussing this short
poem, in order to suggest that it works better as evidence of my
'deconstructive' Didsbury than it does for Kennedy's notion of a Dids-
bury who merely problematises referentials. This will at the same time
illustrate the kind of dangers which are inherent in the aesthetic of
what I called earlier 'looking away', and will focus some of my reser-
vations about the effects achieved in a-chronotopic writing. 'Building
the *Titanic*' reads in full:

> The streets are full of air.
> You quit the shipyard on the lunchtime shift
> and we catch you there.
> The gates finish opening and already our hands reach back
> to empty *your* hands, your faces.
> We work a black change on you.
> Resolved into coats and moustaches
> You are free, now, to consort like wolves on the snow.
> We turn you into a thousand German orchestras.
> You'd play for a thousand years
> if we'd half a mind to ask it of you,
> and we might have. We do all this
> simply to hear ourselves say, 'This is what we know.
> This is the lunchtime shift and even the trams are hungry.
> They advertise bread. They will eat you, if you don't make
>   way.'

There is a note on the poem at the end of the volume, which reads:

> The 'Grecian Urn' syndrome. These workers are fixed as irrevo-
> cably, in a well-known contemporary photograph, as Keats's
> 'marble men and maidens overwrought' on the sides of the urn.
> A 'Cold Industrial'.

The poem responds to a frequently published picture by Belfast
photographer R.J. Welch, which shows workers from the Harland &
Wolff shipyard in Belfast streaming out into Queen's Road at the end
of the working day. It is made from plate-glass negative H1555 in the

Figure 5.1 The 'well-known contemporary photograph' referred to in Peter Didsbury's note to his poem 'Building the *Titanic*'. The *Titanic* itself can be seen in the centre background, beneath the squared gantry.

Photograph title and credit: Shipyard workers leaving H&W, 1911: *Titanic* on stocks in background. Reproduced by permission of the Ulster Folk and Transport Museum, Harland & Wolff Collection.

Harland & Wolff Historic Photograph Collection (now stored at the Ulster Folk and Transport Museum), and the catalogue description reads 'Queen's Road and shipyard men leaving work. TITANIC in background ready for launching.' It is dated 'May 1911' (the launch of the ship took place on 31 May). The photograph is reproduced in *Steel Ships and Iron Men: Shipbuilding in Belfast, 1894–1912* (Michael McCaughan, Ulster Folk and Transport Museum, 1989) and the caption informs us that many of the workers 'are boarding trams for parts of the city beyond walking distance'. Tramlines lead towards the viewer and a line of open-top double-decker trams is filling up with workers. Men are seen walking along or across the tramlines ahead of the trams, and the leading tram has an advertisement across its front for 'Inglis' Bread'.

As we look at it today the photograph is imbued with layers of retrospective significance. At one level it can be taken as suggestive of Britain at the height of its industrial power, for in this period Britain was the world's major shipbuilder, and fourteen thousand men were employed at this yard alone. In today's post-industrial Britain, by contrast, men would only be seen streaming out of gates and walking together in such numbers after a football match. Another element which contributes to the power of the photograph is the fact that the ship shown ready for launching is the *Titanic*, and this serves as a reminder of how fragile this industrial supremacy proved to be, and seems emblematic of the beginning of a long period of British industrial decline. There is also the strong probability that many of the men shown in the photograph died a few years later on the Somme, so that we feel their vulnerability, as individuals and as representatives of a whole social class, in the face of high-level blunders which will destroy them and their work. But for the fragile moment shown in the photograph (the moment of the 'cold pastoral') an uncomplicated patriotism and national pride, of a kind no longer possible today, is evoked even by the place names: the shipyard is on Queen's Island, and the men are streaming out on to Queen's Road. But, of course, on second thoughts, the patriotism is not uncomplicated at all: this is sectarian Belfast and these names are highly divisive, actively disaffiliating the Catholic section of the community, which was generally excluded from this particular workplace right through to present times. So the photograph also suggests the distant roots of present ills. How then does one particular viewer, the poet who wrote 'Building the *Titanic*', react to it?

In the poem the cityscape is evoked by proxy, by referring to elements in the photograph: we see the shipyard gates, the men streaming out in their 'coats and moustaches', the trams with their painted advertisements. But the poem mainly seems to celebrate not the industrial power which the photograph depicts, but the power of the authorial imagination, without which, it seems to say, there is nothing here at all; hence the opening line 'The streets are full of air'. Indeed, the poem is robustly 'post-Fordist', registering the demise of heavy industry and its replacement by the poet's own form of cultural production. In that sense it is an ironic celebration of the changes mentioned in the introductory chapter whereby the new cultural, entertainment and service economies have supplanted the old industrial economy represented by the photograph. And whereas a Seamus

Heaney might look at these men and feel twinges of something like guilt (because a poet doesn't do 'real' work like this), Didsbury seems to have no such feelings. The helplessness and powerlessness of his subject matter is insisted upon repeatedly, and is even embodied in the grammatical forms used, so that the people in the picture are in the object case, caught up in the web of authorial power as soon as they appear at the gates and come into the frame of the picture ('we catch you there'). They are worked upon, for instance, by quasi-divine hands which reach into the picture to manipulate them 'The gates finish opening and already our hands reach back/ to empty *your* hands, your faces'. So the poem seems to celebrate and assert an old-fashioned authorial omnipotence, and this angle is stated and re-stated as the poem goes on, so that the poet becomes a kind of alchemist ('We work a black change on you') or a whimsical tyrant ('We turn you into a thousand German orchestras./ You'd play for a thousand years/ if we'd half a mind to ask it of you, and we might have'). The conclusion seems to elevate the poem and place it beyond the literalist assumptions of this line of questioning, seeming to mock the idea of any epistemological certainty at all being possible:

> We do all this
> simply to hear ourselves say, 'This is what we know.
> This is the lunchtime shift and even the trams are hungry.
> They advertise bread. They will eat you, if you don't make
>   way.'

But the reader's confidence in the poet's ironic assertions about 'what we know' may well be shaken by the number of casual 'misreadings' of the photograph embodied in the poem. First, this is not the 'lunchtime shift' at all but the end of the day. Shipyard workers did not, of course, go home for lunch (on trams to distant parts of the city). If it looks rather light for the end of the working day, then that is because it is late May and this is a northern city. Second, the trams are not threatening to mow down workers who won't make way (as the line 'They will eat you, if you don't make way' implies); in fact, they are not moving – the driver's seat of the first tram in the line is unoccupied. Third, the poem seems to take the picture as a snow scene ('you are free, now, to consort like wolves in the snow'), but though the contrasty appearance of prints made from plate-glass negatives makes the roofs and road surfaces appear white, no footsteps are visible in the 'snow', and the late May dating of the picture would seem to make a snowfall unlikely. Of course, from Didsbury's artistic perspective such things are unimportant. He has taught himself to look elsewhere in cities ('Upstairs') and does not believe that 'telling the truth about the world' is the best way of getting some things down ('The Flowers of Finland'). All the same, a reader aware of these casual inaccuracies necessarily begins to realise that the poet's attitude towards the photograph might be emblematic of his attitude to every-thing which he regards as merely his 'material'. In turn, the way Didsbury uses this photograph might be taken as emblematic, too, of how poetry sometimes (mis)conceives its relationship to the 'real' and perhaps even explains why there is a decline of general interest in it. In this poem he is, so to speak, distancing himself from photographer R.J. Welch and asserting strongly of himself (and on behalf of poetry in general) that, unlike Isherwood's narrator in *Goodbye to Berlin*, 'I am not a camera'.[8] Here, then, is an attitude to the urban which is the opposite to that embodied in Roy Fisher's declaration 'Birming-ham's what I think with'. The apparent assumption here is that the poet will just think and imagine, self-sufficiently, intransitively, so to speak, and not in partnership with 'material' which also has its rights, its claims, and its relative autonomy (claims which are implicitly accepted in the poetic mode I have been calling 'loco-specific').

In any case, does the poetic license rather bullishly insisted upon in the poem really produce such impressive results? Why, for instance, will the poet 'turn you into a thousand *German* orchestras'? I don't know. But I suspect that it is suggested by the name 'Wolff' in the title of the firm 'Harland & Wolff'. (It is the name of Gustav Wilhelm Wolff, a marine draughtsman from Hamburg, who was one of the founding partners of the yard.) In turn the name 'Wolff' probably also generates the 'wolves in the snow' image. But, surely, the main ques-tions to ask about all this relentless imposing of his 'imaginative' perspective on his material are ethical ones. Why is the poet doing this, other than because he can?

My 'daft' line of questioning would continue by asking why the poet is imposing yet another layer of victimhood on those who are depicted in the photograph. 'We work a black change on you', he says gleefully. The only way of accommodating the poet's imaginative 'aestheticisation' of the scene is to say that his own ruthless artistic manipulation of these depicted figures is a deliberate counterpart of the ruthless way they are manipulated by capitalistic forces. Either the poem achieves that rather spectacular mimetic effect (as I think Kennedy believes), or else (and this is my view) the gap between the 'material' and what the 'imagination' makes of it is bizarrely unbridged in this poem, in a way which seems to me characteristic of, at least, Didsbury's earlier work.

Sean O'Brien

Some of the features noted in the work of Peter Didsbury are also seen in that of Sean O'Brien. For instance, the third poem in O'Brien's first book, *The Indoor Park* (Bloodaxe, 1983) is entitled 'Air', and its topic seems related to Didsbury's 'streets full of air' in the *Titanic* poem (air features again in 'The Disappointment' and 'Two Finger Exercise'): 'Air' itself begins 'I shall be writing you until I die' (not 'writing *about* you', notice) and this seems to entail again that potentially tedious insistence on the poet's creative and imaginative prowess. This is 'An empire of affection built in air:/ The air remains, the context of At Last', and the poem ends with the additional assertion that we 'breathed the air behind the air', which seems to designate the zone which O'Brien and Didsbury both aim to penetrate. Indeed, mentions of air, wind and light, seem common in Hull poetry, a producing a distinctly 'estuarial' feel (if I am using this Hull word correctly):[9] likewise, the word 'elsewhere' occurs in O'Brien too, a Larkinesque word which always seems implicated in the ambition of transcending the provincial: in 'Station Song' a mundane 'here' is contrasted ironically with an exotic 'elsewhere', in the opening lines:

> I should have seen you all the time, you ghosts,
> But I was taken up elsewhere
> With getting on, which got me here.

'Station Song' is a kind of dream of departure, as is '*Le Depart*', which begins 'You've been leaving for years and now noone's surprised/ When you knock to come in from the weather', where, typically, someone aiming for 'elsewhere' inexplicably ends up 'here'. All there is to say about travelling is that 'You're halfway there': the would-be escapees end up asleep 'in early restaurants,/ Boastful of such daft endurance,/ And then inspect the shipping lists/ Until the time is right.' In the end the travelling gets converted into metaphor ('Are we not always, always travelling?'), which is, of course, a license to stay put, and the use of the Didsburian word 'daft' seems to ridicule the whole enterprise.

So far I have been emphasising his affinities with Didsbury, yet the overall feel of O'Brien's work is quite different: crucially, there is a realisation that the constant flashing of one's poetic license isn't really a good idea; what is 'In the Head' (to quote from the poem of that name) has to be balanced against something else, and in this poem (which has the Hardyesque scenario of glimpsing and desiring a woman seen in a street or a park) the poet admits 'Her life could not be touched by mine./ I know that she is real somewhere', which draws back from the Didsbury position of assuming total artistic control. Like Didsbury, O'Brien also bases a poem on a *Titanic* scenario ('Those in Peril'), but without attempting to substitute its fantasy for reality: it begins 'We are drunk, or the whole place is tilted absurdly', and the alternatives offered in this line leave open the possibility of a reality which is impervious to the poet's manipulations. The ship motif is a common enabling device for an exploration of cultural enclosure and the ship here figures in knock-about fashion the cultural ambience of 'these Northern lassitudes' (an ironic reference to the 'Polar Bear' pub, much favoured by Hull poets, which is the *setting* here, in a generalised sense, though the Hull resistance to local specifics keeps it at a kind of subliminal level). This is all 'ludic' and 'imaginative' in a perhaps too-familiar way, but poets writing about cities, writing out of cities, or writing cities into their poems, do need that humbling sense of an external reality which is at least as reciprocally indifferent to their manipulations as any nail-paring artist could be to his or her material. And, indeed, this sense of a brute circumambient reality emerges strongly, though in no way photographically, in several of the most successful poems in the collection, including 'The Park by the Railway', 'Ryan and the Historical Imagination', and 'Not Sending Cards this Year'. In the first of these a couple visit a fair in a 'shabby park', and later wait for a train, 'Sitting in the waiting-room in dark- ness/ Beside the empty cast-iron fireplace'. The examined decor of the waiting room reveals an industrial past which is not unlike that evoked in Didsbury's *Titanic* poem; but it is evoked as real, not as a mere site for comical intervention:

> You strike a match to show the china map
> Of where the railways ran before us.
> Coal and politics, invisible decades

Of rain, domestic love and failing mills
That ended in a war and then a war
Are fading into what we are

This seems to me a more truly imaginative act than Didsbury's in his
Titanic poem, for here the past is evoked as real, even though it existed
before we did: the sweep is panoptic and, yes, sentient (words use by
Dunn in his pamphlet in praise of Larkin – see the first footnote), and
the effect is to make the speaker-protagonist seem to doubt *his own*
reality rather that of the lives evoked – the two people in the poem are
merely 'the ghosts of us', and 'We speak, and we've gone'. This sense
of personal transience is reflected in the representation of the city in
the poem as a hybrid place, the park an 'industrial pastoral' of 'grass
under ash', with its 'half-dismantled fair': it is a 'city beyond conser-
vation', a place 'Of in-betweens, abandoned viaducts/ And modern
flowers, dock and willowherb,/ Lost mongrels, birdsong scratching at
the soot/ Of the last century'. In 'Ryan and the Historical Imagination'
(Ryan is an alter-ego or persona figure sometimes used by O'Brien) the
first two stanzas suggest the end of a relationship, but the last records
the end of something else:

We never photographed the streets
Before they tore them down.
The clearing she undressed in aged fifteen
Discovering boys were more useful than horses
Is part of a motorway pillar.

And the poem ends with the italicised line '*Life imitates the art we
cannot make*', which is an ambiguous pronouncement, of course, but
does seem to concede that there is a limitation of some kind on the
autonomy of the imagination. 'Not Sending Cards this Year', finally,
is interesting because of the way it reverses the usual Hull progression
of beginning with a 'locatory pre-amble', set 'here', and then making
a fairly rapid transition to an 'elsewhere' which is an amalgam or
hybrid made up of historically inflected worlds and imaginative
scenarios. This poem does it the other way round; it starts off in the
exotic, cross-temporal world:

Consoled by the dead with their tea-things
In somebody's lodge in the snowed-under forest,

> We listen with them as the end of the world
> Comes six months late by pigeon post

I am tempted to say 'and so on', for I think it is easy to over-estimate the poetic valency of this kind of writing. My difficulty is that I cannot see what difference it would make to the poem if the end of the world had come (say) a year late and on a tractor, or by second-class mail and with a 40p surcharge. In other words, it is not clear to me how the image is *earned* (so to speak) if the 'imagination' faces no braking friction at all from its 'material'. The central section of the poem, indeed, is partly about this 'earning' process, for it seems to concern the practice of intensely honing the fabric of a poem ('the death of the definite article', 'We watch them tune their metres down/ *Revise*. *Revise*'), a process which is essentially concerned with enabling the encounter between the unstoppable force of the imagination and the immovable object of the 'material'. In this case the poem becomes exciting when it swings back to the mundane, ending with:

> Let's go out now, to where we live,
> The dead harbour, the pub and the station buffet,
> North of the Word, where it rains in your face.

It is a relief – can I be alone in feeling this? – to escape the slightly stuffy atmosphere of the a-chronotopic imagination and get out 'to where we live', where you can feel the wind and rain of commonplace reality in your face. Going out to where we live, going 'North of the Word', my point is, is the *real* challenge to the imagination. Of course, like Didsbury (like all poets), O'Brien sometimes get tired of the 'truth' of 'where we live': in 'From the Narrator's Tale' the narrator (for it must be he) says 'I am tired of telling this prickteasing truth/ That I cannot invent or abolish', but at the same time 'the detail' remains fascinating, and stakes its claim: in 'The Amateur God' he says 'There's nothing but detail/ And leisure to name it', and in 'Walking' the opening lines are 'I am in love with detail. Chestnut trees/ Are fire-damaged candelabra./ Waterbirds are porcelain'. Here the hand-me-down Martian metaphors, it is true, aspire to an instant aestheticisation, making the object all percept. Even when done well, this technique will hog the reader's attention distractingly, as in 'The Exiles' where we find 'Out on the park/ The grass wears week-old snow/ Like unchanged bandages, half-off'. Yet at least it allows a notional initial parity to 'here' and 'elsewhere', in the instant before the showy metaphor occludes the former, and being in love with detail is a useful safeguard against the temptation always to look elsewhere. Part of my point here is, again, the evident affinities between 'Hull' work of the early 1980s and the genres favoured in Motion and Morrison's *Contemporary British Poetry* anthology. But O'Brien seems (to me) markedly more successful than Didsbury in integrating 'imagination' and 'material', without the violent swerves to one extreme or the other which are seen in the latter's early work.

HMS Glasshouse (OUP, 1991), O'Brien's third collection, maintains the precarious balance. Indeed, what holds him to 'here', and prevents him leaping off with Didsbury into the imagination, is what amounts, almost, to a love for and a fixation with the physical infrastructure of the 1950s, and its concomitant psychological processes: this always seems to hover in the 'ruined districts' his work so often returns to: in 'Betweentimes', for instance, (in *HMS Glasshouse*) 'you can study the dust in the windows/ Of incomprehensible premises, guess/ ... At all the further streets these streets conceal'. Frequently lives of 'quiet desperation' (Thoreau's phrase) are glimpsed, for instance, in this poem, that of the 'old man re-reading the paper' in a drab pub: 'You'd think they had built this around him,/ Brick and varnish, optics, disappointment'. Fear of such disappointment drives people 'elsewhere', to a life as a sailor, for example. Thus, in 'Dry Sailors' a 1950s dockscape of ships' funnels is glimpsed above warehouse roofs and across vistas of streets:

> The White Star, the Black Star and Ellerman Wilson –
> Their funnels behind the back roofs
> Of an Atlas of cities,
> Those Grimshaws of rigging and smoke
> In which all the best streets come to nothing.

Here the speaker measures his own life unfavourably (he is a 'dry sailor' who can only 'sail theoretical oceans') against the lives of those who sailed the oceans for real, but in him the sense of personal dissatisfaction is induced by *images* of the sea in art and literature, for instance, by Atkinson Grimshaw's glamorous moonlit dockside scenes, and by the sea stories and narratives of Conrad, Melville, Coleridge, Poe and Verne, all of whom are cited in the poem, either by name or by a well-known motif from their work. But the sailing of anything other than theoretical oceans has been rendered virtually impossible by Britain's maritime decline, including the collapse of Hull's fishing industry, as 'Cold' recalls, with its mention of trawlers ('The dozen or so not sold off or scrapped').[10] Now the new brutalist bus station is the only pointer to 'elsewhere' for 'those who have nowhere to travel', who would once have been drawn, perhaps, to Arctic waters with the fishing fleet. Hence, the poem evokes a stark world of down-and-outs suffering rejection and 'rolelessness' (such as 'the comics/ Not even their mothers would book' who 'freeze tonight// On Blanket Row and Beggar Lane'). The roar of the river outflow, audible from where they doss down, is something 'they can almost remember/ From childhood, an atlas of oceans/ That sounds like a mouthful of stones'. This is a 'Boyhood of Raleigh' in which the boy inspired by the fabulous tales of old mariners grows up to find the docks derelict (or, more likely, turned into a marina or a shopping mall). This, of course, is a scenario which, give or take a detail, fits the whole of post-industrial Britain, or 'junk Britain', as Tom Paulin calls it in a well-known essay about contemporary poetry (in his book *Minotaur: Poetry and the Nation State*, Harvard University Press, 1992). Here, indeed, is a Hull which can truly stand in for the whole of England, an *indicative* city, representative and summative of the whole, just as a particular hill or a patch of meadow would once have been taken by Housmann or Edward Thomas as embodying an essential 'England'.

This is sometimes implicit, sometimes explicit in comments on the city by Larkin and Dunn, and a familiar motif in many of the poems. *HMS Glasshouse*, for instance, contains 'Working on the Railway', which is one of the most loco-specific pieces in the whole of O'Brien's *oeuvre*. In his comprehensive listing of local places mentioned in Hull poetry, John Osborne notes[11] that this poem cites the Station Hotel, the Botanic Crossing, Stepney, Stoneferry, Wilmington and the North Eastern Railway's Victoria Dock Line, one branch of which went to the dock ('here') and the other to the local seaside ('elsewhere'). The O'Brien persona is in a nostalgic reverie induced by a photograph in *Lost Railways of England* (the treatment of the photograph contrasting markedly with Didsbury's use of the Harland & Wolff picture). He imagines the trains packed with soldiers in the 1940s, or seaside trippers in the 1950s, with the waiting railway carriages standing in the summer heat, 'with their headachy air/ Full of dustmotes, their pictures of elsewhere:/ An hour of silence that seems to be England'.

There is an unusually overt Larkinesque quality in these lines, especially in the easy flip-over from the loco-specific to the panoramic, as we glide from 'here' to 'elsewhere' (via the photographic scenes of railway holiday destinations displayed above the seats in the compartment) and suddenly hit an 'England of the mind'. At these moments Hull becomes a 'generic city' (what I earlier called an 'indicative city') which claims a unique authority that stems from its very *lack* of uniqueness. This is a place whose vast empty skies provide the poet with an empty canvas to project on to, whose true essence is nothingness (the 'air' which occurs so often and so strangely in their poetry), the estuary so wide it yawns onto mere emptiness (that 'estuarial' feeling – a recurrent Hull poets' word), not on to a clearly visible 'other side' which provides scale and a sense of mutual definition in other cities.

The related poem which follows 'Working on the Railway' is 'On the Line', where again an intense interest in local industrial archaeology (such as abandoned factories or machinery) can facilitate a sense of awe and the uncanny, an urban equivalent of the feelings evoked in Wordsworth by mountains, conferring on beholders a sense of belatedness and inferiority as they contemplate installations that must now seem, in the post-Fordist, post-industrial Britain of service 'industries', to be 'the work of giants', of another race, now vanished, like the iron men in Didsbury's *Titanic* photograph who built the iron ships:

> The red factories stand
> With their decoys of steam, on short time
> In a soup made of old grass and water

The remnants of this world are now an 'elsewhere' of the past, rather than a 'here', and as often in Hull poems, we glimpse the moment (as in Didsbury's 'Drainage') of stepping from one to the other, from the real to the imagined – 'I'll step over/ The line that divides my own place/ From the one where the map has no answers'. Characteristically, though, this other world in O'Brien's case, unlike in Didsbury's, is not the product of simply playing the surrealist joker and then revelling in the ludic: rather, the poet remains in a kind of *rooted* fantasy, of a recent past ruthlessly stripped away, rather than a completely deracinated imaginative zone. What gives his poetry the edge over Didsbury's is its retaining an element of 'social realism'. This may enable us to speculate about the precise difference between a 'deconstructed' and a 'problematised' reality in poetry, by suggesting that the latter has some of the elements noted in O'Brien, such as retaining a 'here', which is problematised by not being the 'here' of now, but of a fictionally reconstructed 1950s: or else, by a 'here and now' which is suffused with the kind of literary and artistic representations typified earlier by Atkinson Grimshaw, Poe and Conrad. Hence, the poem strives, albeit with a kind of desperation, to bring the real and the reconstructed worlds together:

> And though twenty years' growth
> Says the line is abandoned, I'll still
> Put my ear to the track, and a penny, then sit
> On the bankside, on cinders not cold enough yet
> To undo the conviction that if I go up
> And look hard the far signal will change.

This is not necessarily great poetry, but the syntactical braking which allows the lexically quiet final line to work effectively is impressive, and the educated, bookish register of the lines ensures that the 'sentience' doesn't degenerate into sentimentality. Trapped in his 1950s nostalgia there is nothing the poet can do except ensure that his own verse, like the structures he depicts, and to which he imparts resonant metonymic status, is built to last. The same kind of held-in-check nostalgia is evident in 'Coming Home', which is related to 'Cold' and portrays more 'theoretical voyaging' to Arctic waters ('white shores receding/ And gone, with the last light still ghosting the eye'). The opening is registered by an eye not disdaining to be photographic, or at least, not scrupling about a throw-back to the matter and manner of *Terry Street*:

> These cold nights I catch it all clearly –
> the terrace, its front rooms unlit
> And kept only for coffins, the streetlamp
> Grown cloudy with breath, where the children swing,
> And the footprint set down in fresh snow
> On a doorstep, as if by a template, still perfect.

The seeing eye then 'goes estuarial', as it were, slipping out to where 'A lightship intones that it too is a place', and where the river outfall meets the salt of the North Sea: as often, the mundane 'here' is counterpointed with the exciting 'elsewhere', suggested by 'the atlas you gave me, a place/ Made of names which are cold and exciting to say'. An atlas is a gift usually made to a child, and the poet regresses to childhood ('the first thing I want is a story') as the poem progresses towards its end, through the moment of parental death ('high in the darkness a crane waits/ To build the infirmary you'll die in'), and back to 'the moment I entered the world':

> While the dead in the house with their teacups
> Complain that the door is left open, I'll wait
> With the snow and the sirens, as long as it takes.

While again here the poem is characteristically bifurcated into a present 'here' and a past 'elsewhere', the elsewhere is 'anchored' and the transition between the two adroitly managed, without the yawning semantic and conceptual gap which often seems characteristic of Didsbury. The intertwining of a personal remembered past and a vanished industry provides images of a larger-than-life kind of manliness (the trawlermen who, at sailing time, 'sprint from their taxis,/ Still dressed up, still drunk and still broke') and the result is to inspire in the poet, not feelings of unlimited artistic empowerment, but something much more like a regretful sense of personal belatedness.

Douglas Houston

If Didsbury is unusual in writing so little about family or forebears and seeming to prefer the ludic to the overtly personal, then Douglas Houston, the final Hull poet I will consider, seems to combine O'Brien's air of rootedness in personal history with Didsbury's imaginative sweep. Houston's first book, *With the Offal Eaters* (Bloodaxe, 1986) contains a remarkable variety of work, of which the most immediately impressive part is the 'core' of elegiac poems in memory of his father ('For My Father', 'Here's tae Us ...', 'Remembrance Day Photograph' and 'In Llanbydder'), the only survivor of a Second World War shipwreck, who survived because a rescue boat's searchlight happened to pick him out after hours in the North Atlantic. While the father's unquestioning confidence in his ultimate survival is recorded, the son's reaction is an abiding sense of his own fundamental precariousness ('You sink beneath a scanning beam/ On rollers close to cancelling my birth', in 'For My Father'), and this is reflected in the shifting styles and modes of the poems in the book. There is, quite simply, no single characteristically 'Houstonian' manner here, but a whole range of evanescent poetic identities, beginning with the jokey, Hippyesque bard who opens the book with 'To the Management' (a list of surrealistic suggestions to the local bus company, evoking a kind of 'happy-hippy city' not dissimilar to that of Roger McGough's 1960s Liverpool, where pleasurably subversive activities are always likely to break out on buses). In an interview in *Bête Noire* Houston refers to this aspect of his poetic identity, which sees writing as a form of free expression, as 'the Beat thing in some ways'.[12] In his personal memoir in the same issue he dismisses this phase as a time when his work was 'stuck in some post-hippy crevasse and reluctant to shed its Late Romantic flab' (p. 182). He also uses a heavily ironic manner, a kind of cod eighteenth-century diction, as seen in 'Lines on a Van's Dereliction', a manner perhaps related to the tonal experimentation seen in poems like Didsbury's 'Eikon Basilike', which Houston greatly admires, with its Defoe-esque opening 'During the late and long continuing cold/ I went for a walk in the empty heart of the city'. Other poems are 'confessional-autobiographical' in mode (like 'Case History' or 'On the Beach'): others record states of intoxication or drug-altered awareness, somewhat in the mode of Baudelaire's 'Hymn to Absinthe' (such as 'From the Corner', 'Nightown Revisited', 'D.T's on the Koningsallee' and 'Going Downstairs'); others are highly crafted poems which meditate intently on a simple material object (such as 'The Clasp', which is about a gift from the dying Lesley Dunn, and 'Holly', which finely and minutely describes the culling of a single twig of that plant). Poems of this kind seem to lie at the opposite (ultra-disciplined) pole to the 'post-hippy crevase', and might be imagined as provoking from Houston's older poet-friend Douglas Dunn, the kind of reaction he gave to 'From the Corner' when he 'just sort of smiled and shook his head enthusiastically over it' ('Memoir', p. 183).

What I am emphasising here is the crucial mutual influence of a *community* of writers (quite a different thing from a *school* of writers, which these poets insist, quite rightly, they have never been). Such a grouping is quintessentially urban, and vital to the individual's development, both as stimulus and sustenance. Even when books have been published, and reputations have been established, these networks provide a vital spur, and work widely approved of will not satisfy the writer if it fails to pass muster at that ultimate tribunal. The lack of that kind of writers' network brought Houston back to Hull in 1978, and is a source of some regret since his second departure in 1982. Houston's Welsh exile from Hull is perhaps lamented in his poem 'The Welsh Book of the Dead' in O'Brien's anthology *The Firebox* (1998, p. 327). It should be read in conjunction with its companion poem 'The Hull Book of the Dead', published in *English*, autumn 1999.[13] The network continues to exist in diaspora ('I can pick up the phone any night now and talk to Sean [O'Brien], Peter [Didsbury], or Douglas [Dunn], read a poem if I've got one worth the trouble, continue conversations started years ago, mostly about poetry', 'Memoir', p. 183), and, presumably, in reflective encounters which continue in the mind of the individual writer as a remark or a reaction continues to resonate in the mind. But at a certain stage of development, as Houston realised, the process requires a common place of residence, and will probably be rooted in earlier collective membership of some connected enterprise, such as (and as in the case of this group) a university or college department.

The mark of Hull on Houston's poems, then, is in one sense pervasive, for it lies in the emphasis on craftsmanship which was very strong in this group, generating a strong sense of the need to 'earn the lyric' by intricate and detailed shaping of material and effect. As anyone who has been involved in such groupings will know, their effect is often to stimulate a high consciousness of craft: your writer-friends take it for granted that you have something to say, and that this something is significant, and what they focus on is the otiose phrase, the imprecise image, the words whose running order is muddled. The end product can be the 'fully crafted' poem, like 'The Clasp' or 'Holly', where the tightly interlocking phrases always threaten to seem just a little too finely honed for their own good. The poet seems in these poems to be a little too totally in control. But 'The Clasp' and 'Holly' are not typical Houston poems, and generally the learned 'ordering' reflex is fruitfully countered in his work by his 'generational impulse', as it might be called, the 'post-hippy' thing which allows the appearance of informal spontaneity and flow in an utterance – the 'father' poems, for instance, have this not-quite-all-under-control element, for the feelings, the image-lines, the viewpoints and the registers which feature in them are not so tidily sorted out – like Coleridge's 'Conversation Poems', they record perennially unfinished business, and this lets the reader in as co-possessor of the poems, ultimately raising them above the super-crafted pieces. The craft pieces, by contrast, don't really need *readers*; they need – which is different – an *audience*, which will watch the expert verbal sword-play in awed silence, or suspended fascination, as a knife-throwing act is watched, with relief at the end when the subject emerges more or less unscathed by all this sharp wit. The 'post-hippy' impulse which can allow a loose end to hang is one which Douglas Dunn, five years older, and hence (I think 'hence' is justified) more dominated by the Movement's poetics, sometimes seems to lack. Developing in early isolation as a poet (by his own account), Dunn lacked the kind of contact with a community of writers which might have helped to counter-balance his 'natural' tendency to hew and shape, which leaves the 'seeing eye' (and 'I') too habitually in control. In Houston, though, we should add, the purely *technical* crafting is usually fairly conservative, the poems being stanzaic, each line beginning with a capital letter and flush with the left-hand margin, and most being more-or-less end-stopped. Also very marked is precision of observation and diction, accompanied by the tight interlocking of phrasing already mentioned. In 'Holly', for instance, where it is seen at its extreme, the speaker on waking notices the scratches which the holly-hunting has left on his hands; they are described as 'fine red striations, / ... / hatched on one hand at the base of the thumb', where the scientific coolness of 'striations' (rather than the everyday register of 'scratches') and the precise indication of the location of these marks almost suggest the forensic exactitude of a coroner's report.

The emergence of the poems out of a 'writing community' which has a powerful collective investment in these values is suggested by the dedications and allusions to other members of the group, suggesting ways in which skeins or networks of poems by various members need to be read cross-textually as a group: 'Gardens', for instance, is dedicated to Peter Didsbury, and refers to his poem 'Eikon Basilike' (in Didsbury's second book, *The Classical Farm*), but is a specific response to Didsbury's 'The Residents, 1840', which is dedicated to Houston and appears in *The Butchers of Hull*, Didsbury's first book. Houston's 'The Rest' has an epigraph from Sean O'Brien, and the poems which describe rooms seem to evoke implicitly 'Up in Duggie's Room', which is about Houston, in Dunn's second book *This Happier Life* (Faber, 1972).

But the physical presence of the city of Hull itself is residual in the book (rather like that of Liverpool in the work of Deryn Rees-Jones, discussed in the next chapter) since Houston moved from Hull back to

Wales in 1982, four years before his first book was published. His
own recollection of the distinctly 'Hull' poems in the collection notes
the presence of the Hull Royal Infirmary in 'Ward Seven' and 'Mr W.'
(and in 'After the Anaesthetic', according to John Osborne's list of
Hull locations in Hull poetry); of Hull's Spring Bank Cemetery in
'Case History' and 'Cemetery'; of city centre locations in 'Gardens'; of
the waterfront in 'Devotions' (where 'Victoria Pier was vaguely
present ... but not really specific', Osborne quotes Houston as saying);
the outskirts of the city in 'Driver' ('the journey out along Beverley
Road through Beverley to the coast', says Osborne); and in 'Sic
Transit' 'Walking through fallen blossoms in Chanterlands Avenue',
according to Osborne, and confirmed by Houston in conversation. In
many ways the itinerary is a familiar one: the cemetery and the infir-
mary feature in Larkin's work (and the latter was the scene of his final
illness); Spring Bank, as Houston points out, is the scene of Dunn's
'Winter Graveyard'; the pier appears at some point in the work of all
Hull poets, and the public parks and gardens are prevalent especially
in Sean O'Brien. All specific locations, though, even when (or even
especially when) named, seem peripheral in Houston's work. In 'Devo-
tions', for instance, the mock purification rites after drinking take
place 'underneath the end of the pier', but having been thus 'tagged',
the poem has no further use for the loco-specific (as his quoted remark
above implies). In 'Gardens' there is perhaps a more sustained use of
the cityscape of Hull, complicated by the poem's cross-referentiality to
those of its dedicatee, as already mentioned. The two verses focus,
respectively, on Hull and then on Wales, the cultivated 'civic lawns' of
the former being contrasted with the rustic plots of the latter. The
former connote a network of friendships and connections, suggestive
of the complicated and conflicting duties and allegiances of middle
life: the ground is flat and even, highly 'worked' and bearing the
human impress; nature here is merely implicit in the 'overdetermined'
municipal topiary: the 'civic lawns' are nature colonised to a 'rectilin-
ear hortuan geometry', and the regularly spaced suburban residential
streets produce 'the parallel parceling of demotic gardens'. In the
public squares and gardens friends consult their respective timetables
and allow their paths to intersect for an hour or so, the 'ordered guise'
of the city being the artistic imposition of the poet-archeologist friend
who wrote the poem 'Eikon Basilike', which cuts through and exposes
the layerings of urban civilisation on this ground, so that the city in
this first stanza is viewed with the other's ordering eye. The second

stanza, by contrast, depicts a world where the civic has a more precarious hold, a world of 'mansions dynamited decades ago' leaving rhododendron bushes to run riot 'purpling June/ round Ystwyth'. In the chimney post 'nestings chant/ Ensemble; they are demanding life, more of it', as if about to recolonise the land which had been won by cultivation but is now to be claimed back. The speaker lacks heart for the fight-back, admiring the grass he's meant to scythe, the instrument being blunt anyway, and his attempts at bean-growing inept, and disapproved of by a neighbour who notes the inadequate crafting ('the bad free-verse of our planting') in a negative parody of the network of poets which has now been left behind in the urban centre. There is an anxiety, then, about a loss or decline of talent, and a sense of belatedness and isolation. In the urban/rural contrast, the urban connotes the intellectual stimulus and feedback the poet needs, while the rural is implicated in a sense of being becalmed and idle. Almost anything grows in the countryside, but thoughts, he finds, *don't* seem to grow as easily there as in the city.

The intertextual connections, as often, complicate the matter: the two eleven-line stanzas of Houston's poem 'Gardens' shadow the two stanzas of Didsbury's 'The Residents, 1840', dedicated to Houston. Both poems have an 'urban' first stanza and a 'rural' second stanza. An archeologist by profession, Didsbury's first stanza (*'Menzies at Mosul'*) concerns the Scottish antiquarian Archibald Menzies (1754–1842) exploring the temple inscriptions at Mosul in modern Iraq, a city identified with the site of the Biblical Nineveh: the poem begins 'The mud walled cities. I approve of them./ Law and commerce and scholarship.' He corresponds 'with Farquhar, a long way east,/ about the coathanger scripts of India, but only because I have to.' The second section, *'Farquhar in Bengal'*, shows a kind of renunciation of western values; the study of eastern scripts had led to the adoption of 'eastern' values ('I have given up learning for the necklace of sense/ which my woman brings me in the evening'); there is (as with Menzies) a split between inclination and duty ('In the mornings I do what I have to do,/ the rest of the time I think about myself'). Farquhar will withdraw from the intellectual network which has linked them ('I shan't be replying to Menzies' last). Though oddly aligned, they are also estranged, as each imagines that the other imagines himself to be a god: the Menzies stanza ends 'He sits there painted blue/ and writes he believes he is Krishna', while the Farquhar stanza concludes with 'he knows all I knew now/ and begins to believe he is

God'.[14] In this context Didsbury's poem can be read as a still urban-dwelling Didsbury/Menzies puzzled at the now rural-dwelling Houston/Farquhar's self-imposed exile, and the turn his interests are now taking. At a more generalised level, both poems consider the relative merits of an urban-intellectual collective kind of knowledge on the one hand, and on the other a 'rural' wisdom achieved by withdrawal, isolation and meditation.

As Linden Peach has noted, Houston's post-Hull period results in an increase in the number of poems about rain,[15] and 'The Rural Muse' implicitly endorses, we might argue, an urban poetics, especially when read in the context of Houston's non-poetic comments on his work. Thus the opening, 'Here are all varieties of rain' seems to assert that the countryside contains rather less than God's plenty, and there is again that sense of nature as a circumambient entropic force constantly striving to obliterate traces of human civilisation, like the 'dense hedges that resent the hidden roads'. The roads, moreover, have to negotiate the land (literally) as they 'tortuously thread the countryside', following detours and doublings which the lie of the land dictates, unlike the rectilinear geometry of 'Gardens' which seems to actively facilitate encounters. At any rate, in this poem, what is recorded is not a failure of inspiration, but a registering of an environment which fails to stimulate. Here, says the poet, 'I am given facts of green, not ideas',[16] and what is around him offers only 'glum parables of stark containment',/ Like several frogs trapped in the garden tank/ Where a drowned mouse floats till all are tipped out'. Linden Peach suggests that Houston (who is Welsh by birth) rejects in such poetry the clichéd mantle of the 'Anglo-Welsh' poet whose settings would be predominantly rural and pre-modern, whose poetic stances would be ruminative, static and predominantly univocal, and whose line of ancestry would go through R.S. Thomas and the early Seamus Heaney. This is the outlook vigorously condemned by Ian Gregson (himself a 'Hull' poet, anthologised in A Rumoured City, who is also a Lecturer in English at University of Wales, Bangor) in the 1992 article cited earlier in this book. Strikingly here (and contrary to Derek Mahon's sentiment cited at the start of this book) Houston denies that such rural settings are the places where a thought could grow, for, on the contrary, 'No, it does not make me think, this valley'. In fact, to be blunt about it, the poet seems to be going completely bonkers in all this rural peace, as the rain drums 'like hard boiling' on the kitchen roof, and the rural muse, grotesquely fisting the poet, seems to be trying to rape him rather than woo him as 'Her green fist in my throat, the rural muse/ Would have me believe that nature is enough'. Houston's thoughts grow, then, on pavement and tarmac and under the sodium lights, or just immediately beyond the city, where the ground is flat and featureless and the road sweeps grandly on to the sea, rather than threading the tortuous hills of Ceredigion.

Another constant in the Hull poet's repertoire is the lift and exultation given by the flatness and emptiness surrounding the city, by the abundance of light, air, and space ('The Return' has as epigraph the line from Baudelaire '*Aujourd'hui l'espace est splendide*'). A common motif is when the overburdened heart (that recurrent word) lights out for these territories, where it finds relief. Andrew Motion's 'Spurn', for instance, in *Heartlands: Words and Images from the River Hull Corridor* (ed. Shane Rhodes, City Arts Unit of Kingston Upon Hull City Council, 1998) does this at considerable length, while Houston's more compact version is 'Driver', where the poet is seen 'Driving through the city's sodium-yellow A-roads,/ My own compass set for the marshy coastal flats./ Out there I will be quite at ease, and shivering'. The poet adjusts the degree of isolation to his need: out here he is 'truly alone', personal compass set for the coast, cruising at sixty in a silence which is salutary. The accessibility of this hinterland, the sense it gives of being on the edge of a wilderness while also being in a city, is the psychic bedrock frequently referred to by Hull poets as fundamental to the place. Ultimately it is to do with having a choice which allows easy passage from network and community on the one hand to isolation and self-communion on the other. This is the correlative of the airy, estuarial feel of the urban poetic territory which lies 'North of the Word'.

Notes

1   In his pamphlet *Under the Influence, Douglas Dunn on Philip Larkin* (Edinburgh University Library, 1987) Dunn perhaps gives a hint about the motives for compiling *A Rumoured City* when he comments on reviewers' tendency to over-estimate the extent of his own debt to Larkin, and adds 'Nor was it a constant succession of delights to be thought of as "Hull's other poet." It was even worse for anyone else writing poems in Hull' (p. 10).

2   Didsbury's subsequent collections are *The Classical Farm* (Bloodaxe, 1987) and *That Old-Time Religion* (Bloodaxe, 1994). O'Brien's collections after this first book are *The Frighteners* (Bloodaxe, 1987), *HMS*

Glasshouse (OUP, 1991) and *The Ghost Train* (OUP, 1995). For his account of modern and contemporary British poetry see *Deregulated Muse: Contemporary British and Irish Poetry* (Bloodaxe, 1998), and his recent anthology *The Firebox: Poetry in Britain and Ireland after 1945* (Picador, 1998).

3 O'Brien's work is discussed by Kennedy (see below) in the context of British postmodernism and poetry. Michael Schmidt in his *Lives of the Poets* (Weidenfeld & Nicolson, 1998) gives O'Brien a kind of recognition when he writes that '[Carol Ann] Duffy and [Simon] Armitage (along with Glyn Maxwell and Sean O'Brien) have outrun the pack and are already subjects of undergraduate, M.A. and Ph.D attention: canonical not only in their lifetime but in their youth' (p. 848). It is characteristic of the book that no details of this 'attention' are given. David Kennedy in *New Relations: The Refashioning of British Poetry 1980–1994* (Seren, 1996) takes Didsbury as one of three exemplary British postmodernist poets in his chapter '"Just the Facts, Just the": A Rough Guide to British Postmodernism' (the other two are John Ash and Ian McMillan). In the introduction to *The Firebox*, O'Brien himself cites the 'strange, celebratory excursions of Peter Didsbury' in the context of the 'narrative form' of postmodernist verse also represented by the work of Andrew Motion, James Fenton and Michael Hofmann. In *Contemporary Poetry and Postmodernism: Dialogue and Estrangement* (Macmillan, 1996) Ian Gregson discusses Peter Didsbury (pp. 222–5) in a chapter about John Ashbery's influence on British poets, though his conclusion is that the more overt influence on Didsbury is from Christopher Middleton.

4 Dunn is drawing here, of course, upon the distinction between parochialism and provincialism made current by the Irish poet Patrick Kavanagh. 'Provincialism' is a state of mind characterised by its dependency upon norms established elsewhere. Kavanagh writes 'The provincial has no mind of his own; he does not trust what his eyes see until he has heard what the metropolis – towards which his eyes are turned – has to say on any subject.' By contrast, parochialism is a robust state of intellectual self-sufficiency. The parochial mentality 'is never in any doubt about the social and intellectual validity of his parish', and for Kavanagh all great civilisations are based on parochialism 'Greek, Israelite, English'. For a full discussion of the matter (on which I am drawing closely here) see chapter 6, 'Parochialism', in *Patrick Kavanagh: Born-Again Romantic* (Antoinette Quinn, Gill and Macmillan, 1991). The distinction was taken up Seamus Heaney, and used as the basis for an overview of Irish writing in his prose collection *Preoccupations: Selected Prose, 1968–1978* (Faber, 1980), especially in the specific essay on Kavanagh, 'From Monaghan to the Grand Canal', and in the well-known piece 'The Sense of Place'. Kavanagh had described his move from his native countryside

to Dublin in 1939 as 'the worst mistake of my life' (p. 122), and parochialism as defined here seems an implicitly rural value system. Heaney makes it explicit in the final sentence of 'The Sense of Place' when he writes 'And when we look for the history of our sensibilities I am convinced, as Professor J.C. Beckett was convinced about the history of Ireland generally, that it is to what he called the stable element, the land itself, that we must look for continuity' (p. 149). The direct relevance of Heaney's *Preoccupations* to the Hull poetry of the 1980s cannot be doubted – the Kavanagh essay had first appeared in the collection *Two Decades of Irish Writing*, which Dunn had edited for Carcanet in 1975, and the influential 'Englands of the Mind' saw Larkin as voicing an 'essential' England, cognate with Rupert Brooke's Grantchester and Edward Thomas's 'Adlestrop', in which an underlying pictorialised, almost mystical 'deep essence' of England ('The shadows, the meadows, the lanes,/ The guildhalls, the carved choirs', as Larkin says in 'Going, Going') is being obliterated by 'concrete and tyres' (Larkin), by 'houses and roads and factories', as Heaney summarises it (p. 168). By cities, in other words, which this potent rhetoric 'de-essentialises', as far as the notion of 'England' is concerned. The word 'English', in the kind of thinking and feeling which such writing stimulates, collocates 'naturally' with words like 'village' or 'meadow' or 'landscape' – to say nothing of lanes and carved choirs – while 'British' collocates with 'city' or 'army' or 'motorway'. Part of my point in this book is to assert that a street is just as English as a lane.

5   The *locus classicus* here is Leavis's famous (and suspect) detection of a special 'English strength' in the couplet of Keats's 'Ode to Autumn' in which the poet says of autumn that 'sometimes like a gleaner thou dost keep/ Steady thy laden head across a brook': Leavis believes that 'In the step from the rime-word "keep" across (so to speak) the pause enforced by the line-division, to "Steady" the balancing movement is enacted' (*Revaluation: Tradition and Development in English Verse*, Chatto and Windus, 1936, rpt 1969, pp. 263-4).

6   Ian Gregson takes the opposite view and argues for the solid presence of Hull in Didsbury's work: 'In Didsbury's case', he says, 'the city of Hull and its environs provide a stable underpinning to his fabulatory flights into the exotic, and a contemporary ground for his archaeological delvings into the ancient' (*Contemporary Poetry and Postmodernism*, pp. 231-2). He then contrasts this with another British poet he sees as postmodernist, Ian MacMillan, whose 'poems are solidly grounded in the territory of social realism – set mostly in Yorkshire, they refer to mines and factories and to a landscape where the industrial and the rural meet' (p. 232). Ian Gregson is himself one of the nine poets in the *Rumoured City* anthology and these comments seem again a reification

of the familiar Hull dichotomy between the eye and the imagination. The 'territory of social realism' is the feared locale of Terry Street (see footnote 8), lacking in the intellectual 'airiness' (see footnote 9) to which third-generation Hull poets aspire.

7 'Secret narrative' involves the use in poetry of obliquely told, often fragmented and unanchored narratives, emotive but obscure in character, often with highly coloured colonial or historical settings. The name comes from Andrew Motion's 1983 volume *Secret Narratives* (Salamander Press). For more successful poems by Didsbury in this manner see 'A Priest in the Sabbath Dawn Addresses his Somnolent Mistress', which is the opening poem in *The Classical Farm*, and 'A Man of Letters Recalls an Incident in His Youth' from later in the same volume.

8 The 'anti-visual' stance may be related to Douglas Dunn's formulations about the nature of poetic creativity, in which 'merely' looking is placed very low down the scale. Dunn is clearly anxious that *Terry Street* might have seemed limited in precisely this way. For instance, in his Larkin memoir he writes of the Terry Street locale that 'Documentary film crews poked the snouts of their cameras around these streets'; he adds:

> all Larkin knew of that side of Hull's life was what he felt on his eyes, but those lines in 'Here', and perhaps his poem 'Afternoons', contributed to my own attempts to explore the effects that living in Terry Street had on me, at times, I hope, at a deeper level than that of observation. As an outsider observation, however, was as much as I could expect of myself in depicting the other people who lived there; and it was probably Larkin's influence that convinced me that my poems of that time should take the form of testimony and, where I could manage it, of objective realism, if that is ever possible. (p. 10).

Indeed, we might see the whole character of Hull poetry since the 1980s as formed by the desire (and the need) to steer clear of Larkinism, as represented first by Larkin's own work, and subsequently by Dunn's first (and only Larkinesque) book. The 'disparagement of the eye' is an index of the fact that Hull poetry was never in the 'neo-modernist' camp. Roy Fisher, though a poet generally admired in Hull, is very far from the Hull aesthetic (which self-consciously foregrounds the 'imagination', as if this had nothing to do with looking) when he confesses his addiction to 'living too much by the eye'. His long poem *City* shows how radicalising this addiction can be.

9 In the *Rumoured City* introduction (p. 14) Dunn writes of Douglas Houston's poem 'Driver' that it 'embodies the estuarial feeling by which several of the poets who have written in Hull have been tantalised', and Houston (in conversation) uses the term 'airy' to indicate the abstract,

intellectually ambitious quality of the kind of Hull poetry under discussion here. I should record here my gratitude to Douglas Houston for supplying me with data, information and insights about the Hull poets, though he is in no way responsible for the opinions expressed here.

10 Figures on Labour Market Trends, published by the Office for National Statistics, show that the British fishing industry is now virtually dead, with 'only around 5000 fishermen left, fewer than one-tenth of the number of couriers', *Observer* (Business), 15 November 1998, p. 6. The decline in the fishing industry is still accelerating: – it is now 25 per cent smaller than it was four years ago. The only trades with a faster rate of decline in the same period were the leather and footwear industries. The effects of such figures on towns and cities once wholly identified with a single, now vanished, industry are incalculable.

11 In the Hull magazine *Bête Noire*, double issue 12/13, autumn 1991/spring 1992, pp. 69–92.

12 *Bête Noire*, 12/13, p. 185.

13 Both are uncollected at the time of writing, but will presumably be included in Houston's forthcoming new collection from Seren.

14 In Didsbury's poems people often think themselves someone or somewhere they are not: 'The Experts' opens with 'A man who knows nothing about pigeons/ is talking to a man who thinks he's a Roman', while in 'Venery' (also in *The Butchers of Hull*) the 'old retainers' who 'move in the dark recesses of the rooms' 'seem to believe/ they are somewhere else'.

15 'Optimism in the Night: the Poetry of Douglas Houston', *Bête Noire*, 12/13.

16 The title 'Gardens' and the line about 'facts of green' is presumably a covert reference to yet another Hull poet, Andrew Marvell, whose 'The Garden' contains its well-known line about 'a green Thought in a green Shade'.

6 'The hard lyric':
re-registering Liverpool poetry

Since the 'Liverpool Scene' of the 1960s Liverpool poetry has hardly regis-
tered nationally as a distinct entity, but there is now, at the millennium, a
considerable body of work in existence from newer poets associated with
the city. The variety of this new work is striking, in contrast to what was
seen as the homogeneity of tone in the work of the 1960s generation, but
I want to argue, first, that the homogeneity of that earlier work is often
exaggerated, and that on the contrary, the linguistic register used by the
earlier generation was often both extremely fluid and shifting *within* indi-
vidual poems and markedly varied from poet to poet. Second, I want to
suggest that the newer poets, while differing just as much from each other,
operate on a much-expanded stage, registering the impact on (and in)
poetry of the anxieties of more troubled times, when industrial collapse,
social conflict and contested national and regional identities prevent the
growth of that unquestioned, pervasive local rootedness which is seen in
the 1960s material. I will make some attempt to relate my perception of
these changes to the shifting urban environment which provides the mate-
rial of these poems, and will take three 1960s poets and then three from
the 1990s. I will, though, be treating the two groups rather differently,
using, in the main, just a single representative poem from each of the three
major 1960s figures, and not making any direct, cross-generational poet-
to-poet comparisons. As a bridging figure between the 1960s and the
1990s I will consider aspects of the work of Black Liverpool poet Levi
Tafari.

The work of both generations, then, needs to be seen against a back-
drop of violently fluctuating civic fortunes. In the 1960s, following the
success of the Beatles, there was something of a cultural renaissance in

Liverpool which led to an explosion of activity related to pop and folk music, painting and poetry. In 1965 Allen Ginsberg famously declared Liverpool to be 'at the present moment the centre of the consciousness of the human universe',[1] and this period of cultural confidence and optimism is epitomised by Adrian Henri's poetry collection *Tonight at Noon* (Rapp and Whiting, 1967); by the Penguin Modern Poets volume *The Mersey Sound* (1967), containing poetry by Henri, Roger McGough and Brian Patten; and by *The Liverpool Scene*, the collection of poetry and photographs edited by Edward Lucie-Smith, and published in 1967. The Liverpool poetry of this period was widely regarded as 'performance poetry', related to that of the American Beats and the cognate British 'Children of Albion', and associated with pop music and art 'happenings', rather than with 'mainstream' British poetry, which in contemporary terms meant Larkin, Hughes and the 'Movement' poets, with Eliot and Auden as the presiding older generation.

A significant exception to the general vow of silence which the academic establishment seemed to have taken about such writing was an early book of Jonathan Raban's entitled *The Society of the Poem* (Harrap, 1971) which examined then recent and contemporary poetry from an unusually broad social and literary-historical perspective (as his title implies), devoting a few highly critical pages to the Liverpool poets. Raban saw these poets as finding an alternative to 'negotiating and compromising with the full force of literary tradition, as well as with immediate social circumstances' (p. 115). They are representative of poets who find 'extreme solutions' 'through regional groups and poetry readings' intent on 'finding a speaking voice for the poem'. But the result is a 'whimsically impoverished speech, an attempt to get a local, private, dispossessed language into verse, to talk straight, bypassing poetic convention, to the audience' (p. 116). The style, he says, is 'curiously bastardized', owing something to 'the ad-libbed backchat of the stand-up comic, something to the language of movie dialogue ... and something to the mesmeric relationship between the pop singer and his public'. This accurately identifies some of the linguistic elements in the dialogic mix of 1960s Liverpool poetry, and Raban goes on to suggest that several of the poems are knowing, ironic reversals of set genres like the Epithalamium, the Elegy, the Ode, the Nursery Rhyme, the Moral Tale and so on. Such poems deconstruct the boundaries between different linguistic terrains – patter and poetry, chat and verse.[2] However, in Raban's view this is undercut by inherent limitations of outlook and subject matter. Henri, McGough, Patten and Henry Graham, he says, have 'a tedious sentimentality directed variously at small children and pubic schoolgirls' (p. 117), and yet 'this determined childishness, the sustained *faux naif* pose, does release a speaking voice which is able to talk freely from inside its retardations. It announces itself, as do so many of these puritan, minimalist styles of contemporary verse, as the nearest thing to an honest voice that we have in a society of corrupted and compromised adults' (p. 118).

Roger McGough

Raban's criticism cannot be entirely discounted, but it is not quite the whole picture, for the voice in the poems, as well as possessing a distinct linguistic mobility which takes it across registers seldom combined in the same discursive structure, is often more culturally complex than Raban suggests. For instance, in 'Limestreetscene '64' (*The Liverpool Scene*, p. 15) McGough shifts register, and indeed genre, as the poem progresses. He begins with an apparently inconsequential denotation of the speaker's peregrinations through the urban scene, fiercely 'loco-specific' and clearly addressed to a readership to whom the streets and the buildings mentioned are familiar:

> Turned left into Lime Street
> felt small
> like a pelota ball
>
> St. George's Hall
> black pantheonic
> like a coalman's wedding cake
> glows in the neonic
> presence of Schweppervescence
> and 'Guinness is Good for You'

Here the 'exotic' and culturally-specific pelota ball is puzzlingly chosen for use in the simile, rather than (say) the more familiar tennis ball. The difference seems at first to add little, in a way precisely analogous to the moment when Eliot's Prufrock expresses his sense of the triviality of his own life by saying 'I have measured out my life in coffee spoons' – why, the reader might wonder, doesn't he just say '*tea* spoons'? The answer is two-fold, for the image is skilfully over-deter-mined: first, coffee spoons are smaller than teaspoons, so the idea of smallness and triviality is thereby given extra force. Second, coffee spoons are distinctly genteel in comparison with tea spoons, and they therefore evoke the social milieu in which Prufrock's life will be lived out. McGough's pelota ball has the same kind of double-denotative charge: first, it is smaller than a tennis ball (just a little bigger than a golf ball, and weighing about four-and-a-half ounces), and hence intensifies the notion of personal smallness; second, and more complexly, it has an effect equivalent to the way the coffee spoon connotes gentility. 'Pelota' is the Spanish word for 'ball', and it is used as the name of the Basque team-game version of hand-ball (*pelota vasca*, or 'Basque ball'). The ball is 'handmade of virgin rubber, layered with nylon thread and two goatskin covers', and according to *The Guinness Book of World Records* it is the world's fastest ball game, 'a thrilling, dangerous, high-speed game played with a rock-hard ball traveling at over 150 miles per hour'. It is difficult to say whether these connotations of speed and danger are brought into the poem by the word 'pelota', but certainly the use of the word functions as a social-status indicator, just like the genteel connotations of the coffee spoon, for the effect is, first, to construct a speaker (and hence, of course, an audience) of fairly wide education and awareness to whom this game is known; in other words, the *faux naif* air which Raban complains about is immediately revealed to be precisely and knowingly that, when it occurs in the linguistic vicinity of such a word. Second, it imparts a cosmopolitan air which cuts across the conventional notion of a provincial city as a place narrow in outlook (an association which, I think, underscores Raban's comments on the Liverpool poets), linking later in the poem with the mention of such things as Irish linen, Chinese cafes and Viking whalers to suggest the cultural and ethnic complexity of the city.

These linguistically implied elements of cultural sophistication recur in the next lines: in the mid-1960s St George's Hall (a Victorian neo-classical building whose immense bulk confronts the visitor emerging from Lime Street Station) had not yet been sand-blasted clean, and its 'black pantheonic' presence dominates most city-centre views of the period. Its Roman (rather than Greek) style is used as well in the adjoining complex of buildings comprising the William Brown Library, the Walker Art Gallery and the Liverpool Museum, so the coinage 'pantheonic' (referring to the Pantheon in Rome) is historically, architecturally and culturally precise. As an element in a linguistic register, therefore, it is distinctly different from that of the next line, which describes the building as being 'like a coalman's wedding cake', which slips back, from 'acrolect' to 'basilect', as linguists say, that is, to the kind of street chat which coins the irreverent description of the building which has passed into local lore. This kind of humour might also typify the 'ad-libbed back-chat of the stand-up comic', noted by Raban, but it should be said that the comparison is visually precise: the old-fashioned layered wedding cake is typically square, sits on a pedestal or platform and uses fluted columns as supports, a description which more-or-less fits the building as well. The coinage 'pantheonic' is echoed by another word, 'neonic', a couple of lines later, describing the display of neon advertising signs attached to the hotels and other buildings which then faced Lime Street Station. 'Neonic' is an ironic back-formation from the academic register of 'pantheonic', starkly juxtaposing a brash commercial present with an idealistic Victorian past (the neon signs spell out 'Schweppervescence/ and 'Guinness is Good for You'). My point in labouring all this is to draw attention to the cultural and linguistic complexities of McGough's register: you could not accurately say that the poem is either 'chatty' in tone or 'cultured', since it is a dialogic mixture comprising both.

McGough's city does contain more disturbing elements; for instance, there are portrayals of meaningless violence in his work, such as the random shooting in 'The day before yesterday'; but the treatment is predominately cartoon-like, for having been shot in the forehead by a complete stranger while innocently walking down Dale Street, the speaker's parenthetical reaction is that 'it was terribly embarrassing'; he stumbles bleeding into the Kardomah Cafe and orders 'coffee and hamroll', but the girl behind the counter 'explained that I was making a mess of the Danish pastries & could I take my dripping carcass elsewhere'. The point of the poem is nothing to do with contemporary urban angst, even though the killer was 'seeking to prove his existence through an intense traumatic experience'. Rather, it settles into a satire against the pretensions of chic gentility: The speaker is more concerned about ruining his new 'Raelbrook shirt & vertical-striped Italian jacket with brass buttons', and maintains decorum by slipping 'into the gentlemen's' (note the registerial precision involved in *not* calling it 'The Gents') to give up the ghost with as little fuss as possible. Likewise, there is the threat of nuclear destruction in McGough's work, but again the treatment is, so to speak, slickly counter-intuitive, as in 'At lunchtime, a story of love', where the speaker's opportunistic announcement of an impending nuclear strike merely leads to scenes of joyous public copulation on the bus. The 'panic' spreads, so that each day people take erotic advantage and 'pretended that the world was coming to an end at lunchtime'. The poem ends, 'It still hasn't. Although in a way it has', which is a cursive, whiplash ending that re-activates and re-adjusts the sense of the whole poem. Again, then, the point of the poem becomes a satire on the social conventions which keep people separate and encased in their inhibitions. The scenario, notice, is essentially urban: it depends on the crowded commuter bus bringing people into the city for work each day, a social space of unusual intimacy in which strangers sit in close and frequent proximity to each other, but remain strangers.

Brian Patten

Where McGough is overtly 'loco-specific', frequently mentioning actual locations and drawing closely, as here, on their cultural and social implications, Brian Patten's work in the 1960s was much less overtly anchored, even though he expressed perhaps most clearly of the group the explicit aim of putting the city into the poems. In the interview snips which intersperse the poems in *The Liverpool Scene* he says 'I've been trying to get something about the city into my poems. I'm amazed I'm on this, this city with winds and grass blowing through, and it's like being on a planet, and this planet is in this universe, and the clouds are going past me, you know. It's a fantastic feeling. I'm trying to get this in my poems. Mainly lyric, the hard lyric' (p. 63). The detail of this remark would lead us to expect more of what is conventionally 'lyrical' in Patten's work, but it is, as he memorably says, the 'hard lyric', with a kind of underlying toughness, which is typified by 'Party Piece' (p. 62), one of his best and best-known poems in which a couple make love after a chance encounter at a party, and the poem ends:

> So they did,
> Right there among the Woodbines and Guinness stains,
> & later he caught a bus, and she a train,
> And all there was between them then
> Was rain.

This is remarkably well-behaved poetry, simultaneously obeying the typographic conventions of prose (it has standard punctuation) and verse (every line begins with a capital letter). It makes tight use of rhetorical tropes like zeugma ('the party-goers go out/ & the dawn creeps in'), neat metaphoric transfers ('let's unclip our minds'), a tight lexical and syntactical balance within the line which is reminiscent of Pope ('& later he caught a bus, and she a train'), and a concluding iambic pentameter within a rhyming couplet structure ('And all there was between them then/ Was rain'). The line break in the pentameter is perfectly placed to facilitate the slight pause in performance which will give exactly the right sense of pathos and finality, and the whole poem is wrought with a fine spareness and concision. As a kind of contemporary, street-wise, troubadour mode this could hardly be bettered, and the tenderness it expresses is credible, proper to the macho protagonist, and salting the lyric, so to speak, with hardness. This is Patten at his best: the verse is virtually allusion-free, and remarkably homogeneous in register, without the shifts of linguistic gear which are common in McGough. There is a verbal dexterity which is like McGough's, but it is seldom used for humorous effect, and to imply that this kind of writing were wholly performance-dependent would make little sense.

Adrian Henri

Adrian Henri's techniques in the 1960s differed very markedly from those of the other two poets in the group. Henri, then as now, was closely tuned in to European and American artistic avant-gardism, looking back to Dada and Surrealism, to Duchamp, to major modernist artists like Jasper Johns and Kurt Scwitters, and to contemporary 'happenings'; to the activities of political groups like the Situationists, and to conceptual art generally. His 'Summer Poem without words' (in *The Liverpool Scene*) typifies this ambiance and is richly redolent of this provenance:

> (To be distributed in leaflet form to the audience: each poem should be tried within the next seven days.)
>
> 1. Try to imagine your next hangover.
> 2. Travel on the Woodside ferry with your eyes closed. Travel back with them open.

3. Look for a black cat. Stroke it. This will be either lucky or unlucky.
4. Find a plastic flower. Hold it up to the light.
5. Next time you see someone mowing a lawn smell the smell of freshly-cut grass.
6. Watch *Coronation Street*. Listen to the 'B' side of the latest Dusty Springfield record.
7. Sit in a city square in the sunlight. Remember the first time you made love.
8. Look at every poster you pass next time you're on a bus.
9. Open the *News of the World* at page 3. Read between the lines.
10. The next time you clean your teeth *think* about what you're doing.

This might be called a poetic statement rather than a poem, for there is an element of conceptual art in the notion of the poem without words: the actions actually performed will be the poem, not the words on this page, which are merely its specification, just as, in what was later known as 'Land Art' (and associated with figures like Richard Long and Robert Smithson) the artifact is the walk itself through a certain terrain, and not the adjustments to the landscape (piled stones, for instance) which are left as the material traces of this activity. The actions listed in the poem constitute a radical reclamation of the most ordinary aspects of day-to-day life, radically extending notions of what the imagination is, in the manner advocated by the Situationist theorist Raoul Vaneigem, for whom 'poetry is the act which reverses the perspective'. He continues 'True poetry cares nothing for poems. In his quest for the Book, Mallarmé wanted nothing so much as to abolish the poem. What better way could there be of abolishing the poem than realizing it?'[3] The chapter from which I am quoting here begins: 'Human beings are in a state of creativity twenty-four hours a day. Once revealed, the scheming use of freedom by the mechanisms of domination produces a backlash in the form of an idea of authentic freedom inseparably bound up with individual creativity.' Henri's poem seeks to embody the ideals of this august Shelleyean rhetoric: it seeks to abolish poetry in the conventional sense (hence, it calls itself a poem without words) and re-embody it in the individual creativity evoked in Vaneigem's text: in doing this he seeks to stimulate the backlash of individual freedom against the scheming mechanisms of domination. Likewise, the cultural artifacts which a high modernism schooled by Adorno would despise as inauthentic – a plastic flower, *Coronation Street*, Dusty Springfield, advertising posters, the *News of the World* – are here salvaged and embraced. They are not so much recommended for study (this is not the syllabus for a cultural studies programme) as for contemplation: what we are asked to read between the lines of the newspaper is not the hidden or implied meanings – much less the construction of cultural, gender and racial identities – but literally the blank spaces. Likewise, we must 'look' or 'hold' or 'watch' or 'listen' – for those crystallisations of the quotidian flux of perception – in the spirit of Susan Sontag's 1966 essay *Against Interpretation*.[4] The plastic flower, for instance, is to be genuinely admired: in another of Henri's poems the first sign of spring is the appearance of plastic daffodils in Woolworth's. The flower is not despised as inauthentic, nor – heaven forbid – regarded as a symptomatic simulacrum of the postmodern identity. Such puritanical condemnations are utterly remote from a sequence of observations which teases us out of thought with the relentlessness of Keats's 'cold pastoral' urn. Other lines in the sequence recommend the experiencing of the senses and of bodily sensations (imagining a hangover, traveling with closed eyes). Such 'deep' experiencing of the simplest everyday act (brushing the teeth, for instance) is the kind which Vaneigem sees as potentially transforming. It attempts to understand an oft-made proclamation, one which teases us out of thought, that in a post-revolutionary situation literally *everything* would be different.

If we were to generalise, then, about the way the city is represented in and suffuses this 1960s-period verse we could argue that it is a kind of urban play-field, always potentially the benign backdrop to the poet's pleasure, enlightenment and fulfilment. As the facilitator of the poet's experiential and personal 'Odyssey', it becomes an urban equivalent to Wordsworthian 'nature' – a point I will come back to later.

If the 'pop' poetry of the 1960s voiced a confident 'regionally devolved' literature in a city which was still very sure of its worth and values, then the contrast with the poetry of the 1990s is very stark. Liverpool's cultural bubble burst and dispersed in the 1970s and 80s, and as industrial decline and civic demoralisation gathered pace, there occurred a series of widely reported disasters associated with the city, including the so-called 'Toxteth Riots' of 1981, the Heysel Stadium tragedy involving Liverpool football fans in Brussels in May 1985, the Hillsborough disaster in Sheffield in April 1989, again involving Liverpool fans, and the abduction and murder of two-year-old Jamie Bulger in Bootle in February 1993 by two ten-year-old boys. Over the same period, from 1983, the Militant-dominated Labour administration of the city under Derek Hatton made Liverpool synonymous in the national media with extremes of left-wing local government. The cumulative demoralising effect on the city of these events is difficult to estimate, but was undoubtedly considerable, and undoubtedly suffuses the later poetry associated with the city.

Levi Tafari

The most successful contemporary Black Liverpool poet has been Levi Tafari, 'born and raised in Liverpool by Jamaican parents' as Benjamin Zephaniah says in the biographical notes to Tafari's most readily available collection, *Liverpool Experience: Collected Poems*,[5] Tafari's choice of the title *Liverpool Experience* and the use of the Liverpool landmark the Liver Buildings on the front cover of his book make strong loco-specific claims, but the work's most immediately prominent affinities are with a national burgeoning of Black politically conscious 'performance writing' which emerged in the 1970s in the work, especially, of Linton Kwesi Johnson (*Dread Beat and Blood*, Bogle L'Ouverture, 1975) and later in that of Benjamin Zephaniah. The term 'dub poetry' was invented by Johnson, and denotes poems primarily written for performance, often in 'Nation Language', which is to say in a style containing lexical and grammatical features identified with Caribbean or Black British English: the term is a coinage by Barbadan poet Kamu Brathwaite, intended to provide an alternative to more traditional labels which denote linguistic hybridity but also contain somewhat negative associations, like 'creole', 'patois' or 'dialect'. Dub poetry often makes use of calypso or reggae rhythms, and often contains a radical political message. (Johnson claimed that it stemmed from the practice of Jamaican radio DJs in the 1970s.)

In many ways, and in spite of its exciting and energetic qualities when staged in clubs and poetry venues, dub poetry is both verbally and conceptually a rather austere mode of writing, which proscribes directly 'confessional' or first-person accounts of 'real-life' experience – in this regard it is quite different, for instance, from the kind of politically conscious poetry associated with the feminist movement, and also from the styles most favoured by Black women poets like Grace Nichols, Jackie Kay and Jean 'Binta' Breeze. Its characteristics can be seen in one of Tafari's most successful poems 'Pat-a-Cake Inna Bakers Stylee' (*Liverpool Experience*, pp. 38–40). Tafari had trained at a catering college and then went into full-time catering, attending the Liverpool 8 writers' workshop in the late 1970s, finally giving up his secure job in 1981 to earn his living as a performer. Hence, one might expect the poem to draw upon this experience, as indeed it does, but in a highly stylised and heightened way, using a 'tall-tale' mode, which, again, has specific generic and cultural affiliations, particularly to the Trinidad form of the 'calypso tale', whose characteristics are such things as the use of subversive irony, melodramatic exaggeration, farcical anecdote, a degree of stereotyping, and dramatic repetition, all of which are seen in the poem. Interviewed for a job as a baker, and asked to demonstrate his capabilities, the protagonist makes a cake in the shape of the Eiffel Tower, then 'twelve dozen loaves/ in less than half an hour'. He then asserts his pride in his ethnic identity by rustling up some 'fried dumplins' ('It's roots food') and then 'juggled them round with one hand/ on seven different plates they did land' The interview/audition ends with a fantastic demonstration of culinary and performance skills:

> Then I put the Eiffel tower on my head
> in each hand stood twelve loaves of bread
> Then I did an African dance around the table
> put them down nice and stable.

The political point of all this is perhaps that although arriving for the interview conventionally dressed 'in a crisp black suit', a Black applicant needs to meet expectations of something exotic, but this kind of political point-scoring is only an undercurrent in the poem: the applicant himself wants to whip up some fun as well as some food, and explicitly rejects the routine of factory work in favour of hotel-style catering, assuming that that it will provide some outlet for such élan. The performance gets him admiration, but not the job, the manager's reaction being 'Friggin Hell son you've got an expert's touch,/ but I'll have to say no because you fuck about too much!'. The poem ends with this rhyming couplet, which wraps things up like the rhyme at the end of a Shakespearean scene. The joke is meant to rebound on the teller, rather than simply implying racial prejudice on the manager's part, or simply making the point that a Black interviewee fails to get the job even when obviously brilliant. Clearly, then, these are not events narrated as they actually happen: rather, they take place in the 'generic out-take' of the oral 'tall tale'. The stereotyping and stylisation pervade the material and take in all the figures portrayed. The protagonist contains elements of a persona-type widely used by Black British poets, which is that of an 'innocent abroad' whose naivety of outlook enables the poet to register impressions of difference (between Britain and the 'Island' culture of the West Indies, say, or Black 'roots' culture more generally). In performance, the 'Island' persona is given marked linguistic features of accent or lexis. Examples of this practice are seen in the work of Jamaican-born poet James Berry, whose 'Lucy' figure, a Jamaican immigrant living in London, writes letters home to her friend Leela (see *Lucy's Letters and Loving*, New Beacon Books, 1982). Other examples of the use of the 'naive persona' are the 'Mama Dot' figure used by Fred D'Aguiar (see *Mama Dot*, Chatto, 1985) and the 'simple immigrant from Clapham Common' who speaks in John Agard's well-known poem 'Listen Mr Oxford don' (in *Mangoes and Bullets*, Serpent's Tail, 1990, p. 44). I have emphasised here the 'extra-Liverpudlian' affiliations of Tafari's writing, although Fred D'Aguiar, in a general chapter on Black British poetry, links Johnson's 1975 breakthrough (introducing politicised writing in non-standard dialect linked with popular musical forms like reggae) to the 'Liverpool scene' of the previous decade: he writes that 'the poems [in Johnson's 1975 collection] had startling resemblances in their social concerns to the best of the Liverpool poets of the decade before, making them anti-establishment in their appeal and popular – qualities unfamiliar to most poets operating in Britain at the time'.[6] Furthermore, the kind of local integration between writers and readers seen in the 1960s Liverpool poets and their audiences continued in the 1980s when Zephaniah was poet/writer-in-residence at the Active Artist's Collective in Liverpool during the years 1988–89, resulting in his booklet *Inna Liverpool – A celebration of the City of Liverpool*,[7] and in the publication of Tafari's *Liverpool Experience* collection with Zephaniah's 'biographical notes'. But the Black poet contemplating this city always remains conscious of its role in supporting the slave trade, and Tafari is quoted in the introduction to *Liverpool Experience* to the effect that 'Liverpool had the biggest seaport once, and here all the slave-trading took place. The slavery connection has put a tarnish on Liverpool, and that is what the city is suffering for now' (p. 9). By 'now' is meant the

Thatcher era of spreading unemployment which hit Liverpool especially hard in the 1980s; as the title poem 'Liverpool experience' says, being Black imposes an extra layer of suffering: 'Yes living inna Liverpool/ is living in hell/ especially if you are/ black as well' (p. 73). However, the five sections in the book each move the focus progressively outwards; the first is about the poetic medium itself, with poems on 'De Tongue', 'De Word' and 'Duboetry'. The second ,'we a guh learn sinting', has poems on school, learning and socialisation (it includes 'Pat-a-Cake'): the third, 'inna land a competition', is on the city itself, the fourth has five poems about women and love, expressing a very traditional set of gender stereotypes and expectations, and the final section, 'people of de earth' looks outward to systems of oppression in the world at large (such as apartheid in South Africa, the power of the American dollar and so on). The general effect of this arrangement is to situate Liverpool in an overall context, rather than viewing it more-or-less in isolation as the 1990s poets considered below have tended to do. But while the affinities with the 1960s poets can, in general terms, be felt, the sense of the city's changing economic fortunes, and the need to voice a radical dissent, is very palpable throughout Tafari's work.

A major source for Liverpool-based poetry in the 1990s is the anthology *Liverpool Accents: Seven Poets and a City*.[8] The editor's brief preface disclaims any attempt at making a representative survey, and makes it clear, too, that he is not attempting to identify and promote a new 'post-pop' Liverpool 'school' or scene. Instead he makes the much more modest claim that 'What these poets have in common is that each has a biographical link with Liverpool. Some were born in the city and have lived in it most of their lives. Others who were born and brought up in Liverpool have moved away to be further educated, to find employment, or for similar reasons. ... Most have written some poems set in, or about an aspect of the place. Some have written a great many more.' In one sense, as this implies, the book represents a kind of Liverpool poetic diaspora. Of the seven poets included, Elaine Feinstein was born in the city but grew up elsewhere. Grevel Lindop, Professor of English at Manchester University, followed the Oxbridge academic exile-path out of the city at eighteen; Jamie McKendrick spent part of his childhood there but is now Oxford-based; Deryn Rees-Jones was born in Liverpool, read English at Bangor, then took a doctorate at Birkbeck College, before moving back to Liverpool to take up an academic post; Peter Robinson himself lived in Liverpool from the age of three, left to study at York and Cambridge universities, and has been an English lecturer in Japan for more than a decade; Adrian Henri, the only one of the 1960s poets included here, has lived in Liverpool for over forty years; Matt Simpson, finally, was born in Bootle, studied at Cambridge, but returned to the city and has had his main career as an academic in Liverpool.

Though the book, then, cannot represent any Liverpool 'group', it nevertheless represents the 1990s, just as Lucie-Smith's *The Liverpool Scene* and the Penguin Modern Poets volume *The Mersey Sound* represented the 1960s. The diasporic character of the later book means that the poets concerned are not generally in direct contact with a more-or-less homogeneous audience through readings and performances, as the 1960s poets were – that culture has gone. Their publishers are predominantly imprints like Bloodaxe, Carcanet and Seren, which publish the bulk of contemporary poetry, rather than the 'prestige' houses like OUP (ironic as that now seems) and Faber (McKendrick is the exception to this).[9] This reflects the fact that these are poets who do not make their primary living from poetry and poetry readings. It may be that the urban cultural homogeneity in which the earlier generation of Liverpool poets flourished is simply no longer possible – that the 'urban bard' that Henri used to be is no longer a tenable option: there is, of course, some truth in this.[10] The most sustained use of the city's landscape and environment is in the work of Matt Simpson, while the poet whose references to it are the most oblique and fragmentary is Deryn Rees-Jones, and I will therefore concentrate on the work of these two, as a kind of 'bracketing' pair (though not confining discussion to their poems in the *Liverpool Accents* volume). I will also discuss a work of a very different kind, Robert Hampson's sequence *Seaport*, which was published, like so much poetry which has later emerged as significant, outside the sphere of mainline publishing houses and distribution networks.

Matt Simpson

Matt Simpson's main collections have all been published by Bloodaxe, beginning with *Making Arrangements* (1982), now out of print as an individual volume, but included in entirety in *An Elegy for the Galosherman: New and Selected Poems* (1990); his most recent collec-

tion to date is *Catching Up With History* (1995). All Simpson's work
draws closely on his autobiography and has a strong narrative thread
which runs from poem to poem. As he says in the biographical note to
Galosherman, 'Most of the poems in this collection have been care-
fully arranged so as to suggest an evolving story, a pattern of forma-
tive moments in the life of a poet who, born into a Liverpool seafaring
family before the Second World War, grew up in the bombed back-
streets of Bootle. ... Progress is mapped from the emotional intensities
of home in Bulwer Street ... towards university at Cambridge, then
half-a-lifetime's teaching, mostly in Higher Education'.

   Several of the poets in *Liverpool Accents* quote the phrase from the
start of Simpson's poem 'Bootle Streets' about the 'ocean-minded
streets' adjoining the docks which were the cityscape of his upbring-
ing. Crudely, these streets had to do for Simpson what the mountains
did for Wordsworth: that is, they had to awaken a peculiarly fraught
and mixed emotion of fascination, intrigue and fear, the sense of some
great force around him which is not wholly benign, and not wholly
understood. The Wordsworthian parallel could go further, for this
poetic enterprise of sustained introspection and retrospection results
in the kind of verse autobiography which we see in *The Prelude*. The
key poem 'Making Arrangements' (*An Elegy*, p. 23) begins with this
sense of the streets as 'lines of force' whose pull cannot be wholly
resisted, even by those whose exile-track takes them to Oxbridge and
the lecture theatre, rather than across 'the thousand miles of furrowed
brine/ of fragrant isles' (mentioned in 'Bootle Streets') which lead to
ports all round the world ('Hobart, Valpo, Montevideo') and the
engine rooms and crews' bars on freighters and passenger ships.
'Making Arrangements', then, constantly promises (or threatens) to
say that 'geography is destiny': if the opening lines are true, then the
poet/speaker, who never went to sea, must be marked, and perhaps in
some way broken, by these forces, in ways other than physical:

> Look at the map. The streets where I grew up
> move in a direction hard to resist,
> lines of force that drag down to grey docks,
> to where my father spent his strength.

Hence, even for the long-time academic, the formative locale of these
dockside streets lives on within him. These streets are not comfortably
in the past, away on the other side of the city, and available as the

topoi of nostalgic reverie, for the whole atmosphere is one of uncom-
fortable, half-understood complicity with the hardness and even
brutality they engender: the poem continues:

> I am making these arrangements into meaning
> to re-inhabit after twenty years some places of
> myself – backyards full of ships and cranes,
> of hard-knock talk, and death – not just
> to mouth at ghosts, unless there's welcoming
> in such a courtesy; not merely exorcise:
> I'd like to talk at this late stage on equal terms,
> declare a kind of coming of age
> to those who have implanted death in me.

The phrase 'some places of/ myself' is striking, and implies that this
is a kind of return to the primeval 'first locale', but unexpectedly, the
'lines of force' are still potent, and the choices made long ago still
demand to be rehearsed and justified all over again. For instance, the
intransitive use of the verb 'drag' is curious, and suggests an omission:

> The streets drag down to the docks – to warehouses,
> dericks, pigeons, and hard men
> that I resisted twenty years ago
> by riding inland, choosing softer options
> they would say.

Here the phrase 'choosing softer options' sounds a note of guilt at the
inevitable severance from that childhood background, and this note is
a constant in all those poets whose trajectory includes social-class
transition (Heaney and Harrison are obvious poetic parallels). In
Simpson it sounds most clearly in 'Latin Master' (*An Elegy*, p. 37),
which is about an archetypal figure in such 'transitioning' lives, that
is, the school teacher who opens the way for the crossing of social
boundaries by general encouragement, or by lending books, or merely
by suggesting books to read. Thus the speaker becomes a spy-at-home,
a class-traitor, a turncoat (to use the emotive inner language used in
the poem itself); 'His Latin verbs put me to work/ inside the fort,/
made turncoat of me in the end'. Hence, gradually the teacher's intro-
duction of Bach or Brahms 'lost us our purchase on the things of
home,/made traitors of us to our kind'. So the anti-localising force of
education counters and defeats the local force, the ocean-ward drag of

the streets 'he altered all our history,/ until the sea/ seemed to lose its dragging power/ and we learnt to hate our dockland streets/ and know ourselves barbarian'. The resulting trans-personal subjectivity envisages a peculiar intimacy between normally discrete entities – person and place, present and past, father and son, even – as if the speaker is somehow beginning to doubt the very bedrock notion of individuality and calling it into question, even though one might suppose that an increasingly sure sense of the self, and a confident possession of its prerogative of existential 'self-improvement', would be one of the products of the life trajectory this personal *Prelude* describes. At one level this inter-generational subjectivity has a 'simple' physical counterpart, for the line 'those who have implanted death in me' refers to the speaker's recognition of a hereditary illness, suggested more explicitly in 'Once', which asserts that 'the dead/ are too expensively alive/ in the bone, the membrane,/ the organ out of tune'.

The notion of the street as a portion of the self, locus of the transpersonal self which collates father and son, place and person, past and present, recurs in 'Blossom Street' (*An Elegy*, p. 75). The poet drives back to familiar streets, pulled by the 'drag' he had long ago resisted, 'It is myself/ I am compiling, re-arranging a town/ for reasons I don't understand'. The 'turncoat' is still sensible of his shame ('What is it that/ accuses?/ I walked the length/ of Blossom Street,/ caught by a name/ from thirty years ago, a terraced street,/ ancestral place I'd never seen before'). The ancestral place is part of his father's life, and 'From here his ruined boyhood comes/ spilling into what I have become./ This is where the sea begins its mutterings.' The mutterings, presumably, are within the speaker and are in the main accusatory. The accusation is implicit here, but explicit in the previous poem, where it receives its starkest and most memorable expression:

> Education, also, exalted and betrayed.
> I was the sailor's son who never put to sea.
> I left the city like
> the Cunard liners and returned
> to find their red and black
> familiar funnels gone from gaps
> between the houses where I'd lived.

One of the most interesting things about poems like this is their inherent assumption of a kind of benign integrity embodied within

these streets, in spite of the embitterment and family cruelty which
they also engender, and which Simpson is keen to depict, for any
merely nostalgic-elegiac rendition of the past is explicitly disowned.
Betrayed and seduced by education, the scholarship boy turns away
from his upbringing, and in doing so loses some vital self, so that in
middle age the *revenant* comes back to these scenes from the past,
seeking something vital which is buried there, which, by his and its
very nature, he can never find, so that the search itself merely increases
his sense of self-disdain because of the earlier act of abandonment.
These 'Bootle dockland streets' are the ones about which precisely the
opposite was speculated in the Jamie Bulger case, where the very
nature of the terrain, it was suggested, now converted to anonymous
high-rise blocks, vast, impersonal shopping malls, and fast urban
freeways, somehow generated the unfeeling sensibility which commit-
ted the crime, or caused ordinary people to fail to notice a small child's
seemingly obvious distress.

Yet the question remains of what world is given in return for the
one which is lost. The answer, in part, is that in place of Liverpool the
poet receives England, for it is Vaughan Williams's *Lark Ascending*
which (in the poem of that name) he imagines being played at his own
wake, 'when everyone's half-canned/ on Scotch and almost out/ of
dissolute affection', and it's difficult to imagine anything more likely
to harden the sneer in the seagull eyes or draw the lace curtains more
tightly shut. For the spirit (his own) which passes to the skies with
the music is 'something perhaps/ (was this what Brooke naively
meant?) embarrassingly English'. This claim to *Englishness* is
extremely unusual in the Liverpool setting, bizarre, even, in the
context of a city whose claimed affiliations are always with anything
but that – with America, with Ireland, but never with its own regional
environment. While the father's voyages always led in the end to
'approaching land,/ rope to bollard, feet again on stone' ('Seagulls'),
the son's departure was like that of 'the last/ Cunarder facing the
horizon' ('The Other Side of the Street') which never saw harbour
again. The educated turncoat can never know home and landfall
again, even in the painful sense of home expressed in R.S. Thomas's
poignant line 'You are home. Come in and endure it'. He is now, as
Thomas puts it, exiled in his own country.[11]

Deryn Rees-Jones

This mention of Thomas offers a transition to the work of Deryn Rees-Jones, who is 'Anglo-Welsh' in background, brought up in Liverpool, spending childhood summers in Wales, subsequently going to university at Bangor, and then on to doctoral study in London, before returning to Liverpool and taking up a university-sector post in Liverpool (at Liverpool Hope, Matt Simpson's former college). Her prefatory statement in *Liverpool Accents* points to the peripheral status of Liverpool in her work, for she writes that 'Only one of the poems in my first book, *The Memory Tray*, refers specifically to a Liverpool geography, but then very few of my poems incorporate real places'. The poem in question, called 'Soap', explores the Liverpool of popular representation ('there are a lot of clichés about Liverpool that I hate – which is what prompted the poem "Soap"'), and against these mono-dimensional images she places a counter-balancing personal image of the city, viewing it as a series of fault-lines where the tectonic plates of several different cultures meet and overlap, with resulting tensions and frictions ('I value being part of a city that contains such a variety of people, that is a place where Wales, and Ireland, and the North meet'). Though, of course, the notion of the city's underlying 'cultural mix' is a common one – almost a cliché itself, in fact – the emphasis on Liverpool as part of a nexus of interconnections is unusual. More often, its uniqueness is stressed, that sense of its being a kind of psychological island which (in John Kerrigan's words in the introduction to *Liverpool Accents*) is 'an international city which was cut off from its hinterland ... somewhere distinctive yet oddly nowhere' and with an 'air of embattled alienation' (p. 3). But the first of the three sections of Rees-Jones's *The Memory Tray* focuses strongly on the figure of her maternal grandmother (to whom the volume is jointly dedicated), and the introduction to her section of *Liverpool Accents* also seems to pivot on this figure, in a way which closely implicates her with the city itself ('She used to work as a secretary at the Liverpool Philharmonic in the 1930s'), and the details cited link her closely to Rees-Jones's notion of the city as containing 'such a variety of people': 'At one time she had a Chinese boyfriend called Willie Chung (a daring alliance in those days, I imagine). Later she fell in love with a Scottish cabinet maker called Alec'. Though only one of her own poems, as already indicated, 'refers specifically to a Liverpool geography' she ends the brief introduction with a moving comment which interestingly

introduces street geography of the loco-specific Matt Simpson kind,
again evoking that idea of an urban landscape which has as much
personal significance to the perceiving and growing subject as
Wordsworthian mountains, and holds and forms the imagination and
the emotions just as tightly:

> Ten years ago, when my grandmother was being taken to
> hospital for the final time, she asked the ambulance driver to
> do her a tour of the city so she could see it all before she died.
> I often think of that and wonder which route they took, and
> whether she saw the places that she wanted to. Sometimes I try
> to imagine it. And hope that she was satisfied. (p.117)

Yet, it is difficult at first in these poems to *see* the city (though it is
heard and felt), for they are very much poems of interiors, so that the
external geography of social space is merely something whose pres-
ence might be inferred in an opening like 'It might be any winter, any
furnished room – / a table with a tablecloth, a pot-plant in a pot' ('The
Chair'[12]); or 'Being girls, we thought it best to love the Greeks/
sedately taught us in an attic schoolroom' ('Loving the Greeks'). Or
else urban geography is the implied hostile or indifferent circumambi-
ence of the consecrated interior space that provides the setting for
tender intimacies:

> A siren flashes blue and mute Like the moon on a bender,
> staggering drunkenly around the room
> As still our bodies sympathise'
>
> ('Interim')

Here the exterior enters threateningly into the privacy of the room,
like a drunk from the streets who has blundered in by mistake. Indeed,
more often, geography is internalised and made merely metaphorical:
this is the world turned inside out, a classic trope of the love poem (as
in Donne's 'one little room' which becomes 'an everywhere'). Hence,
the opening of 'Shadowplay':

> I come to you like a child, as only an adult could
>
> With the silence
> Growing and shrinking

This is it. Infidelity.
These are the strange geographies of hurt.

You hold my head in your hands
As if it were a globe
Rocking me slowly
From side to side. As if love
Were a country, difficult to place.

In what follows the lover projects shadow shapes of animals on to the walls, and the space of the encounter is thus mimed as both 'macro' (a globe, a country) and 'micro' ('the blank walls of the familiar room'), but without that intervening dimension of the local exterior – the familiar *streets*, rather than the familiar *room* – which are precisely the dimension which the love intensity seems to eliminate. The temporal dimension in erotic poetry loses its *middle* in exactly the same way: the lovers live the *now* (the 'micro' element), and are conscious of the brevity of human life in the context of eternity (the 'macro' element), but eliminate the 'day-to-day', that is, the intricate temporal geometry of meals, pastimes and daily work (Vaneigem's 'everyday' life, which cries out, usually in vain, for transformation). Love poetry, it might be suggested, has a natural tendency towards the a-chronotopic. The internalised geography occludes the 'middle element', and the lover is the person who 'taught me at seventeen/ To make myself a body map', and the room and the self float in a 'dislocated space' without a hinter-land, like the Liverpool evoked by several of the *Liverpool Accents* poets. 'Afterward', likewise, remains firmly inside the room ('Here, in the darkness, I might be with you for the first time'), and the poems continue to operate within a scenario which is almost entirely interior, like the hermetically sealed-off interior spaces of the *film noire* genre, where, among other things, passion and menace, once removed from the mundane quotidian, thereby become oddly aligned. The conven-tionally dangerous space beyond the consecrated interior is hinted at, again, in citing the window and the colour blue, as the environment gradually re-materialises in the post-erotic calm ('Later, in a moment of moonlight,/ We are ordinary again,/ Striped by the shadows of the blue venetian blind'). The moment is presented in a strikingly filmic way, since the 'seeing eye/seeing 'I' sees *both* of the people involved ('Our gleaming eyes are beacons'), whereas the homodiegetic persona would see only one pair of eyes.

The two final poems of the middle section of the book (the section
which centres upon intimate, room-based poems of 'erotic *frisson*')
both use explicit cinematic allusions, and complete a kind of progres-
sion which is rather like that of Joyce's *Portrait of the Artist as a
Young Man*; thus, there is a gradual shift from the Part 1 material,
centred on childhood memories, to the room-based intimacy poems of
Part 2, to an altogether more 'public' kind of writing (using filmic,
cultural reference, for instance) in Part 3. Here, the poems contain
'public' events and established cultural icons (Yeats's marriage in
'William and Georgie, 1917', *Star Treck* in 'Lovesong to Captain
James T. Kirk', high art in 'Leonardo', mythology in 'Porphyria', and
so on). In 'Connections' a chance encounter through a misdialed
phone call evokes a kind of self scrutiny from a personal and national
perspective in response to the voice from the other side of the world
which asks her if she is English. She says she is, but uses the Welsh
word for it ('Am I English? *Saesneg*, I explain'). Likewise, her land-
scape is literally both English and Welsh, but the Welsh mountain is
barely remembered, and the Welsh word for it mispronounced ('I have
stars, I say, English stars, A Welsh mountain I can/ Just remember –
mynydd – a word I can't pronounce too well').[13] So the circumambi-
ent cultural geography is bewildering, complex and far from re-assur-
ing, but this time the speaker's turning inwards to the familiar room
boundaries of personal space also fails to re-assure:

> In this room
> I have newspapers
> Three days old. A vase of dying flowers. The radio.
> I have the voices of the politicians. Books. An atlas
> I can't find either of us on.

Here again, then, the middle ground between the micro-scape of the
room and the global macro-scape which contains the two callers is
curiously absent. The landscape of arctic wilderness around the
distant caller is 'placed' with metonymic precision ('the snow has
never been so thick,/ Caking her lonely wooden house./ the gutters
spill water/ the colour of flour). But the corresponding urban 'midi-
scape' around the speaker at the other end of the phone is conspicu-
ously absent, even though the infrastructure which enables its
superstructural expression – newspapers, radio, politics, books – is
directly mentioned. Such things are precisely what makes the wilder-

ness described in the first half of the poem no longer that, even though (the city-bound speaker thrillingly imagines) you might hear from the distant fir woods 'The comforting roar of the hoarse brown bear'.

Robert Hampson

I will turn finally to Robert Hampson's *Seaport*, a work very different in character and provenance from all the material looked at so far. *Seaport* is in four parts, published as a 46-page A4-sized book by Hampson's own Pushtika Press, in what is described as an 'Interim Edition', since Part 4 is incomplete, being represented only by two fragments included as an appendix. The work is part of the 'avant garde' of contemporary British poetry, an old-fashioned term, but one quite frequently used to designate work which is 'modernist' in technique, with provenance and allegiances that include (on the American side) Ezra Pound, Charles Olson, William Carlos Williams, the 'New York' poets, the Objectivists, the 'LANGUAGE' poets, and (to some extent) John Ashbery; and (on the British side) Basil Bunting, J.H. Prynne, Roy Fisher, Allen Fisher and Eric Mottram. Poets working within this sphere have tended to shun conventional outlets and have set up a wide network of alternative literary sociology with its own bookshops, journals, presses, poetry events and conferences.[14]

Seaport makes extensive use of 'incorporated data' of various kinds, including literary sources such as Conrad's sea novels, Melville's *Redburn* (which, of course, itself uses the same model and incorporates extensive documentary material on the port of Liverpool in the middle of the nineteenth century), the Liverpool material in Washington Irving's *Sketchbook*, Defoe's account of Liverpool in *A Tour through the Whole Island*, letter and diary comments from Nathaniel Hawthorne written during his period as American Consul in Liverpool, and so on. These are not just brief 'allusions' lifted out of context and pasted in, as in *The Waste Land*, but identified quotations, more in the manner of Pound's later *Cantos*. A further strand of data takes in material from historical accounts of the growth and development of the port, of the history of race relations in the city, newspaper accounts of local events and local guidebooks. The verse which links or incorporates this material is spare and taut, avoiding any kind of lexical or imagistic embellishment, and apparently acting simply as a denotative 'seeing eye'.

However, though the style and register look at first to be fairly homogeneous throughout, there are in fact four clear stages which indicate different degrees of intervention in the adopted material. I will focus on this technical aspect of the poem, since in my experience the most frequent demand made of the explicator of this kind of writing is for a demonstration (or laying bare) of the procedural or structural principles on which it is organised. The *first* stage, then, is that of minimal intervention; the poet does a simple cut-and-paste job from the sources, and the passages used are set on the page as prose, with label identifiers, like quotations in an academic essay. For instance, page nine has a series of quotations from Quentin Hughes's *Seaport*, and from Defoe. These might be taken as a series of epigraphs, but they are not placed at the start of the work, or even the start of the section, so that the effect is to deconstruct the distinction between the textual and the paratextual (in Genette's sense; that is, boundary-marking features like titles, sub-titles, epigraphs and so on). Implicitly, this raises fundamental issues about where things begin and end. Did the notorious murder of Charles Wooton by a white mob in Liverpool in 1919 (see Part IV of the poem) begin with Liverpool's involvement with the slave trade? Did the arrest of a seventeen-year-old black youth for dropping a chip-paper in Granby Street, Liverpool, in July 1981 (also in Part IV) begin at the same time? And has it ended yet?

The *second* stage involves slightly more intervention in the source material: sentences are selected and taken out, rather than text being lifted in paragraph-sized blocks. They are then isolated into significant phrase-units, and arranged on the page so that it begins to look like, say, the notes from reading which a lecturer might make in preparing to speak on a topic: this, for instance, is the start of page sixteen (I have numbered the pages through, calling the title page page one):

> between 1846
> and   1855
>   nearly three million people emigrated from Britain
>
>   the majority   from Ireland to North America
>   by way of Liverpool.
>   the famine of 1846
>   (more fully reported in Canada
>   than in the British press)
>   was followed by typhus in 1847

The *third* stage takes the source material into a minimalist poetic register, whereby words and brief phrases on a carefully sculpted page are made to resonate strongly because of the unusual spacing and grouping. Words are isolated by space markers of various sizes, indicating reading pace, degrees of emphasis, and units of breath: the page is composed as a spacial entity, not just as a linear sequence, usually with minimal punctuation and capitalisation. These procedures are part of a clear line of development running from Williams's 'variable foot', Pound's 'ideogrammatic method', Olson's 'Project Verse' and Eric Mottram's 'mosaic' style. The opening page, for instance, is 'perch rock' (named after the New Brighton fort which is the innermost landmark for ships approaching the port of Liverpool):

ships   move in
                    from the bay
close to the flat   coastline of crosby
                    into the narrows

perch rock   stands
                    to starboard
the close
          vestibular   landline
              runs
              from   the point blocks
                                      of flats
to the graceful lines
              of dark-brick
                    terraced houses.

In this instance the technique has been to draw out latent poetic qualities from prose sources by editing and re-spacing the material, so again the process of composition is deliberately pared down, and the scope for poetic 'flights' is crafted out, just as a modernist building would present a plain surface which can be part of an overall compositional massing, but is not allowed to provide a frame for decorative embellishments. All the same, the effect is now distinctly 'poetic', whereas the effect in the first two stages was distinctly 'prose-like'.

Finally, in the *fourth* stage the poetic effect is heightened further, to such an extent that the material might be mistaken for personal observation. This is from part IV, 'The Leaving of Liverpool', which concerns the 1960s cultural boom period referred to earlier, and page thirty is headed 'you can't dance to art (merseybeat 1962–64)' and reads complete:

> a suburban
> music shop
> youth in a
> collarless
> jacket
> fingers the
> chord
> A minor
> on guitar
> cuban-heeled
> boot rests on
> tiny amp
> Vox AC30
> (amp &
> speaker
> combined)
> you could
> carry it
> yourself
>
> the simplicity.

Here the period is marked by sharp metonymic details, like the collar-less jacket, the cuban heels, and the now quaintly modest-seeming audio equipment; the poem has an iconographic quality whereby its slim line suggests, perhaps, the neck of the guitar, or the slimness of the youth himself. Likewise, its ultra-cool tone makes no attempt to impress us with emotive, evocative, sensitive or ingenious diction – the poem simply isn't in that sort of game at all – and hence mirrors the assured self-possession of the guitarist who will use his minimal resources (the three-chord trick, so called) to produce magical effects. *Seaport*, then, offers another version of the 'hard lyric', providing a large-scale vehicle of surprising flexibility which can accommodate the overtly political, the archival-historical and radically pared down versions of poetry's more familiar affective modes.

I have polarised the 1960s and the 1990s work pretty starkly throughout, though the 'bridge' section, I hope, may suggest possible accommodations between them. A different chapter could easily have been written which would emphasise throw-backs, anticipations and continuities between the Liverpool poetry of the two periods (providing a proleptic view of the 1960s, juxtaposed with an analeptic view of the 1990s).

Henri, McGough and Patten are major writers and performers still, and their work has, of course, not remained fossilised in the long-ago moment of 1965 when Liverpool was the centre of human consciousness. Thus, Henri appears in the 1990s *Liverpool Accents* anthology, and '1990s' poet Matt Simpson actually belongs to the same generation. The benign, 'pastoral' city of the 1960s produced a body of work whose tone never dwindled to a narrowly provincial monologia, even while it celebrated its vigorous loco-specificity. In the 1990s, as the city emerged from its traumatising 1980s decade, it has produced a much more troubled and troubling kind of writing. It has, in both senses, re-registered its poetic claims. What links the poets of the two decades is their realisation that poetry can be written (in Patten's phrase) 'Right there among the Woodbines and Guinness stains', that 'this city with winds and grass blowing through' is potentially the site of poetry. This seems elementary, but realising it is always a breakthrough, for the rural, neo-Georgian carapace of poetry has proved amazingly resistant to change.

Notes

1 *The Liverpool Scene*, ed. Edward Lucie-Smith, Rapp & Whiting/ Andre Deutsch, 1967, p. 15.

2 Raban's broadly sociological approach to poetry, and his tendency to view it as a public institution, anticipates much more recent trends in literary criticism. The word 'public', for instance, is currently popular in book titles, such as Richard Salmon's *Henry James and the Culture of Publicity* (Cambridge, 1997), Paul Magnuson's *Reading Public Romanticism* (Princeton, 1998), and Lawrence Rainey's *Institutions of Modernism: Literary Elites and Public Culture* (Yale, 1999). Ultimately, however, Raban's residual allegiance to New Critical ideals seems to make him disappointed that poetry cannot interface with public discourse without being interfused by it.

3 Raoul Vaniegem, *The Revolution of Everyday Life*, trans. Donald Nicholson-Smith, Left Bank, 1983; the quotation is from Chapter 20, 'Creativity, Spontaneity and Poetry'.

4 *Against Interpretation and Other Essays*, London, Deutsch, 1987 (first published 1966).

5 Edited by Cristian Habekost and published by Michael Schwinn (Neustadt 1, Germany, 1989). Tafari was also included in Habekost's anthology *Dub Poetry: 19 Poets from England and Jamaica*, published by the same press.

6 See Fred D'Aguiar, 'Have you been here long?' in *New British Poetries: The Scope of the Possible*, ed. Robert Hampson and Peter Barry, Manchester University Press, 1993, p. 54.

7 Published by AK Press, 33 Tower Street, Edinburgh, EH6 7BN, Scotland.

8 Edited by Peter Robinson and published by Liverpool University Press in 1996.

9 This has turned out to be an advantage, of course, since OUP made its notorious decision in 1998 to withdraw from the publication of contemporary poetry.

10 Though it *is* possible to identify elswehere poets who seem to aspire to that '1960s' urban pop-bard role, such as Ian McMillan, the 'Barnsley Bard', who tours with 'The Circus of Poets' and 'Yakkety Yak'. He has a local status and career pattern which ressembles that of Henri, McGough and Patten in the 1960s, and in a town which has suffered industrially (it contained the Headquarters of the National Union of Miners before the drastic run-down of the coal industry in the 1980s) in ways reminiscent of the fate of Liverpool.

11 These phrases occur in 'The Lost', one of the poems in Thomas's *No Truce with the Furies* (Bloodaxe, 1995): 'We are exiles within/ our own country/ "Show us",/ we supplicate, "the way home". "But you are home. Come in/ and endure it."'

12 All of Rees-Jones's poems cited here can be found in *The Memory Tray*.

13 Rees-Jones is one of the younger Welsh poets praised by Ian Gregson his controversial article in *New Welsh Review* (No. 27, winter 1994, pp. 22–3) entitled 'An Exhausted Tradition'. Gregson sees her as representative of fractured postmodern, multiple identitities, exploring 'mixed Welsh and English ancestry alongside other issues – especially those of gender and the extent to which identity is destablilsed by sexual desire'.

14 For general accounts of this area of activity see such books as Hampson and Barry's *New British Poetries*; *Out of Dissent: Five Contemporary British Poets*, Clive Bush, Talus, 1997 and the anthology *Other British and Irish Poetry Since 1970*, Richard Caddell and Peter Quartermain (Wesleyan University Press, 1998).

7 'Take your shoes off in King's Cross':
envisioning London

Topographical epics

The London writers discussed in this chapter might be called 'visionary historiographers', for all three are acutely aware of the city as a palimpsest, a document constantly over-written, not just by successive eras of history and development, but also by natural and geographical forces. The effect is to emphasise flux and change, seeing urban space as constantly deconstructed and reconstructed, always part of a dynamic, in which everything bears the marks of its previous stage of evolution. The resulting 'mythic geography' or 'psychic geography' is presented within large-scale, epic-length works. The three poets, and their poems, are Iain Sinclair's *Lud Heat* of 1975, Allen Fisher's *Place* of 1974–77 and Aidan Dun's *Vale Royal* of 1995.[1] In what follows I discuss each work in general terms and comment more closely on a short extract from each. I begin, however, by listing seven characteristics which these poems have in common, the seven types of continuity, as it were, between them. First, all three are works of poetry on an epic scale, rather than collections of short personal lyrics. Second, all three centre explicitly on the geography of London, Sinclair predominantly upon parts of the East End, Fisher mainly on South London, and Dun upon the region of King's Cross. Third, all three works have an over-riding concern with mapping and re-mapping their territory in terms of such things as associated myths, historical traces, geo-physical forces, electro-magnetic energies and even psychic agencies, a process for which the poet and critic Eric Mottram used the term 'locatory action'. Fourth, all three pile multitudinous data into their poems, in relation to all these elements; the information load is so great that this kind of poetry seems to require its own label: I call it 'content-specific' poetry, seeing the data and the poem as built into each other, in the way that an art installation is built into its exhibition space in 'site-specific' art-work.[2] Fifth, all three poets blur the boundaries of recognised discourse types, producing what might be called *discursive-hybrids* or *generic-hybrids* which mix together poetry and prose, diary extracts and poetry, jottings and poetry, letters and poetry, sources and discourses and so on. Sixth, all three share (though not in equal measure, and I will make a slightly different connection in the case of Aidan Dun) a mainly American recent poetic ancestry: thus, operating on an epic-scale takes its cue from Ezra Pound's *Cantos*: large-scale local mappings of sharply delimited territory is seen in William Carlos Williams's *Patterson* and Charles Olson's *Maximus Poems*: the use of a diary format within the context of concerned ecological speculation and investigation is seen in Gary Snyder's *Earth Household*, and so on. Finally, all these poets share an ambition to understand the way apparently separate 'systems' (such as sociology, psychology, politics, mythology and history) interact and interpenetrate each other, a quality which Eric Mottram, again, called 'the imagination of synthesis'. It should be added that the data is often presented in such a way as to mock the synthesising ambition, while remaining at the same time driven by it.[3]

In spite of these 'continuities', readers of all three poems will also be struck by the differences in the mental universes they represent, and a figure or device found at the start of *Lud Heat* can be used to encapsulate one of the ways in which they are different. Part One of *Lud Heat* is sub-titled 'The Muck-Rake', in reference to an incident in Bunyan's *Pilgrim's Progress* which Sinclair quotes in his epigraph to the poem. The Pilgrim is shown an image of 'a room where was a man that could look no way but downwards, with a muck-rake in his hand'. A figure above the man's head offers him a celestial crown in exchange for the muck-rake, but he doesn't look up and doesn't see this. This image seems to encapsulate the sombrely pessimistic topography of Sinclair's London vision, as he must have intended when he selected this as his epigraph. His 'psychic geography' is typically ground-based, obsessively scrutinising a dense network of urban streets, his sacred text being a London *A to Z*, rather than (say) a historical or scientific treatise, as might be the case with Fisher, or editions of the poems of Blake, Shelley and Chatterton, as it might be with Dun. Though I see him as one of the London historiographers, Sinclair's work progressively sloughs off the kind of intensive, bibliophile preoccupation with textual traces which is found in Fisher, for his overwhelming bias is towards the annotation of obsessive field-work. Hence, the amount of verbatim quotation from written sources declines in his more recent work. Typically, he is not in his study, but on the stump, *A to Z* in hand, engaging in a distinctly masculinist ambulatory ritual with one of his select group of street-walker companions – usually the film-maker, journalist and novelist Chris Petit, or the photographer Marc Atkins. These rites of urban passage involve setting off early in the day, and pausing mid-morning for a 'full English' at a proper caff, and then a pint or two round lunchtime at a pub with a river view.[4] All this has become familiar to a very large public in the 1980s and 90s, but in prose works rather than poetry. The take-off point for Sinclair's wider reputation was probably the publication of Peter Ackroyd's novel *Hawksmoor* in 1985, with its prominent acknowledgment of the materials from Sinclair's *Lud Heat* which it drew upon. The walk-ritual is ruminative, reflective and goal-orientated: there is always intellectual prey to stalk (Sinclair some-times uses the 'stalker' image in introducing his readings, though with apologies), but the truth is always *out there*, so to speak, in the terri-tory, not within some written source: it is revealed in a shift of the light, a faded advertisement, a message encoded in the names of streets or the location of a steeple. The fieldwork, in other words, subsumes the archival work, which, for a historian, rather than a visionary historiographer, would loom at least as large. Sinclair, then, is a terri-torial scrutineer, a close-reader whose text is the streets, the viewpint usually eyes-down and locked within a very tight framework of close-knit data, rather than seeking to open up broad new horizons of ideas. The muck-rake seems an appropriate emblem.

Allen Fisher, by contrast, and again using the image from Bunyan, can be seen as seeing and accepting the offer of the crown, since his poem embraces an enormously wide range of concerns, is voraciously textual and archival, and constantly strives towards forms of intellec-tual enablement. But he wisely insists on keeping his muck-rake as well, refusing to give it up in exchange, so that his poem retains the detailed topographical 'grounding' – the *A to Z* element – which is the source of much of its fascination. (Fisher's own name for the muck-rake is 'the topological shovel'). In other words, the street names, the chance encounters and the faded advertisements are as fascinating to him as they are to Sinclair, but in Fisher's case this 'fieldwork' element is complemented by a widely ambitious range of archival back-up –

typically, the texts he writes have extensive fragments from several other texts embedded within them, like the debris from a head-on textual collision, and his own texts interpret them, speculate upon them and bring them into new juxtapositions. The result is that Fisher is by far the most demanding of the three writers discussed in this chapter, because the demands made upon the reader are so disparate. The 'crown' image I am using here is meant to suggest a looking outwards to much wider intellectual horizons, sometimes outwards into an intellectual mist through which the light thrown on to the topography is only intermittent.

Aidan Dun, finally, going back again to the Bunyan image, seems more straightforwardly to accept the exchange of the muck-rake for the celestial crown, so that there is a rather different single-mindedness in his poems, a tendency to leave the visionary elements of the poem too conspicuously 'ungrounded'. The implement he mainly uses is without a name, but on the analogy of the muck-rake I call it 'the sky-scrape'. The risk of exclusive reliance on this implement is that the visionary overlay often obscures the contemporary topography, so that the most recent layers of the urban palimpsest disappear altogether, the blend of history and geography, archive and fieldwork, tipping too decisively towards the first element in these dyads. This may imply that Dun's model is really more David Jones's *The Anathemata* than Williams's *Patterson* or Olson's *Maximus Poems*, for while both these Americans superimpose a complex historical and mythical overlay on the locales they write about (the towns of Patterson, New Jersey and Gloucester, Mass., respectively), the contemporary reality of each place is also fully present in each poem, so that history and geography are in counterpoint throughout. The situation is different in Jones's British version of the topographical epic, for here contemporary London has some difficulty in emerging through what Jones calls the 'deposits', which is to say the great mass of historical material – medieval, Roman and Celtic. In 'The Lady of the Pool' section of *The Anathemata*, for instance, comprising some forty pages of densely annotated text, the lavender-seller who meets a ship arriving at the Pool of London speaks a sustained, *tour-de-force* monologue which is a kind of poetic equivalent of Molly Bloom's soliloquy at the end of Joyce's *Ulysses*, except that it is densely loaded with Celtic and Saxon lore, references to Greek and Roman mythology, allusions to obsolete fragments of Christian liturgy and medieval trade practices, and much more. The effect is as if the accumulated local experience of the ages is downloaded and replayed, at high speed and in fragmented form. But what cannot emerge through it all is any real sense of contemporary realities, for the balance between what is *seen* and what is *envisioned* – the tension between the two which provides the energy of 'urban-visionary' writing – is missing. Aidan Dun's Kings Cross is, likewise, more 'crown' than 'muck-rake', and the reader must approach it with that expectation, though I will go on to suggest that it has many compensating qualities. Dun's high-energy recitation style (he commits his long texts to memory like an actor) performs the poem in a lilting, lyric over-drive (very evident in the reading of the poem on the CDs which accompany the text) and is reminiscent of the headlong energy of Jones's epic. It should be added that his 'visionary overlay' of London has several strata which are fruitfully in common with Jones's.

The muck-rake: Iain Sinclair's *Lud Heat*

The first of these works, *Lud Heat*, is some 140 printed pages in the Vintage Paperback edition of 1995. The work is in nine long sections, some poetry, some prose: parts one, three and five are prose 'out-takes' which were written after the rest of the material. The remaining six sections are made up of journal entries, prose commentary and verse, and were written between May and August 1974, when Sinclair was employed by the Greater London Council as a gardener. The original publication was by Sinclair's own Albion Village Press in 1975, and in its original format the photographs interspersed with the text reinforced the loco-specific aspect of this work, though they also seem to have the effect of highlighting questions of factuality in a direct way, making us ask whether what is said about Hawksmoor's churches is truth or metaphor. This slightly inconvenient question seems more easily sidelined in the absence of these mundane photo-graphic prints of the Hawksmoor churches as they are today, these original illustrations being engagingly amateur 'snaps', not heightened art images like Marc Atkins's photographic essays in the 1999 *Liquid City*.

The book, then, is dominated by the idea, expounded in the first section, entitled 'Nicholas Hawksmoor, His Churches', that Hawksmoor's eight London churches (built in the late seventeenth century) exert over London an 'unacknowledged magnetism and control power' and channel into it energies which have their ultimate source in ancient Egypt. Sinclair sees these energies as generated by the pyramid motif which all three churches contain, and by the churches' positioning across the map of London, which imposes these pyramids on the city's geography. This scenario compares interestingly with that of *The Waste Land*, where, again, a network of Renaissance churches is imposed upon the contemporary topography: but they are predominantly Wren's churches in Eliot's poem, and the influence seems essentially benign, whereas Sinclair envisages a malign web of negative influences. The one Hawksmoor church in *The Waste Land* is St Mary Woolnoth, which marks the centre of the contemporary necropolis; those whom death has undone are seen flowing over London Bridge, then up the hill into the City, the heart of which is by the Bank of England close by St Mary Woolnoth, 'with its dead sound on the final stroke of nine'. This use of the ambulatory scenario and the church overlay puts the two poems in dialogue with each other.

Sinclair sees evidence for the 'negative magnetism' of Hawksmoor's buildings in the fact that many notorious acts of violence have taken place in their vicinities, and he cites the Ratcliffe Highway murders of 1811, the Jack the Ripper murders of 1888, and the Kray Brothers' murders in the 1960s. He sees ritualistic and 'Egyptian' undertones in all of these, for example in de Quincey's account of the Ratcliffe Highway murders, in which the killer's energies are said to jump up 'like a pyramid of fire, and the blood of the victims is referred to as 'the silent hieroglyphics of the case'.[5]

One way of looking at this bizarre imposition of sinister meanings onto his own locale is to suggest that it is a way of 'appropriating' urban territory by patterning it. The act of appropriation is essential for the city dweller, since (as Robert Harbison puts it in his book *Eccentric Spaces* (André Deutsch, 1977, p.132)):

> Cities have always violated the bounds of individual conceptions: though cities are entirely human products, they express most clearly the sense of human divergences which no single observer can comprehend entirely.

Harbison sees the detective as the archetypal urban hero, because he 'powerfully re-assures us when he finds the mystery of the city a calculable quantity'. Like fictional detectives such as Poe's Dupin in Paris, Chandler's Marlow in LA, and Paretsky's Warshawski in Chicago – who perceive a pattern in the apparently random violence of their cities – Sinclair's recuperative pattern-making 're-forms' the city so that it again becomes a 'calculable quantity' and falls 'within the bounds of individual conception'. Sinclair's narrative persona is a pattern-maker within this detective tradition, though in his own treatment of the material the detective element remains implicit, if pervasive. *Rodinsky's Room* (Granta, 1999) repeats the basic scenario and proposition that the key to an inner psychosis lies in an outer topographical skein of connections with which it is in sympathetic (if malign) resonance. As is well known, the detective element in Sinclair's material is made explicit by the novelist Peter Ackroyd who uses this data in his novel *Hawksmoor*. Sinclair's patterning, then, re-maps the city in terms of occult and pre-industrial forces. This is how he introduces the Hawksmoor material near the start of the book:

> A triangle is formed between Christ Church, St. George's-in-the-East, and St. Anne's Limehouse. These are the centres of power for those territories: ... St. George's, Bloomsbury and St. Alfege's, Greenwich, make up the major pentacle star. ... These churches guard, or mark, or rest upon, two major sources of occult power: the British Museum and Greenwich Observatory – the locked cellar of words, the labyrinth of all recorded knowledge, the repository of stolen fires and symbols, excavated god-forms; and measurement, star knowledge, time calculations, Maze Hill, the bank of light that faces the Isle of Dogs. (p. 15)

This is Sinclair's basic map of forces, within which he places his detail:

> Yeats in the British Museum, at the time of the Ripper murders, researching into Blake – Blake and Newton, polar opposites. Milton; his early morning walks over the ground where St. George's was to be built. ... St. Luke's obelisk (the church itself is decayed, the roof gone) stands over Bunhill Fields, plague pit, burial place of William Blake, Daniel Defoe, John Bunyan. Plague-year excavations discovering the antiquity of this site as a field of inhumation pre-Roman. ... Milton died here in his house at 125 Bunhill Row. ... Standing here, on a walk along the whole chain of Hawksmoor churches, we notice five minor obelisks in the fenced area beyond Blake's burial slab. (pp. 15--16)

Again, it is interesting that while Allen Fisher mainly works through specific quotations from sources, Sinclair, even at this early stage in his career, often uses more generalised citations like this which legitimise his pattern-making without restricting it. The concentration within his chosen locale of the writerly energies of Defoe, Milton, Bunyan, Blake and Yeats seems to suggest a positive counterpart to the violent negative emanations of the same place. But this is a very polarised 'Jansenist' universe and the same being can simultaneously embody both forces: we can never be sure that the negative forces are confined within a safely exteriorised 'other' – on the contrary, they may both have their source in the same complex of energies. This is the point of a narrated dream of his wife's, which the speaker relays at a crucial point in *Lud Heat*:

> Another of Anna's casually recounted, but vital dreams: that there are two creatures, one is her husband, the supposed protector, who is sitting upstairs in a wicker chair, while the other, also with my face, kicks down the door. (p. 110)

Sinclair's process of mapping out danger points (focused on Hawksmoor's churches) is a common way of coping with the tensions of urban space. Without such personal maps the positive-negative double identity of the city can suddenly flip over: a block too far for the un-streetwise tourist, a thoughtless turning off the main, well-lit boulevard can land the traveller in sudden danger. The mapping reclaims the city, recuperates its mean, chartered streets, and fits them into an ordered, if frightening, preconception. Such reclamations may be imposed on the city itself, as when Baron Housmann, redesigning Paris, imposed the long, straight, diagonal lines of his boulevards across the winding streets of old Paris. Sinclair's 'power-lines', crossing the existing street lines, are very similar to these. They are similar, too, to the lines imposed by the architect A.C. L'Enfant on the city of Washington, DC, which overmap the symbolic energies of federal power on to the city plan in the form of long, wide, diagonal avenues crossing the city's basic rectangular grid-iron, representing the fifteen then existing American states with the fifteen points of intersection between the diagonals: the main diagonal links the 'high-points' of the White House and Capitol Hill with the 'flarepath' of Pennsylvania Avenue running between them. The resulting map looks very similar to Sinclair's frontispiece map of London, with its

diagonal lines crossing between Hawksmoor's churches and repre-
senting a superimposed energy system on the city beneath.[6]

To appreciate the energies thus delimited, the ground has to be
walked, as patriotic American 'pilgrims' are seen walking between the
various Washington sites of national commemoration and celebration.
So the climax of *Lud Heat* is the scheme of 'walking the flarepath of
Hawksmoor's churches by night, in company with two others, taking
drinks in the appropriate cellars and rat-holes'. However, the narrator
is taken ill before the appointed day:

> He crawls out, on the third day, shaded in straw, a photograph
> of the last months of D.H. Lawrence. [Furthermore] One of
> my proposed companions for the night walk did not escape the
> word of the pyramid either: he was opened to receive the appro-
> priate message. He got a varicose vein on the male member.
> (pp. 108/111)

This pervasive sense of night-time menace and claustrophobia in the
prose sections is contrasted with the relaxed, meditative, free-verse of
the poetry sections. These annotate Sinclair's day-to-day work as a
member of a team of municipal gardeners, operating the Flymo round
the lawns and graveyards of the borough. With plenty of time, in the
warmth of the 'bothy', to read Homer and eat sandwiches, these
sections now seem like a kind of idyll to an era of communally useful,
non-alienated labour under the benign aegis of the Greater London
Council. But if this is the 'dominant' culture, then the 'emergent' is the
prelude to a more sinister time, and the notations include ominous
mentions of the steady increase in the National Front vote in the East
End, implicitly seen as further evidence of the negative energies which
permeate the ground. In the sub-section 'The Querent, At Home' he
contemplates these matters from the domestic security of Albion
Terrace:

> in this morning sun I notice
> my finger pads are gouged & cut
> the sharp blade through the green tomatoes
> the onions the green pepper
>
>   no pain no blood
> so we feel inhuman

& dream of blood canceling pregnancies
don't quite understand
        the manipulations of time
but read about them

this eyot
        the privilege
of the streets

'there are still enchanting enclosures, such as
the little group Albion Square, Albion Terrace &
Albion Drive, with fine public houses, the
Duke of Wellington & the Brownlow Arms'

        claims Arthur Mee
in 'London North of the River'

the season the walking
                            out
        the child
finding pleasure in simply
treading the grass

put down the elements
        a bowl
against darker times

here: Hackney South & Shoreditch where
Mr Robin May polled the National Front's
best result   2,544 votes

mechanistic
        sanguine
cloudy engine

        love
moves the sun

This extract is typical of the relaxed free verse of the poetry sections
of *Lud Heat*. The verse is packaged into quasi-stanzaic 'batches' of a

few lines each. Documentary data is slipped in, and the diary-like discursive frame contains such material without difficulty. The first four lines register a conventional speaking persona, a 'unified subject' voicing an essentially autobiographical thought-stream. But having set the scene, the text slips out of this personalised mode into something else: the 'I' becomes 'we' in the second batch, and then a 'pronominal absence' sets in, and the observations seem to emanate from some disembodied overviewer; the exception is the documentary material, which is attributed to its published source, or else quoted verbatim from a newspaper report. The passage ends with utterances with are cryptic, bardic, shamanistic, almost, giving a 'mysticalised' tone characteristic of the 'counter-cultural' poetry of its period, achieved through a species of pared-down, minimalist lyricism. This 'drift' from one kind of discourse to another makes an overall discursive structure which is vigorously heteroglossic, to use another Bakhtinian term.

Lud Heat and Sinclair's later work

Given Sinclair's increasing prominence as a writer about London, it is likely that readers of *Lud Heat* will mainly be coming to the poem already familiar with his later prose works and reading it with, so to speak, advanced fore-knowledge of what followed it. What must emerge from reading the poem in this way is a strong sense of how little Sinclair's basic urban vision has changed in the quarter century which has passed since the writing of *Lud Heat*. Near the start, for instance, we have the detailed yet impressionistic collective descriptions of Hawksmoor's churches; implicitly contrasting them with the elegance and rationality of Wren's, we are told that in Hawksmoor's churches:

> Certain features are in common: extravagant design, massive, almost slave-built strength – not democratic. A strength that is not connected to notions of 'craftsmanship' or 'elegance'. They are not easy on the eye, and do not enforce images of grace ... It shocks every time you glimpse one of the towers. They are shunned. The strength is hybrid, awkward: an admix of Egyptian and Greek source matter – curiosities discovered in engraved library plates. (p. 20)

The peculiarities of Hawksmoor's churches are well suggested by this: their aggressive massing is very striking, especially that of the towers – St Mary Woolnoth's, for example, is reminiscent of heavy items of furniture (wardrobes, chests of drawers) piled one on top of the other. The powerful physical presence of these buildings suggests to Sinclair a presence which is more than physical, and their predominance on the eastern, socially deprived side of the city makes it relatively easy to identify lurid and violent acts which have taken place in their vicinity. From there it is a small step to imagining that something emanating from and between these churches is a contributory factor in such events. The basic elements in this scenario do not change as Sinclair's career progresses. The serviceable auxiliary prose of the *Lud Heat* era becomes increasingly lush, baroque and mannered, but it is always relentlessly sharp and entertaining, curiously phrasal in its effects, consisting of disjunctive, serial hits on successive targets, rather than constituting a flow, as if the lines are really end-stopped poetic images, merely dressed as prose. Always the medium is the matter. Brilliant though he is, nobody, I think, reads Sinclair to find out about the East End of London: rather, we do so for the strange thrill of entering the 'spooked city', vicariously treading those pavements in a dead patrol with Sinclair, Petit and Atkins.

The long-standing continuity of Sinclair's vision can be seen by comparing recent passages in *Dark Lanthorns* (Goldmark, 1999) with passages in *Lud Heat*. *Dark Lanthorns* is subtitled 'David Rodinsky as Psychogeographer' and the substance of this little book (which is in a full-colour facsimile of the binding of a London *A to Z*) is the record of three London walks which trace routes marked out in a real *A to Z* found in a room 'above a disused synagogue at 19 Princelet Street in the East End of London. A room, summarily abandoned years before, [which] was found with everything more or less in its original state, even down to porridge on the stove and the imprint of a head on a pillow. The room's occupant, David Rodinsky, was a reclusive cabalistic Jewish scholar who had, one day in the late 1960s, simply vanished from his home; what became of him no one knew' (Catherine Taylor's on-line review of *Rodinsky's Room* for amazon.co.uk). Sinclair wrote about the topic in the *London Review of Books*, and incorporated it into his book *Downriver*, and subsequently artist Rachel Lichtenstein and Sinclair collaborated on *Rodinsky's Room*.

My point in introducing all this is simply that reading *Lanthorn* makes it clear that Rodinsky is cast as an anticipatory avatar of

Sinclair himself, reproducing the sensibility which generated *Lud Heat*. Thus, scrutinising pages 36–7 of Rodinsky's *A to Z*, which has routes marked out in red biro, Sinclair writes:

> Lines spin out in every direction from South Woodford Station. Wanstead Hospital, the L.C.C Mental Hospital (Claybury) and Dr Barnado's Homes are emphasised as hot spots of special interest. But did Rodinsky's markings trace journeys he had already made? Or were these annotations, laboured over in his Princelet Street attic, his way of uncovering an occulted pattern? Were those wavering lines, sometimes fierce, sometimes faint, the record of a magical act? Rodinsky's fascination with hospitals granted them peculiar resonance. They were potential destinations and sources of obscure power. (p. 12)

The character uncovering occulted patterns and linking prominent buildings of the same generic type (this time they are care-institutions and hospitals rather than churches) is clearly involved in an undertaking closely cognate in character to that recorded in *Lud Heat*, and the diagram described here is obviously a close relative of the one in that volume which shows Hawksmoor's churches linked diagrammatically by lines which demonstrate (as the caption puts it) 'the invisible rods of force active in this city'. On the second walk in *Lanthorn* ('The Dagenham Circuit') the tower of Claybury Hospital is written about as if it was for Rodinsky the centre of a malign and mystical force-field, much as the Ziggurat of St George's, Bloomsbury, or the towers of St George's in the east, are for Sinclair himself in *Lud Heat*:

> And then…I saw it: the tower of Claybury Hospital. The fixed compass-point from which Rodinsky drew his circuits of London. All his maps were based on that sightline. A future vision seen alongside a railway line, behind a fence, in childhood. The dark tower, its past and future selves, was a control beacon, sending out the signals by which Rodinsky – and now his stalking crew – would navigate. (p. 32)

Here the signs are in the street-signs: though out in Dagenham, at the very edges of the known world ('a swamp without restaurants, proper coffee, Japanese hypermarkets or even a branch of Ikea', p. 30), in territory so remote it is innocent of all cultural representation (it is 'beyond *EastEnders*, beyond *The Bill*', p. 30), a waste land of 'trashed motors' where 'civic dialogue is discontinued'), still Sinclair detects a message for his companion Chris Petit, author of the (out-of-print) novel *Robinson* – 'Then I noticed the street name: Pettits Place. Followed by Robinson Road. This was uncanny, *Robinson* being the name of Chris Petit's most autobiographical novel. It was almost as if Rodinsky had set the walk up, as if he had anticipated the particular pair of brogues that would tiptoe across his grave' (pp. 30–1).[7] The urban world posited here (and it is that of *Lud Heat* too) is like a Freudian model of the subconscious, or a Marxist reading of history, a place in which there can be no accidents, no mere coincidences. All is tightly meshed, predicated and predicted like the doubled plot of a typical Borgesian story, where the past anticipates the present, incorporates that anticipation into itself, encrypting its messages into the very topography of the ground, and relying upon a like-minded posterity to decode the planted signs. This overdetermined universe would quickly become unbearably claustrophobic, and perhaps ultimately silly, in the hands of any other writer. What saves Sinclair is that the 'seeing' eye is as acute as the 'visionary' eye, the geography as sharp as the history. The 'triad of signs' which he notes, for instance, is no nexus of occult forces, but 'Pizza Hut, Blockbuster Video, Make Your Will Here' (p. 32), a bizarre and touching metonym of the anonymous, sub-suburbanite 1990s. Back in civilisation, deep in familiar *Lud Heat* territory again, Petit is oblivious to 'the sepulchral figure of John Bunyan in Bunhill Fields' (p. 40) and much more interested in the red lines painted on the tarmac by work-crews from BT or the gas board. In Holborn they note the road-block where the police are 'flagging down all the white vans, interrogating geezers with suspect paperwork' (p. 41). As Sinclair says, they are 'sympathetic to our concept', for they too are 'breaking the map into controllable zones'. This is, in the end, what Sinclair does, inscribing his own mental biro-lines on the tarmac, and then excavating and linking up the marked spots. Sinclair himself, then, is a geezer whose own paperwork, thirty years down the line, and whatever reservations one might have (ethical, rational, political, social, etc., etc., etc.) nevertheless passes muster. Given the *singularity* of his concerns (a word I will come back to), much of this thirty-year progress is anticipated by, and compressed into, his early sequence *Lud Heat*.

The topological shovel: Allen Fisher's *Place*

The contrast between Iain Sinclair and Allen Fisher is very marked. In the 1970s they seemed poets whose projects (urban-centred, London-based, data-packed, making use of 'open-field' poetics, epic in scale and American-influenced) were superficially very similar. Now, in the early twenty-first century, one is known everywhere and the other hardly anywhere beyond a small but enthusiastic set of devotees. Part of the reason is that a career needs a focus, and Sinclair has his focus in the East London materials he has stayed with in spite of major shifts in literary form, from poet, to novelist, to essayist, to film-maker. This degree of focus brings problems, of course, but they are much more likely to be the problems of success. And Sinclair has been able to shift and develop while maintaining the focus, for example altering the balance from history to geography (decisively from, and including, *Lights Out for the Territory*, Granta 1997) and ironising the historical determinism of *Lud Heat* and the novels, so that the occult elements take on paradoxical connotations of cultural 'depth', against which the shallowness of the contemporary scene, with its 'trashed motors' and its absence of 'civic dialogue', can be measured.

In marked contrast to this, Fisher's writing, since the abandonment of the *Place* sequence and its related London-centred materials, has tended towards increasingly abstract and esoteric forms and subject matter. Whereas at the *Place* stage of his career in the 1970s he wrote about, say, an abstract topic like 'process' by studying the processes of one particular city (London), since then he has tended to engage such topics directly, as intellectual abstractions, abandoning with *Place* the inductive, empirical method which alone, I would say, offered him any real prospect of securing a wide and varied readership. In the later work, therefore, the nature of the desired or assumed 'contract' between the writer and his readers becomes increasingly problematical. It just isn't clear what he expects his readers to do, or what kind of person (with what kind of education, for example) he expects them to be. Does Fisher envisage groups of devotees setting up reading groups and meeting weekly to work out ways into, and out of, his cryptic, labyrinthine texts? Does he expect us to trawl in his wake through the lists of cited works on such matters as particle physics or astronomy? In the 1970s I was happy to do this with the more manageable list of *Place* materials, as others were, apparently, for this work (and its satellites) brought Fisher closer than he has ever been since to breaking out beyond a coterie following. The 'Resources' list for *Place I-XXXVII* contains predominantly 'humanist' materials, like works of history, local history, cultural myth and the like, or at least, where the material is scientific the books mentioned were written for a lay audience, and within the ambiance of what we would now call cultural history or cultural geography. In his later work, by contrast, many of the cited books are technical treatises obviously written for a professional audience, and it is difficult to envisage a Fisher readership which could cope with these. The consequences of such factors in terms of Fisher's readership are all too predictable.

The second of these monumental 'London' works, then, is this large-scale project of Allen Fisher's, the parts of which are known collectively as *Place*. This project has now been abandoned rather than completed, though such incompleteness is an honorable condition for the long poem – after all, the work to which *The Prelude* was the intended forerunner was never written. *Place* was published over a period of about fifteen years in a variety of formats, some of them ephemeral and obviously unsatisfactory: it has never received definitive, single-covers publication, though it is partly written in such a way as to defy that possibility. The overall structural plan of this work is complex and (to me) elusive, and one might ask whether, like the city itself, it can really have a plan, except one which is provisional, contingent, retrospectively imposed and endlessly improvisatory.

Place explores aspects of South London using the 'over-mapping' techniques already discussed in the case of Sinclair. It differs from *Lud Heat* in that the 'data-input' is much more varied and demanding, perhaps a partial explanation – as already implied – of Sinclair's greater commercial success. As Fisher once said in an interview, 'My concerns are not singular' – a dramatic understatement. The demands which *Place* makes on a reader's time and energies are very considerable. In a real sense, also, the book is not simply about a securely exterior world, but also about the linked processes of reading and thinking by which that world is constructed. The urban space is 'recuperated' intellectually and emotively through complex and wide-ranging reading, like Sinclair's urban space, only more so. Fisher constantly has a double, triple and quadruple vision of the city, and what he 'sees' is part mythical, part historical, part historiographical.

For instance, a source he uses in looking at his South London territory is the Victorian popular historian Walter Besant (whose own *South London* remakes and extends Stowe's Elizabethan *Survey of*

London, just as Fisher reworks and extends Besant). Besant's reconstructive, synthesising historical imagination is of the confident Victorian kind which reconstructed from fossil evidence the impressive but inaccurate full-sized dinosaur figures which loom from behind trees and bushes round the lake at Crystal Palace Park in South London. At one Besant-like moment in *Place* the speaker looks across the Thames to the container-ship berths at Tilbury; this, at least, is what he is *looking* at: what he is *seeing* is *Llyn-dynas*, the 'settlement on the lake' at the time when London (in this discredited Victorian etymological speculation about the name) was a dwelling in the midst of a great tidal lagoon, before the formation of what is now the Thames basin. This reliance on written sources is typical of the historiographical emphasis of *Place*: in this work, it might be said, historiography constantly ousts history, which is to some extent true of all three works discussed here; all three enter a highly constructed world, not a 'given' world. Likewise, the ousting of *looking* by *seeing* is another major trope which they have in common.

   One major aspect of the historiographical material used in *Place* concerns the many now-buried rivers which flow beneath London: Fisher uses data from Nicholas Barton's book *The Lost Rivers of London*[8] which links the presence of these underground rivers to such things as the incidence of bronchitis in nearby houses, the incidence of house-dust allergy, and even the phenomenon of hauntings and psychic apparitions (where the ghostly event is often preceded by a sound usually described as being like the swishing of a silk dress along a polished floor – these sounds being attributed by Barton to underground movements of water).

   Fisher's *Place* (in accordance with the 'readerly' focus attributed to it earlier) is at its most typical when dealing with interactions between various 'systems' or paradigms of this kind – history, economics, sociology, psychology and technology. One of his emblems for this kind of interaction is the notion of osmosis, the process whereby contiguous systems seep into each other at a rate which can be investigated, and according to factors which can be identified and delineated. In a letter (incorporated into *Stane: Place Book III*) to friends whose house suffers from a defective damp course he writes with impressive precision about osmosis in relation to this problem, seizing on the point at which the abstract scientific notion of osmosis becomes a part of everyday reality and experience. The dead-pan technical discussion of 'passive osmotic systems' and 'electro-osmosis' has its abstraction

defused by contextualisation within the familiar notion of rising
damp:

> The efficacy of the 'passive osmotic-system', which involves, as
> you know, drilling holes in the wall and fitting a continuous
> copper conductor – centres on finding a theory for understand-
> ing the phenomenon of rising damp.[...] it might be useful to
> know that slow corrosion of copper electrodes introduces
> copper hydroxide, which slowly chokes the pores and reduces
> the permeability and that the release of fine particles are filtered
> off by porous mortar, slowly choking it. It is known, for
> instance, that if there is a balance at the rate at which moisture
> evaporates from the surface of the wall and the water, then the
> height of the wet line will not change with time.[...] My reason
> for interest lay in my concern for the once relevant habit of
> lining walls in balance with the earth's electric currents, and my
> thought – now I think subdued – that this electro-osmotic
> system was somehow connected. Anyway, it might be amusing
> to consider some of this.
>   Hoping you are both well, and the kids etcetera,
>   Much love,
>   Allen

(In another work, *The Topological Shovel*, this interest in osmosis,
and the desire to 'ground' the abstract in the actual, leads him to inves-
tigate the origins of the tea-bag, a strangely neglected academic topic.)
For Fisher, this interest in osmosis is cognate with his interest in the
buried rivers of London: in both, thinking about the movements of
water – a topic which ultimately encompasses almost every field of
geophysical investigation – becomes a way of thinking about thinking.
As Fisher said in the interview already mentioned, 'I used the rivers as
a metaphor for thought', and this gives a useful way into the material.

I will try to suggest the nature of the experience of reading *Place* by
looking closely at a brief passage. The following section occurs imme-
diately after the letter just quoted in *Stane: Place Book III*, where
Fisher broadens out from the 'lost' (that is, buried) rivers material of
Part IV and considers the course of the Thames itself, with the aim, as
already suggested, of using the river as a metaphor for thought. In
other words, he is another example of a poet who sees urban topog-
raphy as a facilitator of thought, not a barrier to it. Here he uses an

'open field' poetics, describing his following of the Thames upstream
to the locks round Teddington, engaged in that process which he calls
using the river to think with: in this passage the river is seen as an
interface between ecological systems; it is available for human use, but
it has to be worked *with*. Like Sinclair walking the 'flarepath' of his
churches, Fisher 'walks the ground', anticipating the London 'Ambu-
latory' writing of the 1990s, along tow-paths, and passes along this
stretch of water by boat:

> I joined the main flow at London Bridge
> joined in with it
> rode it from the Temple
> away from sea tide
> tired
> upstream to the locks
> I, not the navigator but led
> by edges of course-lines blurring with boat lap
> with boat rudder
> led indeterminately
> in one channel   the Thames   certainly in this flow
> until my navigator called and we stopped dropped ropes and the
> anchor hooks mud
>
> 'the river of life' a teacher gave me / asked me
> the river of life, well at Teddington now
> I am reminded by its lock
> flash doors flush against Go
> the water edge holding these fish   seed pods   milk bottles
> at the gates of choice
>
> the river begins to connect again through the boundaries of weirs
> seeping through the flash   flow sparking light flecks
>
> In the year-book of Edward I, 1294:
> If one have common in another's water,
> although that water
> be turned into another channel, yet he may always follow
> the water wherever it run, in order to enjoy his common.

Listening the- the gush behind this dam turntabling a barge
                              this mill
                              this pool

            engineered to increase flow
                         by accumulation
                              increase the force of it

mill that grinds flower to flour
                         muthos to mythos
                         fish bones into chalk

      at this watermill   a pool where the biggest fish were weaned
                         pulled here pooled
                         by concentrations of flow of food

Place, in contrast to *Lud Heat*, uses a continuous verse framework of
the above kind throughout, sometimes inserting 'prose blocks' of
extracted data from one of the sources into the flow, but not using the
alternating verse/prose sectioning ('auxiliary prose') favoured by
Sinclair. The verse is much more directly 'Olsonian' in feel than
Sinclair's, in the sense that the pages are constructed 'spacially' or
'visually',[9] so that rather than having a basic orientation of lines to the
left-hand margin, words are arranged in 'blocks' which are sometimes
to the left of the page, sometimes to the right, and sometimes with
lines crossing from margin to margin like prose. On the other hand, as
with the quoted section, the material sustains a unified 'I' more consis-
tently than Sinclair's does, though with the same heteroglossic 'drift'
into source material, into related reminiscence, and into a kind of
'bardic' poetic voice, one which is much taken with word play ('flower
to flour/ muthos to mythos', and so on). The remembered phrase 'the
river of life' hints at the way this tracing of the river is an attempt to
understand intellectual systems and processes: some of the factors in
the process are: thinking about how a 'mainstream' of thought or
sensibility is produced and identified, and what it flows from and into;
how 'keying into' this flow is not exactly a matter just of active
navigation, but of following the 'edges of course-lines'; how the intel-
lectual 'mainstream' is prone to silting up and blockage; what is meant
(if anything) by 'intellectual property rights' (consider the passage
'If one have common in another's water ...'); how the flow of the

mainstream should be 'managed', and the kind of sustenance we can expect to derive from it.

Place will look dauntingly complicated and lengthy to anyone encountering it for the first time and comparing it with more familiar kinds of poetry. Yet in comparison with most of what Fisher has written since the 1970s, it is a uniquely focused, concrete, and 'grounded' work, as suggested earlier. Briefly, since abandoning the Place sequence and its related London-centred materials, Fisher has tended towards increasingly abstract and esoteric forms and subject matter. There have been gestures in an explicatory direction, but they have been carried through only half-heartedly. For instance, under the promising overall title Scram, or The Transformation of the Concept of Cities, Issue 10 of Paul Green's poetry magazine Spectacular Diseases[10] presented representative extracts from four phases of Fisher's work from the 1970s, each section with a brief introduction. But the issue offered no real clues as to the overall nature of Fisher's whole project during this period: for example, it mentions, but does not elucidate, the crucial distinction between 'procedural programmes and processual plans' (p. 11). It isn't that readers want to have the material explained, exactly. On the contrary, what is needed is just an explicatory start, no matter how tentative and speculative, which might help the baffled reader to begin to make some headway. Fisher has a following, but there is an absence of what might be called an interpretive community in which committed readers and critics would begin to build up a body of 'readings', so that gradually some specific commentary would exist on all the significant pieces in the oeuvre. This kind of interpretive community and body of critical material does exist, for instance, for Fisher's namesake poet, Roy Fisher. Allen Fisher is anthologised frequently in avant-garde collections, and given reverent mention, in restricted-circulation secondary materials. But there is seldom any detailed or enlightening textual engagement with his work, and the inevitable result is that his readership, always restricted, and static, I would say, since the 1970s, is aging now. It need not be so, for the re-issue of Lud Heat, and the appearance of Aidan Dun's Vale Royal, creates an ideal set of 'co-texts' for the renewed availability of Place to complete this great London poetic triptych which emanates from the 1970s.

The sky scrape: Aidan Dun's *Vale Royal*

The third of these 'London' poems is Aidan Dun's *Vale Royal*, which came out in 1995, the author's first published work. Iain Sinclair was instrumental in securing its publication, and the poem was reviewed in the *Observer* on 18 June 1995 and in the *London Review of Books* on 5 October 1995 (by Sinclair). The work begins with a Blakean vision of the King's Cross district, about which Dun said 'This is holy ground – take off your shoes in King's Cross' (quoted in the *Observer* review) – hence the overall title of this chapter. Though published in the 1990s, it is based on materials compiled in the 1970s, and was published by Goldmark, the imprint of former dog-meat salesman Mike Goldmark, after a protracted and bizarre series of events which are related in the *Observer* review; it is accompanied by two CDs of the author reading the entire work. *Vale Royal* is Dun's name for the valley of the Fleet river, which still runs beneath King's Cross, but now mainly underground, having been bricked in, diverted, and over-built across the centuries. The Fleet has its source in the seven springs of Kenwood, and then flows down in two arms from Highgate and Hampstead to Camden Town. The valley of Vale Royal is formed by the seven hills of North London: Barrow Hill, Primrose Hill, Parliament Hill, St Michael's Mount, the Penton, Ludgate Hill, and Old Tot Hill at Westminster, which was levelled in the nineteenth century. This 'epic geography' of London is taken from Dun's notes to the poem; Dun calls this valley 'royal' because (quoting the notes) 'King's Cross has exerted a magnetic attraction down the centuries. The artists, the poets have made this forgotten place royal with their presence.' He continues, 'Vale Royal is a geographical vessel, a symbolic container of the quiet mind, a perfect place to realise the vision of oneness'. The choice of the word 'royal' is perhaps unfortunate, for it now has distinctly tacky associations in the British public mind (for this reason a British airline recently decided to stop calling its premium class 'Royal Class'); but the intention, at any rate, is clear.

The speaking persona is a multi-layered being referred to as the 'Sunchild', and one of the layers of this composite figure is the teenage martyr St Pancras (patron saint of truth, children, and dancing, says the note) born near Troy, and in Dun's poem 'symbol of the martyred poets of Vale Royal'. But this composite figure also comprises the poets Blake and Chatterton, with echoes of Shelley and Keats. Of course, we are already familiar with this scenario: the composite figure in *Vale Royal* is similar to the 'familiar compound ghost', made up of Yeats and other poets, who falls into step with the speaker in Eliot's *Four Quartets* and with him 'trod the pavements in a dead patrol' during the London blitz. *Vale Royal*, like *The Waste Land*, *Lud Heat*, and *Place*, is also ambulatory in character, 'walking the ground' of named London streets and landmarks.

Vale Royal, however, is much more homogenous than the other two poems discussed in this chapter, and looking more closely at a short section of it is perhaps the best way to indicate its main qualities. This extract is from page 47, roughly the half-way point: the speaker is tracing the course of the Fleet River:

> The sacred river flows under the city at Farringdon   (1)
> From Mount Pleasant it falls to oblivion in Clerkenwell,
> and winds as a sewer under Saffron Hill.

> In Holborn the Fleet is a secret ditch,   (2)
> the kingdom of typhoid, a conduit of bad air,
> inching green slime and dog-flesh down to the watergate.

> Along the lost river in Brook Street, he hides away.   (3)
> He is safe. A utopian city is built again.
> Nobody knows his whereabouts in the rooftops.

> Certainly now the Palladian lines   (4)
> will bend more dramatically towards the unknown.
> He will trace the sunken river back to her source.

> He tiptoes on the parapet of Mrs. Angel's attic   (5)
> and scans the curve of the northern heights through haze.
> Troynovant circles in trains of ancient fable.

> Through the Chronicles of Britain, like a phantom city,   (6)
> she rises from the fogs on her slow river,
> sister to the old half-mythical Iberian Tartessus.

> Troynovant, great forerunner of London on the Thames!   (7)
> Over ten-thousand rooftops the green-headed Penton rises
> with other high skylines of the ten-mile ridge,

the good walking-country of the long crescent curved   (8)
through Islington and Highgate to Jack Straw's Castle,
the semi-circle of high land round vale royal.

The evening extended with cooler airs   (9)
calls him out into the Fleet valley, lost world
up along the River of Wells, beneath high places ...

He bathes his burning eyes at Black Mary's Pool   (10)
and takes the Pantheon turnpike north,
turning a myth of prior cities in his mind.

It can be seen from this that the poem is an intense fusion of three
modes of urban writing discussed in the introductory chapters, the
urban-generic, with its 'hushed' lighting effects and its rather more
generalised level of urban evocation; then the loco-specific, with its
named streets and its specific cartography; and finally the Audenesque
urban-symbolic, where the city's geography is translated into an over-
arching geometry of ideas about civilisation, society and community.
It is also worth stressing the 'content-specific' nature of this poem: it
is, like the other two, a high-density verbal construct which can surely
yield little to the unseen close reading method which insists on treat-
ing it as 'available surface'. On the contrary, the notes supplied with
the poem are very much integral with it, in the manner of 'content-
specific' poetry, and not a mere optional supplementary adjunct. The
new-critical notion that using the notes might in some way detract
from the impact of the poem 'itself' is unsustainable, for the notes are
like the 'auxiliary prose' which several of the writers discussed in this
book (Iain Sinclair, Roy Fisher, Ciaran Carson) incorporate into their
work as a kind of integral, built-in co-text. The notes do not simply
supply extraneous factual information (for one thing, the information
is not always factual), but help to build the imaginative fabric which
constitutes the poem, exactly as David Jones's notes do in the case
of *The Anathemata*. The latter poem without the notes could hardly
be a poem at all, since the reader who would not need them is incon-
ceivable.

First, then, the 'sacred river' at the start of the quoted extract is,
primarily, the Fleet, which rises in Highgate ponds: but Coleridge in
middle age lived at Highgate and (according to Dun's note, which
adjusts 'true' geography to 'psychic geography') wrote 'Kubla Khan'

there. So the sacred river is also 'Alph, the sacred river' from that poem, which is emblematic of the poetic process, says the main critical tradition on this poem, but also, on a Lacanian (LaKhanian?) reading, emblematic too of the complex skein of desire and lack woven into its poetic fabric. Coleridge's river runs 'through caverns measureless to man', just as the river here flows under the city at Farringdon, and then to oblivion at Clerkenwell. So the Utopian city built again in stanza three of the extract, and the phantom city rising from the fogs in stanza six is also Xanadu. Hence, the passage begins to construct a palimpsest of cities inscribing and re-inscribing the same mental ground: likewise Schliemann, excavating the alleged site of the city of Troy, found successive settlements one on top of another, uncovering a growth-by-layering which is characteristic of cities.[11] Dun's procedure here is also 'layered': so London is Troynovant (New Troy) at the end of stanza five and the Iberian mythical city of Tartessus at the end of six, itself a supposed outpost of Atlantis. So the place which the speaker looks at is London, but the *space* which he makes it into is another 'familiar compound ghost', and the process involves, as he says at the end of the extract, 'turning a myth of prior cities in the mind'.

The Sunchild, at the end of this section of *Vale Royal*, goes north from King's Cross, on the Pantheon Turnpike (that is, the Pentonville Road), barefoot and unmolested, his unprotectedness, as it might be said, his best protection. In this version of the city mythologised, the energies generated by the urban 'geographical vessel' are benign, mystical, inspiring, and healing. (Black Mary's Pool in stanza ten is a healing pool just south of King's Cross.) Here, then, is a contrast to Sinclair's reading of the East End as a vortex of negative energies – where Vale Royal is a geographical chalice, Sinclair's East End is a geographical cauldron. Sinclair's vision is perhaps too dangerously complicit with Victorian images of the East End as 'darkest London', and with the territorial demonisation implicit in the social use of the term 'inner city', conjuring up a Tory nightmare place where sink-schools are run by mob-rule and house insurance costs an arm and a leg.

This isn't to say that Dun entirely ignores the physical degradation which the naked eye (as opposed to the 'seeing eye' mentioned earlier) sees in North London. The visionary city has always occupied the same site as the 'kingdom of typhoid' of stanza two. In Dun's King's Cross this juxtaposition is becoming more obvious by the day, as the neo-brutalism of the migrated British Library (Sinclair's 'locked cellar of words' and source of occult power) flourishes next-door to the pinnacles of Gilbert Scott's St Pancras (a railway station yearning to be a cathedral), adjacent to the epicentre of London prostitution. For Dun the sacred river is hopelessly polluted, 'a conduit of bad air/ inching green slime down to the watergate', and while Jack Straw's Castle, mentioned in stanza eight, is now a pleasant pub for people who work in television and like to do a lot of shopping (how William Empson once described the readership of the magazine *Horizon*, more or less) 'Jack Straw' is also the sinister 'Wicker Man', the giant made of straw in which the Druids performed human sacrifice by burning (so Dun's note tells us; I am not sure whether this is romanticised Druidism or the real thing).

As three epic-scale ways of 'doing' London these three works, I would say, work best when viewed as a multi-authored urban triptych, or composite, embodying the 'moment' of the 1970s. They are oppositional in their politics and their sociology, and make substantial demands of their readers, asking them, in fact, to go beyond the familiar stance of the individual speaking subject found in conventional lyric poetry, and learn a new style of 'thinking with cities'. Given the complexity of the urban subject matter – its characteristic way of defying individual conception – they work best as a group viewed in generic-triplicate, as a rich web of urban co-textuality.

Notes

1   Basic publication data on these three works is as follows: Iain Sinclair's poetry-and-prose sequence *Lud Heat* was first published by his own Albion Village Press in 1975, and republished by Vintage Books (with the related work *Suicide Bridge* in the same volume) in 1995. An extract from *Lud Heat* appears in the anthology *A Various Art*, ed. Andrew Crozier and Tim Longville, Paladin, 1987, pp. 343–9.

Allen Fisher's monumental *Place* project comprised five main books, listed here not in chronological order of publication, but in the order of the five books: *Place Book One (I-XXXVII)*, Aloes Books, London, 1974, republished by Truck Books, St. Paul, Minnesota, 1976: *Place Book Two (Unpolished Mirrors)*, Reality Studios, London, 1985: *Place Book Three (Stane)*, Aloes Books, London, 1977: *Place Books Four and Five (Becoming)*, Aloes Books, London, 1978. Much of this material appeared in various small-press journals, and there were several items related to the Place project published in the late 1970s and early 1980s.

Aidan Dun's 'London epic' *Vale Royal* was published by Goldmark (Uppingham, UK) in 1995, with two CDs of the poet reading the entire work.

2 I explain further the term 'content-specific' in the chapter 'Allen Fisher and "content-specific" Poetry' in *New British Poetries: the Scope of the Possible*, ed. Robert Hampson and Peter Barry (Manchester University Press, 1993), pp. 198–216.

3 Of these seven characteristics it should be said that the first four are equally characteristic of all three poets, while the last three apply most to Allen Fisher and least to Aidan Dun. The appropriateness of the 'Americanist' label is obviously disputable. An alternative (and British) genealogy for the large-scale, geographically centred poem might be found in the work of David Jones, especially for Dun, whose concerns are the most overtly 'visionary' and 'mystical' of this group. (This note responds to a useful comment from Bill Oxley.)

4 'Breakfasts are everything on these occasions; they define the day. The ingestion of the full fry (£2.20) is a necessary ritual. The fearsome sight of Atkins mopping up his double helping of luridly dyed beans. The white coffee mugs shaped from lavatory tiles. A puritanical reward, a break from the journey; scoff that has been earned by sweat and tears.' *Liquid City*, Marc Atkins and Iain Sinclair (Reaktion Books, 1999), p. 62.

5 De Quincey's phrase 'jumps up like a pyramid of fire' is an allusion to Milton's *Paradise Lost*, Book II, lines 1013–14, where, as Satan crosses the abyss of Chaos and heads towards Earth, we are told that he 'With fresh alacrity and force renewed/ Springs upward like a pyramid of fire'. The implication of the phrase, therefore, as used by Sinclair quoting De Quincey quoting Milton, is of the unleashing of destructive, Satanic energies.

6 The Washington diagram is from 'Geography is Everywhere: Culture and Symbolism in Human Landscapes', by Denis Cosgrove, in D. Gregory and R. Walford (eds), *Horizons in Human Geography*, Macmillan, 1989. This item is representative of a range of material relevant to this kind of poetry from within the discipline of Human Geography. Other examples are: Sharon Zukin, 'Postmodern Urban Landscapes; Mapping Culture and Power' in S. Lash and J. Firedman, *Modernity and Identity*, Basil Blackwell, 1992: J. B. Hartley, 'Maps, Knowledge and Power' in D. Cosgrove and S. Daniels (eds), *The Iconography of Landscape*, Cambridge University Press, 1988. Much directly relevant work within the discipline of English and American Studies is about the novel rather than poetry, for example: Hana Wirth-Nesher, *City Codes: Reading the Modern Urban Novel* (Cambridge University Press, 1996): see the introductory chapter 'Reading Cities'.

Other relevant work is primarily about particular cities, such as: Peter Brooker, *New York Fictions: Modernity, Postmodernism, the New Modern* (Longman, 1996), though the first chapter, 'Companion Cities of the Other Side' links London and New York within a trope of modernity.

7 Petit's thriller *The Psalm Killer* (1997) has been a significant success in the 'noir fiction' genre. It concerns a serial-killer called Candlestick who commits bizarre and lurid murders on the streets of Belfast and is pursued by a detective, Cross, who seeks to decode the pattern of the killings. An annotated bibliography claims a degree of authenticity for the events and for the implied complicity between the authorities and crime. The affinities between this and the world of *Lud Heat* are quite marked.

8 Reprinted 1992 by Phillimore & Co.

9 *Place Book One, I-XXXVII* is approximately 'portrait' A4 size in format: *Place Book Three, Stane* is A4 size, but in 'landscape' format.

10 Based at 83b London Road, Peterborough, PE2 9BS, UK.

11 Not surprisingly, this motif of Schliemann's Troys is fascinating to Allen Fisher too, who uses it in *Place*.

8 'Birmingham's what I think with':

Roy Fisher's cities

Roy Fisher and the fulcrum between 'mainstream' and 'margins'

One of the early signs of a thaw in the Cold War between the poetic 'margins' and the poetic 'establishment' was the publication of Roy Fisher's *Poems 1955–1980* by Oxford University Press in 1980. The appearance of this volume from OUP (along with that of Basil Bunting's *Collected Poems* in 1978) was part of the process of the 'deregulation' of the poetry scene discussed at the start of this book. Of course, some division between 'margins' and 'mainstream' exists in all the arts in one form or another, but it had been particularly entrenched and embittered, and mutually impoverishing, in British poetry in the 1970s. We can, perhaps, date its formal constitution in post-war British poetry from the 'International Poetry Incarnation' at the Royal Albert Hall in June 1965, and the publication of its associated Penguin anthology, *Children of Albion: Poetry of the 'Underground' in Britain*, edited by Mike Horovitz in 1969, events which in combination gave the 'margins' a collective 'counter-cultural' identity.[1] It would be difficult to deny that Roy Fisher has been a major symptom and beneficiary of the poetic détente (however it is defined) of the 1980s and 90s, acquiring a more varied readership than any other former 'small-press' poet. In theory, at least, publication by OUP helped him to make the transition from reliance on readers addicted to his method (as he put it in the Jasula interview, see below) to a more general kind of currency. But in Fisher's case the roots of his ambivalent status (is he now a 'mainstream' poet or isn't he?) go back quite a long way, back at least to Donald Davie's seminal 1973 essay in his book *Thomas Hardy and British Poetry* (Routledge and Kegan Paul), which links Fisher with Hardy and Larkin.[2] Before his move to OUP, the jacket-flap of the 1980 volume tells us (without irony, I think), 'his commitment to modernism and post-modernism isolated him from the mainstream of British poetry'. The implication of this is that he subsequently compromised this commitment and thereby gained entry to the bigger league formerly represented by OUP. A growing body of work about Fisher, published within the academic community at large rather than in small-press outlets, is further evidence of his 'transitional' status.[3] Yet this breakthrough to the 'mainstream', which OUP's jacket note complacently constructs itself as constituting, was consolidated in 1986 by *A Furnace*, the first volume of new poems by Fisher to be published by OUP, and one which gave little impression that he had compromised much with the 'mainstream of British poetry' – on the contrary, the book contains the most obviously difficult, sustained, and ambitious work Fisher has ever published. His final OUP collection, *Birmingham River*, was published in 1994. By the time of the collapse of the OUP poetry list in 1998 all the OUP material except *Birmingham River* was again out of print and Fisher had already made the move to Bloodaxe, who published *The Dow Low Drop: New & Selected Poems* in 1996, thereby becoming the third publisher (after Fulcrum and OUP) to publish a Roy Fisher selected/collected poems. Fisher's record of being kept continuously in print by a succession of presses is remarkable for one who is, reputedly, a 'poet's poet', whose paradoxical fame is that he is scandalously neglected. Indeed, the neglect, according to the Hull poetry magazine *Bête Noire*, has of late become 'an offence against public decency'. Another magazine, *The Rialto*, was so annoyed that nobody seemed to want to review the new book that it commissioned Fisher himself to do so. The resulting piece appeared anonymously in Issue 35 of the journal (1996) and was reprinted, with the cover blown, so to speak, in Bloodaxe's own 1997–98 catalogue (pp. 34–5). The piece is actually a masterpiece, constituting a powerful statement of a personal poetic wrapped within a characteristic irony which is oddly both self-deprecating and self-assertive at the same time. So far from being regarded as part of any mainstream, Fisher (says Fisher) was seen by the *Times Literary Supplement* reviewer of the 1980 volume as in charge of 'his own off-shore island in the middle of England'. This remark protests at his usual categorisation as a poetic inner émigré whose elective affiliations are entirely transatlantic.

In fact, his identification with American avant-garde poetics seems to have been set up more-or-less by accident, when early publication

in a magazine called *The Window* led to an invitation from Gael
Turnbull to contribute to an issue of Cid Corman's journal *Origin*,
which Turnbull was then guest-editing. Bizarrely, another of the
invited contributors was Philip Larkin, though Larkin countermanded
his acceptance, by registered post (a nice touch, that), when he realised
the company he would be keeping.[4] By contrast, Fisher claims in his
review of himself in *The Rialto* that when the organisers of the
Cambridge Poetry Festival asked invited poets to list the names of
other poets with whom they would not wish to share a platform,
Fisher was the only poet to send in a nill return. What I am stressing
here, is the element of chance in the formation of the best-known
groupings and the way this is not incompatible with powerful
antipathies between different groups. It may also suggest an underly-
ing 'deep structure' in which these fissures between 'mainstream' and
'margins' were always more apparent on the surface than the under-
lying realities warranted.[5] Subsequently, Fisher was involved with
Turnbull and Michael Shayer in the formation of Migrant Press
(Worcester, UK) which, as he said in the most recent of the recorded
interviews, 'bridged various things that were happening in America
and in this country' (Tranter).[6] Again, the notion of 'bridging' is
notable here, as is the idea of interfusion and cross-fertilisation
embodied in the very names of the early presses which published Roy
Fisher (names like 'Fulcrum' and 'Migrant').

Furthermore, the interaction between Shayer and Fisher (as the
former facilitates the latter's entry into a sphere in which work had not
previously appeared) is itself a 'cross-fertilising' scenario which seems
to reproduce that of the production and publication of *The Waste
Land*, for Shayer acted as the Ezra Pound figure who, Fisher says in
interview, took in hand 'my great heaving mass of odds and ends that
I was writing about Birmingham, which was Rimbaud at one end,
and, say, hard prose at the other, and saw that this material could be
used as a kind of collage work; which he could see and I couldn't. So
he shook it around a bit and produced the first draft of *City* which
was published in 1961 as a Migrant pamphlet' (Tranter).[7] This was
followed by a period of abortive attempts to write prose, resulting in
a long period 'on the rocks' (Tranter), that is, with severe writer's
block, till around 1970. In the interim period Stuart Montgomery's
Fulcrum Press was set up, publishing mainly avant-garde American
material (Zukovsky, Duncan, Snyder), but including Basil Bunting on
the British side of the transatlantic fulcrum, followed by Fisher's

(perhaps oddly named) *Collected Poems* (1968), the first in the
sequence of Fisher 'collecteds' which still continues. As he has said,
each of these books tends to recycle the previous ones, and his descrip-
tion of *A Furnace* in the Tranter interview seems to sum up his
method, which is in the main to produce a palimpsest in which the
same poetic ground is worked and then re-worked, with older bits
recycled, and newer ones added cumulatively, a process of cultural
accretion which mimics the way cities themselves grow and change.
Fisher describes *A Furnace* as being 'built very much on the lines of
other modern long poems, it's a collage of various sorts of experience,
some of them what I can only call cultural, some of them autobio-
graphical, some of them a working over of what I think now about
things I've written before'.

Fisher's composite urban epic

One of the great mysteries in the career of Roy Fisher is where his
major urban sequence, *City*, came from. In some ways, of course, the
answer to this question is obvious, and has been given explicitly by
Fisher in interviews and correspondence. Thus, we know quite a lot
about the double literary provenance of the piece, that is, about its
relationship to both American and European literary treatments of
urbanism. Yet it is so unlike anything else in Fisher's own work, since
the rest of his output suggests so little taste and tolerance for the kind
of large-scale, easy-paced, predominately 'scopic' writing that we see
in *City*. Furthermore, the interviews reveal a rather uncomfortable set
of circumstances surrounding the work, including: the selection and
arrangement of the material for publication by somebody else; the
subsequent somewhat inhibiting realisation that although *City* wasn't
quite the way he wanted it to be, nevertheless, it was finding readers;
the strong consequent desire to produce something more substantial in
prose; an inability, in the event, to produce this great prose work, and
a dissatisfaction with his poetic methods when he returned to them –
which events, in combination, produced a writer's block of several
years' duration which seemed to make it impossible to write again, not
just in the *City* way, but in any way which might look like a natural
evolution from that of *City*. Fisher's reader, therefore, is compelled to
think of *City* as a large and anomalous 'singleton' within the *oeuvre*,
so that those who liked it, and thereby acquired a taste for his work,

had to break the addiction, and develop a taste for other aspects of it, if they wanted to go on reading him.

Yet the *City* materials have a gravitas and an immediately recognisable breadth of significance which other aspects of his output do not necessarily possess. For one thing, they are, I would say, the most powerful literary account we have of the almost nationwide experience in mid-century Britain of urban loss and destruction, a loss brought about by a combination of bombing during the Second World War, and wholesale 'redevelopment', 'slum clearance', and (as we might call it) 'motorisation' in the 1950s and 60s, followed by de-industrialisation in the 1970s and 80s. Notoriously, this sudden obliteration of the past was greater and more sweeping in Birmingham than in any other British city, and the new cityscape which replaced the old more brutalist and alienating than anywhere else. The resulting change was quite different in its psychological effects from that of the continual piecemeal development, which (in contrast to the countryside) is an expected fact of urban life. This kind of gradual change means that the citizen, middle-aged or younger, walking along a street familiar since childhood, will note shops which have changed hands, or changed function, or changed into offices, or have even been replaced altogether by a new building. This is merely 'cumulative' change, for which we can console ourselves with the Tennysonian thought that though the individual (shop or house) is prodigally squandered by the forces of urban change, the species remains, and seems to be protected.[8] But no more, for in the 'transformative' change to which British post-war cities have been subjected, the middle-aged revenant will often find that the street itself no longer exists, nor the district in which it was situated, and that a new urban freeway makes it hard to be sure exactly where the street was, since what had been a densely built-up area of closely packed terraced streets now seems to consist mainly of grassy knolls and is open and empty to the far horizon in every direction. This is the kind of experience, among other things, which is captured in *City*. The reaction to such experience (of change-without-continuity) may, indeed, be an almost frantic and helpless nostalgia, feeding that virtual industry of books and postcards of 'Old Birmingham', and the like. But it can also result in a desire to research and understand the past, to secure thereby some permanence for it, and some renewed sense of place. What was wrong with the notion of 'the poetry of place' (the category under which Fisher was often classified in the 1970s, and which he came to dislike) was its tendency to forget that 'place' must also be a verb, an active, elective 'placing' of the self, as well as a noun denoting the locale of the already-given. Curiously, the spur to undertake such acts of 'placing' is often a sense of continuity with the previous generation, set in motion (as, apparently, in Fisher's case) by the death of a parent whose life we wholly identify with it. In Fisher's case, the mystery of *City* is that, given the evident intensity of his personal act of self-placing within Birmingham, it is puzzling that it should seem to have no apparent analogue in his work, and must always be discussed separately from everything else he wrote.

I cannot claim, of course, to have entirely solved the mystery, but I can see a way of approaching his work in a more integrated manner, while still acknowledging the centrality to it of *City*. This approach involves seeing *City* as the first part of what I would call a 'composite-epic' of urban material, a sequence which has its own overall structural logic and coherence. The composite sequence begins with the major work *City* in 1961, and continues with 'Handsworth Liberties' in 1978, which is a kind of late 'coda' to *City*. It then enters its second major phase with *A Furnace* in 1986, and concludes (at least for the time being) with 'Six Texts for a Film' (a kind of coda to *A Furnace*) in the 1994 volume *Birmingham River*. The composite has two phases, with a major work and a shorter work in each. A distinct shift in the nature of the content is also evident between the two phases: in the first the focus is exclusively urban – the scrutiny reaches the suburbs in 'Handsworth Liberties', but goes no further. In the second phase the focus broadens, both historically and geographically, becoming, for instance, urban/regional rather than just urban, with a strong sense of the interaction between the city and its hinterland. The focus also becomes conceptually and ideologically broader, looking, for instance, at the idea of the city, at the notion of 'centredness', and at the interaction between 'place' as a construct and the 'givens' of geology and terrain, as well as broadening the historical perspective – you have to go back further than *City* went to understand how the city got to be the way it is now. Second, there is also, between the two phases of the composite, a distinct shift in technique. This technical shift can be summed up by saying that *City* and 'Handsworth Liberties' represent two technical extremes, those of 'maximalism' (to coin a phrase) and minimalism. These are bracketing shots, so to speak, representing the 'thesis' and 'antithesis' in the dialectic of technique which will generate the 'synthesis' of *A Furnace*. The latter solves the problem of how to continue to work with *City*-type materials without becoming involved in the mere compulsive repetition of a successful formula (a process that *City* itself memorably calls a 'cemetery of performance'). *A Furnace* shifts the ground to a vastly extended content, using a much more heavily impacted technique, which, however, realises the difference between minimalism and compression, moving away from the slightly arid minimalism of 'Handsworth Liberties', but without going back to the 'maximalism' of *City*, with its extensive sections of 'auxiliary prose'. *A Furnace* thus becomes pivotal, marking the achievement of a mature 'poised' mode which seems to combine the loose documentary discursiveness of *City* with the minimalist, imagistic indirectness of 'Handsworth Liberties'. This latter poem had threatened to abandon the method of *City* entirely and re-adopt as his standard the 'ardent obliquity' (J.H. Prynne's phrase)[9] of most of the rest of his work except *City* itself (and except the quirky, humorous, ironic, self-deprecating pieces, of which there are a surprising number). My approach here, and the notion of the 'composite sequence' of urban material, re-integrates the apparent anomaly of *City* into the *oeuvre* as a whole, identifying these four long urban/regional pieces as its epicentre, and seeing *A Furnace* as the major piece of his later career, balancing *City* and going beyond it.[10]

In this chapter, then, the aim is to emphasise the process whereby the city – one particular city – becomes something the poet thinks with across the whole span of his career, as Dickens thought with London, Joyce with Dublin, and Balzac with Paris, for I believe that Fisher's claims to lasting status depend crucially on this urban and regional material. Furthermore, the Preface to *A Furnace*, establishes a strong sense of continuity between that volume and the earlier major urban piece (while also vividly expressing the 'phase two' extension from urbanism to regionalism):

> I have, indeed, set one landscape to work with another in this poem, more by way of superimposition than comparison: Birmingham, where I was born in a district that had not long since been annexed from the southern edge of the old county of Staffordshire, and the stretch of hill country around the northern tip of the same county where I have been living recently; about the same size as Birmingham, and, in its way, equally complex. (Preface to *A Furnace*, p. vii)

Also, Fisher himself makes the kind of linking between that poem and *City* that I am suggesting here when he begins *A Furnace* with 'Introit: 12 November 1958', which (the Preface says) 'identifies the poem's preoccupations in the sort of setting in which they were forcing themselves on me at the time I wrote the pieces which were to be published as *City* in 1961' (p. viii). This extraordinary initiating retro-gesture seems to voice a desire for the kind of 'composite' thinking about these urban materials which I am suggesting here. Indeed, Fisher himself seems to have this kind of connection in mind in the interview with John Tranter. Tranter makes the point that the 'influence of place' is of crucial importance in Fisher's work:

> particularly Birmingham, where you grew up. Now you live out of Birmingham, in the country. I can't imagine two more opposite environments – Birmingham, busy and industrial, completely different to where you live now, which is very quiet, farming country way up in the hills in the middle of England where a car might go by every five minutes. (Tranter, p. 11)

Fisher acknowledges the difference, but then makes it clear that the force of his imagination – the habitual processes of perception imbued in him by learning to think with Birmingham – make him see the countryside itself as industrialised, and hence cognate with the city, for he says that 'I don't seem to be able to go to any bit of country without finding traces of mining and industry and people's lives in it. When I was living in Birmingham, which I did for forty years, I suppose I was stuck with it like a child out of Wordsworth'. He then talks of how his family had come into the city from the countryside only two or three generations before, so that he feels a kind of affinity with it. He goes on again to stress the 'industrial' history of the countryside, its pre-industrial traces which go back to the Bronze Age, and the geological deposits which shaped its subsequent use, development and patterns of settlement (p. 12). Essentially, this is the formula or 'menu' for his long poem *A Furnace*, cornerstone of the second phase of the composite. 'Brought up in the city', he says, 'rather as if exiled in it, but exiled from what I was never told! – I thought of the city as something to question' (p. 12). Here the Heaneyesque notion of the 'inner émigré' is strong, but it expresses the typically working-class experience of possessing a vague ignorance about even immediate forebears. The advantage of this condition is that the need to question and interrogate one's own ground is thereby very much strengthened. But what constitutes for Fisher the disturbing, 'Wordsworthian' element in his Birmingham environment, that is, the element which is equivalent to the 'huge and mighty forms' which disturb the thoughts and dreams of the boat-stealing child in *The Prelude* (Book 1, line 398)? Surely it is the massively scaled industrial architecture vividly described in *City*, in passages commented upon by almost all who have discussed the poem, namely the 'arrogant ponderous architecture that dwarfed and terrified the people by its sheer size and functional brutality'. This is an image of industrialism cognate with Blake's 'dark Satanic mills', whereby industrial installations are viewed with a frisson that sees them as virtually the work of the devil. Thus, in poem seven of *City* we are told that the pre-1960s city brought 'midnight and its trappings out/ into the sun shadows', where the Wordsworthian sense of the brooding circumambient 'presence that disturbs' is very strong.

It might be sensible, finally, to comment on what will seem to many a conspicuous omission in Fisher's extensive Birmingham materials, namely that he does not refer at all to the patterns of post-war immigration which have significantly affected the character of the city. Though he strongly denies any element of 'nostalgia' in the *City* materials, the material as published might well lend itself to a nostalgic way of viewing this urban past, taking its bearings from a 1930s working-class childhood where home and place-of-work were side by side ('I'd been brought up in the Thirties in a docile working-class environment, five doors from an enormous railway-wagon factory which employed, at some time or another, most of the men in the district. My bedroom window looked out into it', Lester, 23). His own father, however, is not a factory worker, but 'a poorly-paid craftsman in a small jeweller's in Pitsford Street for most of his life' who felt it 'socially degrading, when he was moved to a large factory on war work, for three or four times the money' (Lester, 24). This awareness of the social gradations within the working class is telling, and likewise the emphasis upon the trauma of the Second World War which begins to break up this world. The break up is completed from the late 1950s onwards, with widespread demolition programmes and the creation of 'overspill' housing estates. Though he is fascinated by the process of urban change and transposition, the next stage of it does not seem to feature at all in Fisher's work: thus, Fisher writes, as if with a degree of nostalgia, about Handsworth as a respectable white working-class district, but not about its transformation into an inner-city district with a significant Black population. Likewise, Allen Fisher and Iain Sinclair represent similar parts of London, and from a similar perspective (that is, with an emphasis on successive cultural 'layerings'), without any significant registering of a black presence there.

Reading 'Six Texts'

Fisher's 1994 collection *Birmingham River* contains a sequence called 'Six Texts for a Film', commissioned for a documentary film about him made by Tom Pickard in 1991. The six parts of the sequence are of unequal length, with the first two together being over twice the total length of the remaining four; further, the first (at nearly six pages) is three times the length of the second. This implies a work of epic-scale ambitions which are rapidly scaled down and reined in practice. At any rate, the work is just over twelve pages long, and is concerned with cultural, industrial, and historical connections between the city of Birmingham and its regional environment, and with the poet's personal history in so far as these things impinge upon it. The first section (entitled 'Talking to Cameras') is broadest in scope, beginning with the arresting, manifesto-like statement in the first line – a 'Bakhtinian declaration', Sean O'Brien usefully calls it in *The Deregulated Muse* (p. 112):

> Birmingham's what I think with.
> It's not made for that sort of job,
> but it's what they gave me.
> As a means of thinking, it's a brummagem
> screwdriver. What that is,
> is a medium-weight claw hammer
> or something of the sort, employed
> to drive a tapered woodscrew home
> as if it were a nail.
>
> (*Birmingham River*, p. 11)

One of the remarkable aspects of this remarkable announcement is the way it figures poetry-making as a craft, but not an old rural craft (as it is figured, for instance, in Seamus Heaney's poem 'Thatcher', in *Door into the Dark*, where the act of making a poem is implicitly paralleled with the ancient country craft of thatching). In fact, it might be more accurate to say that it sees poetry-making as a trade rather than a craft, the kind of urban trade which is carried out with screwdrivers, woodscrews and bradawls ('a small tool with a pointed end for boring holes by hand', says the *Concise Oxford*), and in this sense it is broadly aligned with Barry MacSweeney's image, cited earlier, of the oxyacetylene torch as the implement of the poet. Furthermore, unlike the already-discussed pronouncements of Mahon and R.S. Thomas, Fisher's work does not write off cities as places where thoughts might grow. On the contrary, it recognises the city as an implement and a site of hermeneusis. A further striking element in this statement is the way it takes for granted that that the poet makes heuristic use of whatever material is 'issued' to it by its childhood environment, and of Birmingham he says 'It's not made for that sort of job,/ but it's what they gave me'. Indeed, the lines perhaps see poetry not just as a craft, but as crafty, as a matter of constant *bricolage* and improvisation, so that the tools to hand have to be pressed into service for whatever job needs doing (if you don't have a hammer handy you may have to try to knock in a nail with a screwdriver, and if you are too much of as purist to do that, then the job may never get done at all). This raises the question of what kind of material, what kind of environment, is generally thought to be meant for that sort of job (that is, for thinking with in poetry). In answer, we might say (predictably, by now) that the rural environment in which the poetic sensibility of William Wordsworth was formed remains the archetype of one which 'naturally' fosters the poetic sensibility and is meant for that job. This formative rural environment is not, of course, a 'soft' rural or pastoral setting of the *Cider With Rosie* or *Under Milk Wood* kind, but, rather, one which contains elements that disturb and trouble the mind into thought (the sombre, brooding presence of the lakes and mountains is the formative element for Wordsworth – it is the sublime rather than the beautiful, to use a familiar dichotomy). In such surroundings, we tend to assume, thought grows naturally. Fisher's 'Six Texts' asserts its contrary hermeneutic pre-occupations in its opening lines, and likewise claims a 'Wordworthian' educative potency for the urban. Though he wouldn't use the phrase, Fisher's 'composite sequence' of urban material (of which 'Six Texts' is the latest instalment) also traces 'the growth of the poet's mind'.

The opening block of roughly twenty-five lines is followed by an italicised stretch of triplets and couplets, running to about the same length, and reading as a series of mantra-like injunctions on method

'Eyes down, always down,/ looking for the truth of it// fallen out of
the air, out of/ the vents of animals// flaked from the skin of us all,/our
pockets, the underparts of cars;// landlocked creeks/ of dead ground,
waste oil/ with no dead river to float on' (pp. 11–12). Here the
Bakhtinian switch of voice from the confident declamatory tone of the
opening is very marked: the injunction that directs the gaze down-
wards is reminiscent of the Bunyanesque figure with the muck-rake
which prefaces Iain Sinclair's *Lud Heat*. In cities, as discussed in the
next chapter, the walker's eye usually remains below the level of the
shop fascia, but here, in urban-detective mode, the viewer scrutinises
the ground for evidence of the city-as-palimpsest, for the tracks made
and then re-trodden, and then again re-laid ('/… tarmac, concrete,
crumbled and patched/ causeways; innocence and habit// perpetually
breaking the ways across the earth', p. 12). Typically, in post-war
developments, these older multiply determined street patterns were
obliterated, with a completely new scale of townscape imposed,
frequently cutting across the old as though it had never been there,
obliterating, as it were, the 'fossil record' of the previous occupation
of the terrain. Hence, we lose contact with what seems to be envisaged
here as a layer of energy, of charged air which hovers above the re-
trodden tracks ('A zone of air, ankle-high/ where dead stuff drops or
hovers/ in the taboo'); the result is a kind of obliteration of the local
Feng Shui of the terrain. Yet this is not to sentimentalise: the feelings
expressed are more ecological than mystical, and the passage contains
numerous words connoting death and decay, implying that these re-
trodden zones could themselves prove to be the very 'cemetery of
performance' feared in *City*, that is, a deadening routine of 'innocence
and habit' which takes men like the poet's father along the same road
to the same repetitive work for a lifetime, declining better alternatives
even when they are offered. Something of this narrow world of
cautions and precautions seems to be evoked in the language of this
passage, like a parent's cautionary instructions to a child ('Don't eat
what's been dropped.//Disinfect dirty money if you find it./ Eyes down.
Watch your step' p. 12).

    The voice then makes another major Bakhtinian, or registerial, shift
for the remaining three-and-a-half pages which complete the section,
contrasting the habitual 'eyes down' or 'field-work' method of inves-
tigation of the previous section with a more systematic, book-based
approach to local knowledge, a method which can take in issues of
power and ideology:

    If you get systematic,
    and follow power around, you arrive
    at a bedrock out of a book, Sandstone
    by Keuper, soft, so friable
    it rubs back into sand under your thumb. (p.12)

The local sandstone bedrock is 'out of a book' because it is named
'Keuper Marl' (it is also known as Mercia Mudstone), and it has the
qualities of porousness and friability mentioned which cause notori-
ous engineering problems. Book-learning, education and professional
knowledge provide a complementary investigative route to the empiri-
cist 'eyes-down' method by which an understanding of the city and its
environs can be constructed (a dichotomy we noted earlier when
discussing Iain Sinclair). Thus, with one method imposed upon
another, the investigative process itself mimes the gradual layered
build up of the city:

    Believe the Book of bedrocks,
    as in the end, you must,
    and you evolve Book City, just
    as it evolved itself: rock, water,
    forest, settlers, trade. Then
    property, sewage, architects, poets. (p. 13)

Yet the poet at this point, like so many 'city' writers, seems to be inter-
ested, too, in a process which might be called 'deep reprise', a peeling
back of these successive layers of settlement, development and increas-
ing cultural complexity until a 'primal' layer is reached which is like
encountering the terrain for the first time, as a nomadic people would
('But what is it/ when you're first set loose in it, with only/ your
nostrils, fingertips, ears, eyes/ to teach you appetite and danger?',
p. 13) This obsessive kind of 'peeling back' of time-layers has already
been seen in such works as Peter Didsbury's 'The Drainage', Allen
Fisher's *Place* (such as the passage on his awareness of the prehistoric
London 'lagoon' beneath the container berths), and in James
Thomson's 'Sunday in Hampstead', and it seems, as we said, charac-
teristic of the urban gaze of the inner eye. Looked at thus, what is the
city, stripped down to its primal geological determinants and reprised
by the trans-historic and trans-cultural eye? 'Is it the primal ocean,
condemned/ and petrified? Is it a giant/ lagoon in Tartarus, petrified,/

redeemed, made habitable?' (p. 13). As with Didsbury's poem, the
process envisaged here is an on-going struggle with awesome natural
forces. The vision, again, seems Tennysonian, for he supplied the deep-
toned poetic register used at such moments, for instance in *In Memo-
riam*, where he evokes a panoramic sweep through geological time
which sees the hills as constantly shifting forms which dissolve and re-
form with the fluidity of passing cloud-shadows (see poem 123, 'There
rolls the deep where grew the tree'). If we retain O'Brien's notion of
Bakhtinian multiplicities of register within Fisher's work, then we
might say that writing like this is epic or operatic in scale and tone,
with a poise and grandeur which is achieved through the skilful
deployment of an austere vocabulary within a stark simplicity of
syntax: it requires the full, reverberating, stopped diapason note, and
if this manner poses problems for a poet, then they concern the risk of
bathos, and the difficulty of making transitions to and from other
voices and registers.

The modulation to yet another tone takes place about half way
through this five page opening section, with the announcement
'There's one thing certain: this is/ the centre of the universe' (p. 13),
taking us back to the conversationalist manner which is the more
usual tone of Fisher's writing. The section has a wry statement of
rationale for the locative process he is involved in:

> The universe, we define
> as a place which is capable of having
> a place like this for its centre.
>
> There's no shame/ in letting the world pivot
> on your own patch. That's all a centre's for. (p. 13)

This amounts to a gesture which simultaneously de-centres and re-
centres, radically reinstating the local as the essential provider of a
sense of measure ('how far Clare/ needed to walk/ from High Beech
back to Helpston', p. 13).[11] Here the poet John Clare functions as an
archetype of the deracinated self, his familiar world eradicated and
undone by the Enclosures (and, as Michael Schmidt reminds us in his
Lives of the Poets, he also lived long enough to see his favourite
marshland cut through by the London–Manchester railway line) as
Fisher's is by bombing and redevelopment. In what follows, which
continues to develop the idea of the need to centre any given world,

the exemplum is the Oracle at Delphi, supposed Omphalos or navel of the world, designated by the poem as a 'cultural' centre ('the single centre,// not of the planet, but of the earth's shifting surface, the live map', p. 14), and Fisher then reverts to the time 'when I lived at ground level' (rather than, as now, in the hills), and 'centred the universe/ just beyond the midpoint of the garden path/ of 74 Kentish Road, Handsworth', p. 14). This leads a 'world-as-body' meditation, in which the split stones by the garden path correspond to nipples, testicles, eyes, buttocks, or, even, 'big toes'. What is interesting here is that these are all doubled body features, so that Fisher, 'Playing safe,/ and liking to feel at home wherever I live' (p. 14), offers an image of double-centredness, rather than the Greek image of the omphalos, with its connotations of singularity and confident mono-centredness in a much more literal sense.

At the line 'Again. What can it be?' (p. 14) voice and focus shift radically, assuming a privileged, panoramic viewpoint, giving an overview of the urban terrain from which fundamental questions can be asked about such things as the relationship between geology, the lie of the ground and economic development. Where does the city come from? Why is it located here rather than there? What are the forces that sustain it and make it grow? If the city is like a little universe, then what was the nature of its 'Big Bang', the force which set it going and still sustains its growth? And when its heart finally goes cold and it collapses in on itself like an exhausted star, where then do the forces disperse to (and, we hope, re-form)? Speculative, ontological questions like these are surely what lie behind the epic-panoramic sweep of such writing, which show that Sean O'Brien is wrong to call Fisher an 'anti-foundationalist poet ... rejecting the idea of ends and purposes' (though in a chapter – in *The Deregulated Muse* – which is one of the most stimulating pieces yet written about Fisher's work):

> It's an artefact. A sculpture
> a dozen and more miles across. Everything
> that stands in it now
> the work of one protracted
> moment, and impulse to make;
> a long century, the sort of time
> it took to envisage and carry out
> an unsigned medieval cathedral.
> If a certain mind

could conceive that, and get it done,
the same goes for this work of art. It houses
a spirit that talks in ribbons
of tarmac and brickwork, puzzle-spaces for the people
to clamber on and spill through. (pp. 14–15)

What fuels the urban Big Bang, then, is the 'impulse to make', to bash
metal, as David Lodge has it (Birmingham's post-war prose-laureate,
as Fisher is its poet-laureate). The Jewellery Quarter that Fisher writes
about, and in which his father worked, began as a cluster of manu-
factories of small metal toys. Here is the 'end' of the city (to speak tele-
ologically of 'ends and purposes'), the impulse from which it had its
germination and which provides the force that sustains it. Fisher links
his metal-bashing city – producer of railway carriages, cars, machine
tools, tin-toys, jewellery – with the evidence of ancient metal working
in the quarries of the surrounding region where he himself now lives.
It is, we might say, that simple. And we might think (teleologically) of
all the cities discussed in this book as generated by some such primary
impulse. Thus, if the *raison-d'être* of Birmingham is to make things,
that of Liverpool is to move them about, ultimately setting up ship-
ping companies, establishing trade routes, and becoming the matrix of
commercial networks of import and export. Yet, what so many of the
poets dealt with here seem to have in common is that they confront
their cities at a time when these founding occupations are gone, or
have been superseded in a post-Fordist, post-industrial age, so that the
sustaining impulse must find a substitute, or proxy, or reification.
Partly, the act of cultural 'reprise' or re-creation in which the poets
engage is itself the substitute, and several of the poets express an
explicit awareness of this. Such an admission of belatedness is present,
for instance, in key pronouncements given iconic status earlier in this
book, as when Heaney says of his pen 'I'll dig with it', or when
MacSweeney likens his to the shipyard worker's oxyacetylene torch.
The cities have outlived the lifespan of their own economic base or
infrastructure and must now live primarily by their 'superstructure'.
Thus, such institutions as museums-of-local-life or tourist-related
service industries which recycle and re-package the industrial past
assume a primary role in the local economy. But, after all, this merely
reflects the fate of Britain as a whole, in an age when the largest
contributors to the Gross National Product are not steel production,
or shipbuilding, but tourism, the arts and education. Hence, it seems

appropriate that the passage just quoted ends with an image which sees the city as a kind of urban adventure playground built for the entertainment of adults ('puzzle-spaces for the people/ to clamber on and spill through', p. 15). Likewise, the building of the city is viewed as the production of a work of art, as a kind of gigantic action paint-ing, perhaps ('a spirit that talks in ribbons/ of tarmac and brickwork', p. 15). And, again, the question Fisher goes on to ask of this artefact is the same as the one Blake asks of the natural universe – 'What hand, what eye. Indeed' (p. 15).

The image which follows this is one frequently used before by Fisher, in which the urban brick-and-stone skin spreads across the terrain like a poured liquid which finds its own level, fills up all the hollows, and then overspills on to the next bit of ground ('the by-product of a spastic purpose,/ oozing as miraculous drops/ from a sort of spirit into a sort of matter,/ gathering in pools, trickling to fill/ wrinkles, indentations, then congealing as/ masonry: factories, floods of houses,/ shallowing as they spread, converted/ again to spirit in the understanding', p. 15). This is a remarkably panoramic image, with a kind of mystical or cosmic feel: it views creative energy as the philoso-pher Teillard de Chardin did, that is, as a moving force in which spirit (the 'impulse' mentioned earlier) is bodied forth in matter. But it also envisages a kind of reversible creation, which can move back the other way, from material to spiritual again ('converted/ again to spirit in the understanding' p. 15). This expresses the movement we have been talking about from an economic base which consists primarily of industrial production and manufacture to one in which the primary product is 'cultural', rooted in leisure, entertainment, or education. Thus, the city becomes in the main a producer of 'heritage trails', craft museums, international conference centres, orchestras and universi-ties. Forgivably, too, this reading of the progress of civic development modestly elevates the poet's own production of 'Birmingham' to primary status, so that the generative, metal-bashing impulse which had 'congealed', is now made to flow again, in the form of poetic 'word-bashing', a penetrative and revitalising force which can be like a new nature ('Spirit/ filtered though brickwork. Counter-Nature,/ caught in the sculpture and leased out', p. 15). Thus the poet, the artist generally, is the lessee of the spirit, re-inspiring the whole urban enter-prise, as Gaudi's Sagrada Familia, which is mentioned here, is the epicentre and inspiration of a whole urban boom and renewal in Barcelona which is cultural and artistic – 'superstructural' in the sense

I have been using it here – rather than being founded upon the older urban bedrock of industry and commerce (which, like the Midlands' mudstone Fisher refers to) proved to be so porous and friable.

Indeed, even the artist-creator behind the physical fabric this city has strong avant-garde credentials and uses aleatory procedures ('The artist of the place/ left plenty to chance'), but also more traditional methods, first producing a small-scale model 'on land above the Bull Ring', and then changing progressively while remaining centred on this spot ('And it stays centred/ on the same spot, ignoring superseded/ layouts and the quick turnover of the people; it holds/ the inertia of an authoritative will', p. 15). There is a meditation here on the sources and forces of power and how it is maintained, and in the case of Birmingham, the founding figure of Joseph Chamberlain may again be in mind, as in Section Three, 'Authorities', of *A Furnace*, with which this part of 'Six Texts' is strongly connected in both thought and treatment. Here, the role of the artist as a mere validator and sustainer of a dominant political power is considered ('The artwork's the figure of authority'). The perception is like the child's first realisation that (say) the elaborate but taken-for-granted ironwork on the gates of a municipal park, embodies the civic imperium under whose authority he or she lives. At that moment the child begins to consider its own place and status, and enters a new state of being, as in the primal scene of the Lacanian mirror stage, or the Althusserian moment of interpellation. At such a moment (looking, perhaps, at the civic coat of arms on a school exercise book) the child is interpellated as a social being, as a 'citizen', as a controlled life with a certain allocated scope and a specific role to play. That, at any rate, is how I read these lines:

> The artwork's the figure of authority. Swung
> on a green rail somewhere, with a low brick wall
> under your feet, you hear
> a moment in your life tell you that. (p. 16)

What the moment also tells of, I think, is a different kind of art, a kind which is the direct expression and embodiment of political power, and of a political force which looks to maintain a single, never-changing centre. This kind of art is founded on the static Greek omphalos model again, holding to 'an inertia of the authoritative will' (p. 15), rather than expressing the doubled, or constantly shifting provisionalised centre which Fisher earlier identified with the garden path at 74

Kentish Road, Handsworth, a centre which is highly personal and mainly hermeneutic, the kind of *petit recit* which you must make for yourself, rather than this other kind, the public *grand recit* which others impose upon you.

Of course, Fisher is not simply enjoining repeated shifts of centre. On the contrary, he wants to say that apparent shifts of centre are often an attempt to disguise the pathological stasis of power and power-structures ('suspect repeated shifts of centre', he says (p. 16), a useful counter-balance to the more simplistic Lyotardian injunction that we are to distrust all meta-narratives). He ends the section with an image of centralised political power, which is the notion of the city, and a specific part of it, as the 'hub of empire':

> The Forum of Augustus, sitting firm and new,
> drawing centrality to itself,
> had to have its back to a massive
> curtain wall, set there to mask
> slum tenements behind. That sort of place. (p. 16)

Thoughts of the Roman forum are probably provoked by the presence of large classical buildings like the former Town Hall in the centre of Birmingham (as in other British cities). Classical architecture was felt in Victorian times to be an appropriate expression of imperial power, and in most English cities (Scotland was different) the Roman architectural orders were preferred to Greek ones, reflecting the primary connotations of ancient Greece and Rome, the former being associated with art and philosophy (that is, it had primarily cultural and 'superstructural' associations) and the latter with Empire, power, and conquest (that is, its associations were mainly material and 'infrastructural'). To put it slightly differently: in British use the Greek and Roman orders expressed the desire for cultural and material hegemony respectively. Centres of this kind, which aspire to be permanent still points of the turning world, says Fisher, always need a massive curtain wall behind them to hide whatever is their equivalent to the slum tenements. Mono-centred art, to put it bluntly, is often part of that curtain wall.

The next numbered and titled section, 'Birmingham River' itself, is much shorter and much more straightforward. It contemplates Birmingham's two rivers, the Tame and the Rea, following them into, through and out of the city in a way which is, again, indicative of the

urban/regional focus of the sequence as a whole. The tone now is flat
and prosaic, the antithesis of the high oratorical mode so prominent
in the previous section. The beginning is not just dialogic, but, liter-
ally, a dialogue:

> Where's Birmingham river? Sunk.
> Which river was it? Two. More or less. (p. 17)

Like similar material on London's buried rivers in Allen Fisher's *Place*
sequence, it seems the product of research in local history libraries and
walks on the terrain itself, an ambulatory, antiquarian poetic, easy-
paced, eclectic, and without the slightly frantic, obsessive 'Eyes down'
close scrutiny of the previous section. Indeed, Fisher's whole urban
poetic project has this intellectual eclecticism, believing in the efficacy
of an amateur kind of general reflective learnedness, rather than the
professional's narrower 'single-issue' mode. What is widely available
(which is to say, these days, downloadable) on, say, the course of the
River Tame (to take a typical Fishereque area of interest) is produced
by such people as water-management professionals and urban-renewal
experts, and is written in the technical register which foregrounds their
own professional standing. Fisher's work (like that of Allen Fisher and
Iain Sinclair) embodies a belief in an older and broader kind of
humanist concern with the environment, and a commitment to
informed citizenship. Self-evidently, the efficacy of such discourses
(their survival, even) is open to question, and it isn't really clear in
what part of the public sphere they might now have their place. What
tends to happen is that discourses like these are themselves forced to
migrate to quasi-professional, or at any rate academic, locations.
Thus, to find discussion of urban environments which seems cognate
in its tone and preoccupations with that of Fisher's urban composite-
sequence we have to look in the academic field of cultural geography.

Section Two, then, emphasises that unlike so many cities which are
identified with a single river (the Tyne, the Wear, the Mersey, the
Thames and so on) Birmingham is linked to two, the first being the
Tame, linked here with the first Saxon settlements by the 'tribe of
Beorma', a Saxon settlement, which displaced the Celtic people who
had given the rivers their names. These Saxon settlements spread all
along the river, with the main centre of this Mercian kingdom being at
Tamworth., and its name, 'Tame', meaning the dark river, is linked
with the Black Country, the designation of the Midlands industrialised

countryside stretching between the major conurbations of Wolver-
hampton and Birmingham. The river emerges, finally, on Fisher's
home ground ('From Bescot/ she oozes a border round Handsworth/
where I was born' pp. 17–18). But here the river, heading in towards
the centre of Birmingham, catches a whiff of the city ('coal gas//
sewage, smoke', p. 18) and heads off instead for Tamworth, seat of the
Mercian kings. On its way back out, this river intersects briefly with
the Rea, which actually goes into Birmingham, a river of a quite differ-
ent character, without the ancient, regal, rural aspect of the Tame; it is
referred to dismissively as 'the wash that's run under Birmingham/ a
slow, petty river with no memory of an ancient// name; a river called
Rea, meaning river, and misspelt at that' (p. 18). Here the natural flow
is taken over ('Before they merge// they're both steered straight, in
channels/ that force them clear of the gasworks. And the Tame// gets
marched out of town in the policed calm/ that hangs under the long
legs of the M6', p. 18). The two rivers, as already implied, seem to
represent contrasting principles; the Tame is regional, regal, dynastic,
past-rooted, evoking continuities with a mythologised and heroic
Mercian past, its dark flowing waters emblematic of the restless Saxon
energies which still irrigate the local spirit. This is the outlook repre-
sented in his work by Fisher's fellow Mercian poet, Geoffrey Hill.
Fisher, by contrast, follows not the Tame, but the Rea, which is recent
and urban, much more at home with the coal-gas and sewage, more
closely identified with the industrial face of the city. There is, as Neil
Corcoran has claimed, a certain Romanticism in all this:[12] the dual-
river scenario links Fisher's family background (country dwellers who,
in the past, settled in the city to find employment) with the urban,
suggesting, again, a doubled centre (two rivers, not just one), a duality
echoed both formally, in the shape of the un-rhymed couplets in which
the section is written, and emblematically, in the device of the two split
stones which figured in the previous section. The concluding six
couplets of Section Two consider the complementary role of the two
rivers in sustaining the city – as a source of drinking water, as
providers of power for water mills, and then as the process of indus-
trialisation begins in the early nineteenth century, they provide power
for the pioneering Soho Works set up by the engineers James Watt and
Matthew Boulton. The rivers also become bearers of effluent ('waste
and foul waters … sewage, factory poisons', p. 18). Yet in these lines
there is a sense of a system overloaded, threatening to choke up with
its own waste products, and generating toxicity, pollution, and

entropy rather than energy, (for instance, in the nineteenth century, spreading typhoid through the urban system). Bricked-up and culverted underground, the rivers (as so much in Allen Fisher) are ever an uneasy presence, always threatening an eruption leading to their unwelcome re-appearance on the streets (as happened with the Tame in August 1999, while I was writing this). Thus the rivers were hidden from public view behind the industrial buildings which used their waters:

> Sank out of sight
> under streets, highways, the back walls of workshops;
> collected metals, chemicals, aquicides. Ceased
>
> to draw lines that weren't cancelled or unwanted; became
> drains, with no part in anybody's plan. (p. 18)

Written out of the picture, unmapped and largely unwanted, the underground rivers become unknown, unpredictable, a force without a centre. But they remain barometric indicators likely to return (perhaps literally) to plague us in retaliation for environmental abuse.

The remaining four sections of 'Six Texts' are briefer, with Section Three, 'Town World', taking up less than a page and comprising ten un-rhymed free-verse couplets and a single concluding line. Being shorter, these later sections all consist of the extended development of a single image or moment, this being, in the case of Section 3, a view across the built-up spaces of the city. It seems at first simply to record what the dweller in such places always sees, and sees as 'natural', that is, a horizon where land and sky never meet directly, but always as 'a horizon of roofs', which, in a city like Birmingham which is built on relatively flat land, is never very far away. Hence, what is beyond has to be imagined – it cannot actually be seen, for the sense of seeing into the distance is lost, and all that is actually seen are the breaks in the roof patterns which indicate the presence of roads:

> tarmac roads
> stamped through roof-slates;
>
> tree-heads, ornate school chimneys
> pushed high enough up to imagine over
>
> to the next hard skyline (p. 19)

What stands above the roofs, in the districts of working-class terraced streets in cities, is what rules the lives within them, that is, the schools, the churches and the factories. Each hollow of the land – each 'brick dish' – is built upon, and each has 'another covered river'. Each of these hollows, too, has its characteristic manufacture, producing 'alien// factory-odours', and each is uneasily and threateningly 'other', a place from which noxious vapours are likely to be wafted into 'our' territory, that is, the tribal bastion we call home, and return to, presumably, with a sense of relief whenever we have to venture beyond it into these other places with their 'ancient buses' and their 'black air'. There is a grim local chauvinism here which views with great unease the crossing even of the boundary into another postal district. This world, which has shrunk to a space that can be traversed on foot in half-an-hour, or crossed on buses with a few familiar numbers, is vividly captured here. It is, of course, a long-vanished world, where the local pub, the corner shop, the familiar church and school, and the factory of the local employer provided a self-sufficient universe, one which, Fisher tells us, he exclusively inhabited until well into his teens. The sense of being 'home', and the fear of not being, so important in Fisher (for whom 'home' is a frequently occurring word) is one of the primary referents of this section.

Section Four, 'In the Repair Shop', consisting of seven un-rhymed couplets, takes up barely half a page, and its glimpse of a piano awaiting repair is difficult at first to link with the content of the remainder of the sequence. That Fisher, as a jazz pianist, wishes to celebrate the improvisatory art ('to make music's to recognise what's found', p. 20) is understandable. The massive, furniture-like solidity of the instrument contrasts with the evanescence of its product, and is imaged in terms of a labyrinthine interior with interconnecting stairways and passages within which the paradoxical impulse to make music has been planted ('ordained from the beginning, the sounds/ buried like the veins in rock', p. 20), just as the 'making' impulse is the reason and the spur for the labyrinthine development of the city. Here too the idea of the repair shop (as opposed to the factory) connotes the artisanal base of the city's manufactuary, retaining the human-scale atmosphere of work places designated 'work-shops' or 'machine-shops', rather than factories, the kind of environment in which Fisher's father worked, which can confer a strong sense of the individuality and dignity of skilled work, something which the more regimented regime of the factory cannot not provide.

After the un-rhymed couplets of Sections Two to Four, Section Five (a single page) reverts to the more open, loosely versed manner of the first section, and again takes up that markedly elevated tone, as the 'seeing eye' broods over the city ('Low/ over infinite city/ one urban sky that all its horizons share', p. 21). The aim is to achieve a broadly abstract synthesis of guide-book-like material about the city: the growth of the place is linked with natural growth cycles, like that of coral ('They'll tell you the place developed/ like a coral reef,/ by millions of little and a few/ major ones, cleansing its errors by the day', p. 21). This is 'the idea of a city. The ethical body' (p. 21), which 'Six Texts' introduces, but in the end retreats from (more so than does *A Furnace*), being drawn back to that scopic fascination which rules *City*, a fascination with the sheer plenitude of the city's physical body, or, as it is called here, its 'empirical body', which (especially from a certain conceptual distance) is easily conceived of as a unity, a cell-like, web-like structure designed (like coral) to produce and sustain life:

> the empirical body's a unity: brittle,
> slaggy lacework of roads, bastions,
> breeding cubicles, draped
> on a thin armature of sewers
> threaded with cabling and gas-mains. (p. 21)

This is Fisher's de-personalised manner, the closest he comes to the high Audenesque, urban-symbolic manner; it is his way of looking with the dispassioned eye of the 1920s Russian modernist he once described himself as being, providing us with an almost mechanical 'making strange' with the aim of doing nothing less than bringing about a transformation of everyday life. It is a manner which has changed hardly at all since Fisher began using it in the late 1950s, but then, it is not easy to see what it might shift or modulate into, and it remains a distinct element in his verbal repertoire. It sees the city as moving through a series of pre-set motions, like the intricately crafted metal toys once produced in the Jewellery Quarter. The pieced and charted 'social soil' of sports pitches, pathways, allotments and so on, puts nature to use in intimate assimilation. This kind of looking/thinking valorizes the scopic, abnegating a surface/depth model in which there would be 'underlying' truths to be 'unearthed'. Hence, having cited the 'thin armature of sewers/ threaded with cabling and gas mains' (p. 21) he adds 'Under that frame, nothing/ you can sense, not even empty space'. This is the opposite to the notions of the city discussed in the first chapter, the idea that beneath the material fabric there is always something else, either just history (the 'fields beneath' which, in Blake's vision, live on, but 'lie sleeping' beneath the chartered streets) or else something less tangible, the ghost of its former self by which (says Marx) the city is always haunted. Fisher seems here to draw back from this kind of thinking, in one of those puritanical moments characteristic of him, when he asserts the primacy and sufficiency of the eye. So there is beneath 'nothing you can sense' – which isn't to say that there is nothing, but to assert that what is beneath can only be discovered by searching where the evidence is to be found (it might be a local history library, for instance). Indeed, the lack of concern about 'the fields beneath' may be prompted by what looks to be a settled conviction of the primacy of the urban over the rural, for 'country's nothing but a single island/ lapped in city' (p. 21). 'There', the text continues, 'a local nature hangs on'. Initially the referent of 'there' will be taken as the country, but the details cited are an amalgamation of the industrialised countryside ('dark brick barns and pitbanks') and the urban ('cooling towers, an orphanage,/ a fringe of houses'). Hence the terrain referred to seems to be the suburban interface between country and city, where nature lives on, but under different laws and in transformed conditions, like a 'native' culture in a colonised country. In this hybrid terrain a single sweep of the eye takes in 'a ploughed field … an asphalt playground' (p. 21, a passage reminiscent of the ambiguous territory in Paul Farley's poem discussed in the second chapter). These are different manifestations of the pieced and plotted 'social soil' mentioned earlier in the section. As the ending puts it, 'Hard court,/ grass court; same game'. Thus, the tarmac is not condemned, in a gesture of ecological fastidiousness, as a blot on the face of nature. On the contrary, the poet seems to be looking again for continuity between the lives of his remoter country ancestors and those of his immediate urban forebears.

The final section, 'Abstracted Water', consists of fourteen un-rhymed couplets, concluded with a single-line 'bob'. It is concerned with the use of water, the way it is 'borrowed' from nature for industrial and other purposes. It is 'captured for a while', becoming 'a proposition in hydraulics'; for a while it 'carries coal, parties, makes money' (p. 22), then it returns to nature. It comes 'leaking out of the hills' and is converted into 'a thin gell// flavoured with diesel,/ rust, warm discharges'. But, again, the poem does not encourage us to see industrial use merely as pollution and desecration. On the contrary, that kind of ecological purism seems completely alien to it; it is simply that – in line with the binary theme of the poem – the river has two faces or aspects. In town it becomes 'The Cut', which is 'venture-water' in which the populace dumps unwanted items ('motor-bikes' or 'gondolas from supermarkets', for instance). The new heritage industry is keen to clean all this up and make it into an 'urban trail' of some kind, described in a colourful leaflet available from the Tourist Office. But the half-submerged bikes and trolleys are what the urban-contemplative eye feeds on, and once cleaned up and converted to 'heritage' the river can never live again in the imagination, even if it re-achieves the organic life it had lost in its polluted state and again becomes a trout stream. In its undoctored form, lined with abandoned riverside buildings with bricked-up windows, it enfranchised and empowered the eye, for where 'buildings on a street/ stare you out, here it's you who do the looking' (p. 22). Of course, waterways have to be 'managed' and must be used for something. If they are no longer needed industrially they must be exploited for leisure purposes. But the 'blank, patched-up walls with huge/ secrets that stink and flare' and 'piss out coloured suds' are part of a different economy, being highly productive parts of the urban poetic terrain where a thought can grow, 'left in your peace a little way/ from the backside of it all'. Further, if these places let 'the dead stuff spill out' rather unpleasantly, then it may be that a process of self purgation is taking place, where the toxins are being (literally) worked out, rather than being glazed and fossilised into the eerie unreality of the Heritage Trail. The concluding image of the poem tells how 'Sunlight// under bridges stays enclosed,/ lattices to and fro' (pp. 22–3), a beautiful and forceful image of energy incubating, fermenting, seeking fresh eruption. As Fisher ends by remarking 'There's a law// dirt grows out of', which seems to celebrate the valency of chance, disruption, and permeability between systems, a process which will remind us of Allen Fisher – another poetic user of rivers – and his interest in osmosis and tea-bags. Roy Fisher is interested in the osmosis between states of nature and the manifestations of the 'urban' impulses of making, moving, congregating, and recording, which the poem as a whole celebrates. It is this raw stuff, this untidy and sometimes unsightly seepage and eruption, which urban poets see as the silage which makes thoughts grow as well in cities as anywhere else.

Notes

1 The British situation lagged a little behind what was happening in America, where Donald Allen's *The New American Poetry* anthology (Grove Press, 1960) played a similar role in giving the American poetic 'margins' a focus and a powerful collective identity.

2 Davie's role in Fisher's career has been a crucial one, and, indeed, this critic has done much to break down the sterile stand-off between 'mainstream' and 'margins' which characterised (especially) the 1970s. But Davie's view of Fisher has not been universally accepted. Generally, those who write about Fisher take either the 'Davie' view, which is broadly assimilationist and stresses his affinities with the 'mainstream', or the 'Mottram' view (see below), which is broadly 'separatist', stressing Fisher's differences from the 'mainstream' and emphasising his affinities with American and European poetics. The 'separatist' line itself has three branches, one stressing the American side, as (on the whole) the 1975 Rasula interview does (see below), the second the European side, like the John Ash article (below), while the third branch (which might be called 'integrated-separatism') stresses the claims of both these more or less equally (as does Mottram himself, and Gregson, for instance, in the essays listed in the next footnote).

3 Substantial pieces to date (excluding reviews) on Roy Fisher's poetry are: (1) 'Roy Fisher's Work', Eric Mottram, in *Stand*, vol. 11, no. 1, 1969–70, pp. 9–18. (2) 'Roy Fisher: An Appreciation' in Donald Davie's *Thomas Hardy and British Poetry*, Routledge and Kegan Paul, 1973. (3) Some Aspects of the Poetry of Roy Fisher', J. D. Needham, in *Poetry Nation 5*, vol. iii. no.1, 1975, pp. 74–87. (4) 'A Classic Post-Modernist: The Poetry of Roy Fisher', John Ash, in *Atlantic Review* (New Series), no. 2, Autumn, 1979, pp. 39–50. (5)'Responsibilities and Distances', Peter Robinson, Cambridge doctoral thesis, 1980 (in which Fisher is one of three poets discussed). (6) Chapter 3, pp. 29–55, *The British Dissonance*, A. Kingsley-Weatherhead, Columbia University Press, 1983. (7) 'Language and the City in Roy Fisher's Poetry', Peter Barry, *English Studies*, vol. 67, no. 3, June, 1986, pp. 234–49. (8) 'Fugitive from All Exegesis – Reading Roy Fisher's *A Furnace*', Peter Barry, in *Dutch Quarterly Review of Anglo-American Letters*, January, 1988, pp. 1 – 19. (9) 'Signs of Identity: Roy Fisher's *A Furnace*, Andrew Crozier *PN Review*, vol. 18, no. 3, Jan/Feb, 1992, pp. 25–32. (10) pp. 170–74 in Neil Corcoran, *English Poetry Since 1940*, Longman, 1993. (11)'"Music of the Generous Eye": The Poetry of Roy Fisher', Ian Gregson, Chapter 10, pp. 170–91, *Contemporary Poetry and Postmodernism: Dialogue and Estrangement*, Macmillan, 1996. (12) 'Roy Fisher: A Polytheism with No Gods', Sean O'Brien, Chapter 10, pp. 112–22, *The Deregulated Muse*, Bloodaxe, 1998. (13) *The Thing About Roy Fisher: Critical Studies*, ed.

John Kerrigan and Peter Robinson, Liverpool English Texts and Studies, 37, Liverpool University Press, 2000.

4 For this detail, see the last interview listed in this footnote. There are several widely circulated interviews with Fisher and comments from one or more are usually introduced into discussions of his work. However, some of them appeared in rather ephemeral outlets, and even readers with access to a copyright library may find them difficult to trace. The major ones are: (1) Eric Mottram, 'Conversation with Roy Fisher', in *Saturday Morning* (a short-lived journal published by the London University Institute of United States Studies) no. 1, spring, 1976; the interview took place at the Poetry Society on 22 January 1973. (2) Jed Rasula and Mike Irwin, *Roy Fisher: 19 Poems and an Interview*, Grosseteste Press, 1975, issued as part of *Grosseteste Review*, volume 8; the interview took place at Keele University on 19 November 1973. (3) Robert Sheppard, 'Turning the Prism: An Interview with Roy Fisher', Toads Damp Press, 1986; The interview took place on 7 June 1982. (4) 'Paul Lester and Roy Fisher: A Birmingham Dialogue', Protean Pubs [Sic], 1986. This is not strictly an interview. It consists of an undergraduate dissertation on Roy Fisher, followed by Fisher's response. The dissertation was written in 1974 and the response in 1985. (5) 'John Tranter Interviews Roy Fisher', published in the Australian on-line magazine *Jacket* (issues 1 and 2) in 1997. The interview took place at Fisher's home in the Peak District on 29 March 1989. This is now (in the year 2000) the most easily available of the interviews as it can be freely downloaded for individual study purposes. The interviews are cited as 'Mottram', 'Rasula/Irwin', 'Sheppard', 'Lester' and 'Tranter' respectively.

For a more recent interview see John Kerrigan's e-mail 'conversation' with Fisher conducted between September 1998 and February 1999, entitled '"Come to Think of it, the Imagination": Roy Fisher in Conversation with John Kerrigan', pp. 96–120 in *News for the Ear: A Homage to Roy Fisher*, ed. Robert Sheppard and Peter Robinson, Stride Publications (11 Sylvan Road, Exeter, Devon EX4 6EW), 2000.

A compendium of edited versions of the major interviews, along with more recent material, was published in 2000 under the title *Interviews Through Time, & Selected Prose*, by Roy Fisher, Shearsman Books (Lark Rise, Fore Street, Kentisbeare, Cullompton, Devon EX15 2AD). The compendium includes an autobiographical essay by Fisher, and the self-review originally published in *The Rialto*.

5 See Marjorie Perloff's essay 'Whose new American Poetry? Anthologising in the Nineties' (available at http://wings.buffalo.edu/epc/authors/perloff/anth.html (last accessed June 2000)), which makes a similar point in the American poetic context, showing the malleability of the boundary between 'establishment' and 'countercultural' poetry.

6 Of course, over the period of more than fifteen years covered by these
   interviews Fisher's emphasis shifts, but the picture which emerges from
   this material is a consistent one, which I would sum up as follows: (a)
   Fisher tends to play down his 'Americanist' affiliations (those with Black
   Mountain poetics, with William Carlos Williams, etc) – 'I wasn't ready
   to run with it all the way', he says of Black Mountain (Tranter, p. 4) –
   and instead plays up connections with continental European writing
   (such as Rilke, Stefan George and Apollinaire (Mottram, p. 9), and a
   more extensive list in Sheppard, p. 10). (b) He always comments on the
   period of 'writer's block' (dated 'pretty well '66 to '70' in the Mottram
   interview; see also Sheppard, p. 8) which led him to believe that his
   career as a poet was over. The Fulcrum *Collected Poems* of 1968 was so
   named because Fisher thought that's what it would be. (c) He frequently
   emphasises his peculiar 'rootedness' in Birmingham – that he is 'not a
   traveller' (Rasula, p. 18), and never slept outside the city till he was thir-
   teen, and lived in the house he was born in till he was twenty-three
   (Rasula, p. 19). He also emphasises that his father's death (a man 'closely
   associated with the city, with these areas over a period of forty years',
   Rasula, p. 19) was one of the stimuli which led to the compilation of the
   City materials. (d) At the same time, he also emphasises the 'unrealness'
   or 'subjectivity' of the place represented in the poetry – 'Most of the City
   writing is meant to be about a city which has already turned into a city
   of the mind' (Rasula, p. 12) is a typical statement. (e) Hence, and
   concomitantly, he always denies being a 'poet of place', rejecting a cate-
   gorising label which was current in the 1970s. 'I find the "place" tag is a
   very literal one, and I'm not a literalist' (Sheppard, p. 9). (f) He often
   emphasises the restricted nature of his readership, and implies a prefer-
   ence for that situation. Wider notice, he implies, inhibits him as a writer.
   Of Michael Shayer's version of *City*, produced from Fisher's materials, he
   says 'I didn't like it, but it caught people's attention. The knowledge that
   people were reading the stuff, and that it was not perfect, so far as I was
   concerned – it gave me a screaming fit. I could hardly move out of my
   chair for months. it really upset me' (Tranter, pp. 6–7). The attempt to
   write something which had more 'leverage' – 'I spent ages trying to write
   a massive novel' (Tranter, p. 7) – eventually brought about the writing
   block.

7 In spite of the consistencies noted in the previous footnote, there is an
   overall shift in emphasis between the 1970s interviews (Mottram, and
   Rasula/Irwin) and those of the 1980s (Sheppard, Lester and Tranter) in
   that the later ones are less insistent about the 'subjectivity' of the *City*
   material (the 'city-of-the-mind' idea), and more prone to give specific
   personal data about the poet himself and 'his' Birmingham (as particu-
   larly in Lester). Likewise, information about the circumstances of the

publication of his early work is much more specific in the later interviews
(notably Tranter), though there is some of this, too, in the 1973 inter-
view, under skilful probing from Eric Mottram. Interestingly, the treat-
ment of Birmingham and the Midlands in the poetry itself follows an
opposite trajectory, moving from the concrete loco-specificity of much of
City itself to the greater abstraction and abstruseness which is seen in
'Handsworth Liberties' and *A Furnace*. Since there is little danger of
anyone accusing these works of being documentary representations of
places, there is less need to disown that aspect of his work so frequently.

8 See *In Memoriam*, poem 55, 'So careful of the type she [Nature] seems,/
So careless of the single life'. The thought is immediately rejected in poem
56.

9 Used not of his own work, but of the Chinese Language-Poetry Group
(see *Conductors of Chaos*, ed. Iain Sinclair, Picador, 1996, p. 356).

10 I have indicated in an earlier piece (Barry, 1986 – see footnote 3) that I
regard 'Handsworth Liberties' as a less than successful item, but the deci-
sion not to reprint it in *The Dow Low Drop* is surprising, given its
obvious importance in Fisher's 'composite sequence' of Birmingham
materials.

11 High Beech is the name of the asylum in which Clare was confined, and
Helpston that of his home village.

12 Corcoran (in *English Poetry Since 1940*) sees in Fisher's 'characteristic
note of repining' something which seems 'English Romantic in origin'
(p. 171), and in his 'vanishings and dissolvings' he detects ' a strain of the
late-Romantic' (p. 173). He seems somewhat distrustful of this element,
and of the fact that Fisher, 'out of images from a specific urban-industrial
location', appears 'to want to restore to this place something of the inten-
sity of feeling associated with more "natural" places in the history of
English Romanticism', thereby putting places like Handsworth 'into an
edgy continuity with the Derwent and the Duddon in Wordsworth'
(p. 174). I agree with Corcoran that this is what is happening, but given
Fisher's circumstances (of upbringing and formation) it seems 'natural'
that he should substitute the urban-industrial for the 'natural' in this
way. That is, in effect, the gist of what I have tried to say in this book.
Fisher has to think with Birmingham because it's what he was given. If
he had been born by the Derwent he probably would have thought with
that.

9 'I remember when all these fields were factories':
writing the vanishing city

If the period of the 1970s and 80s saw the depths of post-industrial urban decline in Britain, then this is also the period when the city seemed least to interest the poets regarded as major figures. The most 'hyped' poetic tendencies of the time were 'Martianism', which was the tag given to the metaphorical pastiche writing of Craig Raine, Christopher Reid, David Sweetman and others; and the 'new narrative' or 'secret narrative', that form of teasingly refracted verse anecdote, often with a post-imperial or upper-class setting, associated with such poets as James Fenton, Andrew Motion and Blake Morrison, as already discussed. We need to be wary about accusing poets of being evasive, whether consciously or unconsciously, but it is hard to avoid thinking that these approaches seem to facilitate an avoidance of both the personal and the social, leaving the poet free to indulge instead in free-fall linguistic shadow-play or enjoyable diegetic manipulation. Certainly, these strategies usually occlude or ignore the city. In fact there has always been a powerful 'Thatcherite' tendency in poetry criticism which believes that in poetry there is no such thing as society, that the personal is all, and that history, sociology, science and technology have no real place within it, unless it be as the vehicle of the occasional extended metaphor.

And indeed, it may be true that writing about the city in poetry sometimes means writing in a strategically 'superficial' way, in the sense that doing so often means denotating and annotating the surface, what is 'merely' (or primarily) seen, so that urban poetry is often strikingly *ocular* rather than *oracular* poetry, because the gaze is a markedly urban faculty, and many characteristically urban spaces are so constructed as to facilitate its greatest scope and free-play – one might think here of the Parisian pavement café (there is a considerable literature on the idea of the *flâneur*, the stroller),[1] the tiered boxes of an opera house, or the wide, tree-lined avenues built for fashionable promenading. Of course, the gaze is gendered, and looking and strolling in a city are rights that often need to be re-claimed and struggled for. The gaze of the poet in the city sees people, objects and vistas, and the overwhelming plenitude of things seen leaves no easy route back to personal subjectivity, to that mildly melancholy, meditative tone of, say, Coleridge in his cottage at Nether Stowey (as in 'Frost at Midnight') or Hardy leaning on a coppice gate in Dorset (as in 'The Darkling Thrush'). This tone-of-voice – the keystone of the dominant tradition of the personal-lyric in English verse – is less easy to place in cities, and if this tone goes, then so do the personal themes which have dominated English verse for centuries, themes such as personal romantic love, religious reflections and the detailed observation of nature. Writing which is city-focused often seems to block the route to this traditionally personal dimension: it seems to 'stick' at the surface, writing about roofs, or lights, or faces, things which feature, of course, in other kinds of writing, but which are usually just the access routes to a glide into a deeper level of subjectivity. City poems seem to resist that glide. They are typically 'eye' poems, often with a driving social-thematic which can seem to gloss over the personal. But I am thinking here of a particular type of urban poetry: not the Matt Simpson kind of retrospective confessional writing, where social conscience seems to upbraid the poet for the acquisition of that deeper-level subjectivity through departure and education, but the writing of poets like Roy Fisher and Edwin Morgan, who never left the place they write about, and whose merely personal history is always curiously absent from what they write.

But we should try to be more specific about the nature of the urban gaze. There are, it has been suggested throughout this book, two modes of urban vision, which we have called 'seeing' and 'looking'. 'Seeing' is what seems to happen naturally in walking along an urban commercial street, as the eye habitually fixes and scans at a level somewhere below the fascia which carry the brightly lit names of chainstores, building societies and supermarkets which direct the eye downwards. Looking elsewhere would be like being in a theatre and looking beyond the area which is spot-lit or flood-lighted. The eye tends to remain at plate-glass level and the fascia of the shops mark the usual upper boundary of the gaze, holding attention at the level of the street, thereby, in effect, hiding *provenance*, occluding the diachronic, and instead emphasising the synchronic that is the current (usually commercial) use of each building. At this level the present obscures the past, almost totally. A glance above the fascia immediately opens up a different world with a different timescale – perhaps we notice, for instance, that what is now Burger King was once a dairy, for the name 'Emmet's Dairies' is embossed into a stone plinth between the windows of the second and third storey. Evidently the builders had assumed that this building would be 'Emmet's Dairies' for ever, since the name is built into its very fabric, evoking a commercial world apparently operating on an altogether different set of expectations of permanence from our own. It is also a world of far greater 'stylistic stability' than ours, for even if the building were to belong to Emmet's Dairies for a hundred years there is no expectation that it would ever need to update its image with, say, a new logo or a new form of lettering.

This upward 'diachronic' gaze, then, is the other mode of urban vision – 'looking' rather than 'seeing'. It opens up the urban palimpsest of use and re-use, which, again, has featured prominently in this book, so that now the past occludes the present, for the storeys above the commercial, street-level facade are often relatively untouched by successive tides of modernisation and up-dating, and have survived more or less as built. So, we might notice (if I can develop an actual example in a little detail) that this typical city-centre commercial row – Burger King, TK Max, Boots, Electronics Inc – is actually built on to what was once a terrace of three-storey town houses. It can be dated to roughly the 1830s by noting such features as the raised parapet above the top storey, which hides the slope of the roof from ground level, and by the fact that there are none of the projecting bay windows which became characteristic, from the 1860s onwards, of the Victorian terrace. Visibly sloping roofs and projecting windows had to wait till the architectural battle of the styles between Classicism and Gothicism had been won by the latter, with the significant aid of Ruskin's *The Stones of Venice* (1851–53). Of course, the outcome of that battle was also determined by the whole temper of the Victorian age, by what made Tennyson write his *Idylls of the King* rather than, for instance, an epic about the decline of the Roman Empire, as he might have done had he been born a century before. Looking at the block as a whole we also notice that the upper storeys are some twenty feet further back from the road than the ground-level shops, and from this it is clear that when first built the terrace stood back from the road, and that these were once private houses with front gardens. So this was formerly a 'good' residential address on the edge of town, a place where aspiring 'carriage folk' lived, though now it is deep in inner-city commercial territory. Hence, this literally *unremarkable* block (because 'looking' in this way takes a real effort, though it requires no esoteric knowledge) is a graphic illustration (among other things) of the pace of urban expansion in the later nineteenth century, when people of this class decamped to new, brick-built 'villas' in tree-lined roads and avenues which were then suburban, but have long since succumbed to multiple occupation and are themselves now regarded as 'inner-city' problem areas. All this can be 'read' by the simple process of lifting the eye above the fascia, of 'looking' rather than 'seeing'.

The 'seeing' eye, then, is (in Saussure's terminology) synchronic, since it registers the varieties and patterns of present usage, while the 'looking' eye is diachronic, since it goes back through layers and accretions, perceiving history, influence, development, change. Typically, as already argued in slightly different terms, the urban poet combines these two eye-lines, the supra-fascial and the infra-fascial as we might call them, constantly playing the multi-layered palimpsest of the past, back into the commercial and experiential flux of the present. Together, the two make up the poet's 'visioning' or 'double-visioning' eye.

Ciaran Carson, *Belfast Confetti*

A Belfast poet whose work seems characterised by this kind of awareness is Ciaran Carson, though his debut collection, *The New Estate* (Blackstaff Press, 1976) did not in fact feature the urban very prominently, and drew instead on a much more traditional rural vocabulary and imagery, as even the titles of many of the poems make clear ('The Scribe in the Woods', 'St Ciaran and the Birds', 'The Half Moon Lake' and so on). The reason for this rural focus is, I think, that the 'Nationalist' identity which Carson registers and consolidates in these early poems had long been embodied in rural imagery and symbolism. To be Irish-speaking (Carson's first language and home language was Irish) was to be imbued with a culture of traditional myths and legends, tales and heroes whose antiquity necessarily entailed a mainly pre-urban character. Like Yeats (by residence mainly a Londoner) the Belfast-born Carson dipped into this myth pool, since this was the only vocabulary available. Furthermore, the rural was also the predominant register of the most successful poets of the immediately preceding generation. By 1976 Heaney, for instance, had already published *Door into the Dark*, *Wintering Out* and *North*), and all his early running-motifs (the well, the bogland, the harvest bow, etc.) are rural in character. This is to be expected, of course, since such material reflects Heaney's early background, but what is, if not remarkable, then at least worth remarking, is that Carson (like Ken Smith, whose work was discussed in the London chapter) did not feel free to draw upon what was specifically urban in his own background, and uses instead an acquired conceptual vocabulary of birds, flowers and islands. All the same, the best poems in Carson's first book are, I think, those like 'The Bomb Disposal', 'The Car Cemetery' and 'To a Married Sister', which have a strongly urban focus which is proleptic of his later development. For instance, the first of these is a powerful evocation of the tensions of the Troubles, making effective use of urban motifs – maps, taxis, cul-de-sacs, boarded-up windows. What is striking is that the city itself is envisaged as a bomb, which the inhabitants have to 'decode' daily in order to survive. The configurations constantly change, 'its forbidden areas changing daily' (which will become a frequent motif in his work), so that moving through it is like 'hesitating through a darkened nave'; you have to listen 'to the malevolent tick/ of its heart' till you can 'read/ the message of the threaded veins like print', and daily journeys have to be made by constantly varying routes, in case a potential assassin is watching your movements. Hence, when a crowded taxi accidentally turns into a cul-de-sac a wave of suppressed panic is felt as 'everyone breaks out suddenly/ in whispers, noting the boarded windows,/ the drawn blinds'. The self-protecting element here is that the eye has to be supra-fascial rather than infra-fascial constantly, to 'look' rather than just 'see' all the time, the place becoming a mental map which is could be fatal to misread.

Neil Corcoran, however (in an extremely valuable essay), reads the early Carson rather differently, distinguishing his rural Ireland from that of Heaney, for he is, says Corcoran, 'a resolutely urban poet, even when he strays into the Irish *rus* it is a squalidly depleted one: the Donegal-derelict rather than the Derry-lush of early Heaney of the Armagh-deciduous of Muldoon'.[2] Likewise, Corcoran places Carson's later writing (especially *The Irish for No*, published in 1987, the book which decisively established his poetic reputation) effectively within its

Irish poetic context, seeing him as rejecting the 'well-made-poem'
tradition, which was the 1950s 'Movement' and 'Group' inheritance
of the 1960s poets of Heaney's generation, and working instead in
conscious alignment (as the book's title would suggest) with an oral
and aural Irish tradition of music and story-telling: as Corcoran
writes, Carson was

> playing the oral against the literary, the long lines of his poems
> have something of the sustained, improvisatory panache of the
> Irish story-teller or *seanachie*, always aping the movement of the
> speaking voice in self-involved but audience-aware address,
> repetitive, self-corrective, elliptical; while also, in their sustained
> syntactical ebb and flow, maintaining a control of uncommonly
> sophisticated writerly resourcefulness. (p. 217)

At the same time, however, Corcoran partly recuperates the allowed
'difference' of this poetry by identifying Carson's often predominantly
narrative poems with the postmodern (as Corcoran sees it) 'new narra-
tive' mode of British and Irish poetry in the 1980s. Yet this does some
disservice to the starkness and impact of many of these pieces, which
lack the disembodied, ludic, but perhaps ultimately rather pointless
complexities of this mode of writing (which I have already criticised in
the case of Andrew Motion and Peter Didsbury). For instance, the
poem 'Dresden' in *The Irish for No* is rightly identified by Corcoran
as the best in the book. It is as powerful an icon, potentially, as
Mahon's 'Disused Shed in County Wexford', and speaks as unforget-
tably for the victims of our age, for those whom Mahon calls the 'lost
people of Treblinka and Pompeii'. The central character in the poem
is 'Horse Boyle', bored in Ireland, who moves as an immigrant to
Manchester, but is bored there too and joins the RAF, ending up as the
tail-gunner of a bomber over Dresden, and imagining that he hears
from the blazing city below echoes of breaking crockery as 'store-
rooms full of china/ shivered, teetered/ And collapsed, an avalanche of
porcelain, slushing and cascading'. As Corcoran says, the poem takes
a long time to get to this point and explain its title, and it has several
digressions before it does so, as it apes the confident meander of the
practised *raconteur*. All the same, to call it 'new narrativist' seems to
put it into the wrong tradition, for its chronotope is always clear, its
viewpoint consistent, and all the apparently random details are clicked
into place at the end; the Dresden china, for instance, is linked to the

milkmaid figurine on the mantelpiece of his childhood home, the focus of erotic speculation during the recitation of the family rosary.

I am suggesting, then, that the narrative mode used by Carson is perhaps better explained in terms of those urban actualities which Corcoran earlier acknowledges. It is a narrative style which is the correlative of a city in which the detour and the devious route to a desired objective are not decorative or artistic flourishes, but an often-necessary survival strategy. There is always somebody who may be watching you, trying to 'read' you, anticipating where you will be at a given moment, and you must anticipate this anticipation and so 'out-read' your readers, arriving when and where they had not expected you to. This kind of scenario is seen frequently in *Belfast Confetti*, Carson's other major work which came out in 1989 (too late to be discussed in Corcoran's book) and consolidated the major impact made by *The Irish for No*. The 'out-reading' of the reader scenario just mentioned is seen in the first poem in the new book, 'Turn Again' ('Someone asks me for directions, and I think again. I turn into/ A side-street to try to throw off my shadow, and history is changed'). In 'Last Orders' pressing the buzzer to be scrutinised by CCTV cameras and then admitted into a wire-meshed drinking club is like squeezing a trigger; both those who look and those who are looked at are playing 'Russian roulette, since you never know for sure who's who, or what/ You're walking into'. The result is that one's own identity comes into question ('I, for instance, could be anybody. Though I'm told/ Taig's written on my face. See me, would *I* trust appearances?' In 'Gate' the eye that flicks round the shopping street nervously notes the wear-and-tear of the fascia; the 't' and 'r' are missing from Terminus boutique, due to 'a bit of flak' the speaker assumes, rather than just shoddy workmanship. In the speeded-up commercial turnover of the present, it was Burton's six months ago, but it is, as the speaker says, 'difficult to keep track' in a city where the map is (as constantly in Carson) constantly changing.

Hence, the book is relentlessly loco-specific, raining street names, shop names, the names of churches, districts, pubs, and the brands of urban commodities like – well, like confetti. The narrative drive in the longer poems is leisurely, but always strongly determined thematically, with a logical coherence that in due course assimilates all the details (see 'Bed-Time story', 'Jawbox', 'Hamlet' and several other long-lined poems in the collection). Indeed, all the details which the new-narra-tivist would leave teasingly untied are pushed relentlessly home:

always the narrative is an argument of insidious intent, like Prufrock's, and like his, it is the correlative of the urban streets which he follows, always leading to some overwhelming question.

This is most startlingly dramatised in 'Question Time', which is in the format seen several times already in this book, the poem with auxiliary prose, or the poem-in-prose, exploring the urban palimpsest, flicking through the layers, incorporating data and documents. It opens with a quotation from an 1823 history of Belfast which relates an account of a native returning after a long absence to find the known streets of childhood vanished. A narrating voice (somewhat in a relaxed 'travelogue' register at this stage) universalises this experience:

> That disorientation, that disappointed hunger for a familiar place, will be experienced all the more keenly by today's returning native; more than that, even the little piggy who stayed at home will sometimes feel lost.

This is followed by a prose version of the account of the demolition of the Grand Central Hotel which I referred to in the Introduction, and then by comments on how Belfast is a 'mapless' city, because it is an urban text which is constantly being re-written (by bombers and planners – this is a familiar British urban scenario, but with a difference) and can therefore have no definitive reading ('Everything will be revised'). It goes on, 'No, don't trust maps, for they avoid the moment: ramps, barricades, diversions, Peace Lines'. Do photographs, then, show more, or more accurately, than maps? Like this one of a 1960s Belfast riot, which the speaker identifies as a view 'looking down Bosnia Street', with just the 'nia' of Roumania Street visible. (The street names overlay the ghosts of past – and future – conflicts, like the Crimea and the Balkans on to the present one.) The speaker asks himself, 'Was I there that night, on this street littered with half-bricks, broken glass, a battered saucepan and a bucket?' The photograph lays bare the tenderly remembered locale of his childhood: 'here is the lamp-post where I swung as a child, there is Smyth's corner shop; I can almost see myself in the half-gloom and the din.' The narrative line rambles, but the kind of overall coherence I have been claiming (that is, the new-narrativist tendencies I have been denying) mean that it follows an overt logic. The photograph reminds the speaker of his childhood district, which reminds him of the sectarian geography of that period which prohibited passage along certain streets, like Cupar Street, which is Protestant, and where they are stopped by boys who ask them, of the two flags they hold up, the Tricolour and the Union Jack, '*which of them would youse say was the best?*' These reminiscences about the past lead to a natural desire to go down and take a look at the old place 'when I went out for what I imagined was a harmless spin on the bike … so yes, I think, why not re-trace the route of all those years ago, 1959 or 1960'. The sense of urban dislocation in the post-industrial present is familiar for much of this: 'Eventually I find a new road I never knew existed – or is it an old street deprived of all its landmarks?' As he passes through the once-familiar territory the past is being mentally mapped on to the present and mentally audited for alterations, survivals and blanks ('Charleton's shop is bricked up; Tolan's the barber's is long since gone'). But the by-now familiar scenario of urban loss is suddenly broken: pausing at traffic lights he hears someone mutter something in his ear, turns and is grabbed round the neck by one person 'while someone else has me by the arm, twisted up my back, another has the other arm and I'm hauled off the bike'. At this stage the point of the title ('Question Time') starts to become clear, and he is dragged 'into what used to be McQuillan Street, only it isn't there any more, into one of those hole-in-the-wall taxi places, arms up against the breeze-block wall, legs apart, frisked'. The interrogation which follows is not just an in-depth knowledge test on the long-vanished streets of The Falls which he claims to have lived in thirty years ago. That is just the first paper in the examination: '*What streets could you see from the house? Cape Street? Yeah… Frere Street? Yeah…Where was Cape Street? Again.*', The second paper requires a detailed knowledge of the commercial archaeology and kinship patterns of the neighbourhood: '*Who lived next door? Next door again… Mooreland? Where is that? Stockman's? Where is that? What's next?*' And there are sudden returns to Paper One to check that the answers haven't been changed or faked: '*So where did you live again? Yeah, I know it's not there any more. Just tell me what was there. Again. No. 100. Where was that?*' The staccato lines capture the terror of the moment, as the inner city is re-created and re-peopled, and the inner map of the streets that aren't there any more is put back in place:

> The questions are snapped at me like photographs.
> The map is pieced together bit by bit. I am this map which they

examine, checking it for error, hesitation, accuracy; a map which
no longer refers to the present world, but to history, these
vanished streets; a map which is this moment, this interrogation,
my replies. Eventually I pass the test. I am frisked again, this
time in a regretful habitual gesture.

His life is saved by reciting the litany of streets he learned thirty years
ago, a litany which is (in a sectarian city) as surely coded as Catholic
as the rosary whose beads he also learned to tell in childhood, and in
bringing it back to life in such traumatic circumstances he is re-
enclosed in this inner city which is (like Pompeii) now beyond change
and fixed for ever, as no living city can ever be:

> I was *there*, in my mind's eye, one foot in the grave of that Falls
> Road of thirty years ago, inhaling its gritty smoggy air as I lolled
> outside the door of 100 Raglan Street, staring down through the
> comforting gloom to the soot-encrusted spires of St Peter's, or
> gazing at the blank brick gable walls of Balaklava Street, Cape
> Street, Frere Street, Milton Street, saying their names over to
> myself.

Edwin Morgan, 'Glasgow Sonnets'

The special circumstances of Carson's Belfast make work like this
amongst the most moving and effective examples of urban-specific
writing, but it is not different in kind from urban poetry from else-
where in the British Isles. For instance, the work of Edwin Morgan, a
major Scottish urban poet from an earlier generation, has significant
concerns in common with Carson's. The apogee of Edwin Morgan's
urban writing is his Glasgow material from the 1970s, especially the
volume *From Glasgow to Saturn* (Carcanet, 1973) which contains a
good deal of his best-known work. Morgan's notion of the city, as
he explains in his 1996 essay 'The poetry of the city',[3] is that it is
both heaven and hell at the same time. His essay ends with an emblem,
two evocations of Edinburgh by the fifteenth-century Scottish poet
William Dunbar, one presenting the city as 'a fairly hellish place'
(p. 103), the other presenting it as heaven ('we folk in parradyis/ In
Edinburcht'). Morgan sees this as typical of 'the two faces of the city,
perhaps of any city' (p. 104). This ambivalence about the city very

much reflects the Glasgow of this volume, a place which predates the re-born 'Smiles Better' city of the 1980s public relations industry and has a strong continuity with the place of unemployment, gang violence and sectarianism of the 1930s (which he writes about in 'King Billy', a Glasgow poem from the 1968 volume *The Second Life*). The 'city as heaven' is a moment when effects of light conspire to produce an ethereal visual effect: 'Mercy for the rainy/ tyres and the violet/ thunder that bring you/ shambling and shy/ from chains of Easterhouse/ plains of lights' ('In Glasgow'). This is an urban trope familiar as the 'epiphany' in the early work of James Joyce, when a casual glance at the Custom House clock can trigger a moment of light-headed, exhilarating insight. More frequently in Morgan, though, the poems contrast a grim urban present with an exotic alternative (reminiscent of the dichotomy between 'here' and 'elsewhere' frequently found in the work of the Hull poets) – in 'Shantyman' it's a sailing ship 'plunging without stars/ at midnight' as it 'rolls down to heaven like Rio': In 'Floating off to Timor' 'we'd be shimmering on the Trades ... a pace of dolphins/ to the copra ports', as 'the yellow deck/ breathes, it heaves spray/ back like a shout' (pp. 233–4). Here, as often with port cities, the sense of squalor and entrapment can be intensified by the contrast with the supposedly exotic destinations to which the ships travel. This present more often seems beyond redemption, as in the same poem 'But here we are care/ of the black roofs. It's not hard to find/ with a collar turned up/ and a hoot from the Clyde'.

Morgan's most sustained 'city' piece is the sequence 'Glasgow Sonnets' in this same volume, a set of ten rhymed sonnets which register the plight of the city in the early 1970s, a time when the post-war Keynesian consensus in economics was giving way to the monetarism of Milton Friedman and Bernard Heysenck. Friedman's 1968 article 'The Role of Monetary Policy' had introduced the notion of the 'natural rate of unemployment', defined as the 'level of unemployment which has the property that it is consistent with equilibrium in the structure of real wage rates', in other words, with containing inflation. This began the switch from the primary governmental goal of full employment, which had characterised the post-war period till then of the so-called 'Butskellite consensus',[4] to a new period in which the main aim of government became the control of inflation. The city depicted in Morgan's sonnets is suffering from the rapid de-industrialisation which is the consequence for a city three hundred miles away of decisions taken in Whitehall in pursuance of this anti-inflationary goal. The resulting sense of helplessness, anger and despair comes through powerfully in the poems, as major industries like shipbuilding disappear from an area which, in 1936, had launched ninety-one ships, and that was considered to be 'a bad year'. Thus, the wind which opens the sequence is the 'ill wind' of metaphor, as well as the economic wind which blows through a bleak terrain of condemned tenements: 'A mean wind wanders through the backcourt trash./ Hackles on puddles rise, old mattresses/ puff briefly and subside.' Here the hyper-intensified urban gaze discussed earlier is much in evidence: this is the eye in a troubled city, ever alert in a dodgy district for a stray movement which might indicate danger. In other ways the poetic means being used here are conventional in the extreme: thus, the narrative tense used is the 'observer-present', as it might be called, a grammatical feature characteristic of, and exclusive to, poetry, whereby the present tense denotes a once-only action from the past which is now being re-lived in an imagined present, rather than a repeated or habitual action, which is what the present tense designates in ordinary speech.[5] Morgan's sonnets poems use the 'Italian' sonnet form which gives two 'abba' quatrains followed by a sestet in alternating rhyme, and this formal poetic elegance twists the knife of cruelty, like viewing squalor through a gilded frame ('Roses of mould grow from ceiling to wall./ The man lies late since he has lost his job,/ smokes on one elbow, letting his coughs fall/ thinly into an air too poor to rob'). The scenario in sonnet *ii* is like the graveyard of capitalism ('Late shadows lengthen slowly, slogans fade'): the gaunt tenements are tomblike, and have repeated cycles of defeat and deprivation built into them:

> No deliverer ever rose
> from these stone tombs to get the hell they made
> unmade. The same weans never make the grade.
> The same grey street sends back the ball it throws.

Sonnet *iv* debates the poet's own stance in relation to all this, trying hard to work out how to 'place' it and what a poet's stance towards it might conceivably be, for historically, the extreme poverty seems like a grotesque return of the 1930s ('Surely soup kitchens have gone out? It's not/ the Thirties now'). In his poem 'Glasgow 1960' the then senior living Scottish poet, Hugh MacDiarmid, had evoked the city in a jaunty and yet accusatory way, condemning it for its materialism and anti-intellectualism, and fantasising about a great turn-around in sensibility which would make a poet's pronouncements on a foreign poet's 'abstruse song' big enough news to electrify the city and sell the evening editions of the newspapers like hot cakes. The implication of this self-indulgent scenario is that the city has a duty to the poet, to recognise him, and accept his authority. But Morgan rejects this, since 'Hugh MacDiarmid forgot/ in "Glasgow 1960" that the feast/ of reason and the flow of soul has ceased/ to matter to the long unfinished plot/ of heating frozen hands'. He adds 'We never got/ an abstruse song that charmed the raging beast'. Here the 'beast' seems also to refer to a set of poems called 'Glasgow Beasts' (1961) by Ian Hamilton Finlay, which anticipated Tom Leonard in its use of Glasgow vernacular, but was violently denounced by MacDiarmid, as John Aberdein writes (in connection with Polygon's re-issue of the work):

> Hamilton was the avant garde, reviled by the Scottish Renaissance leader Hugh McDiarmid, who wrote a pamphlet eight times the length of *Glasgow Beasts* simply to rebut it and refute its author's credentials: 'language of the gutter' etc. The point at issue was that Finlay was refining an aesthetic, whereas MacDiarmid had a programme for wholesale cultural regeneration.

Morgan, while avoiding the vernacular route of representing the city by reproducing its dialect, uses Scottish words when appropriate (like 'weans' for children), but otherwise accepts the helplessness and marginality of poetry – 'poets words are ill/ to hurt ye', he says to the districts of the city which are suffering under the bulldozers, and then ends the poem in a 'high' poetic idiom which is a compound of metaphor and lyricism: 'On the wrecker's ball the rains/ of greeting cities drop and drink their fill'. In sonnet *v* the political policies which have closed the shipyards (essentially a refusal to counter 'Pacific Rim' competition with a measure of subsidy) are themselves presented in terms of silencing one idiom ('We have preferred/ silent slipways to the riveters' wit'), and substituting for it a vacuous language which expresses an unfelt regret ('Ministers' tears might well have launched a herd/ of bucking tankers if they'd been transferred/ from Whitehall to the Clyde'). Yet issues of tone and appropriate expression remain crucial. When a 'work-in' at the condemned Upper Clyde Shipbuilders was organised by union leader Jimmy Reid in 1973 the stance of jaunty, boozy defiance was excluded ('"There'll be no bevvying" said Reid/ at the work-in') and a tone of dignified resistance was set, but to what avail, asks the poet, 'while distant blackboards use you as their duster'. What had happened to Glasgow, to Scotland, was the product of even more distant forces. The 1973 OPEC meeting had quadrupled the world price of oil, among other things rendering obsolete most of the ships produced by the vanishing shipbuilders of the Clyde. The economic value of west-coast heavy industry was in steep decline, and the oil field discovered off the east coast now tilted the economic map of the whole of Scotland in a new direction: as sonnet *vi* begins by putting it, 'The North Sea oil-strike tilts east Scotland up,/ and the great sick Clyde shivers in its bed'. Glasgow then becomes, like Liverpool, another west-coast port city stranded on the wrong side of the map. The pain of de-industrialisation in Scotland is compounded by the fact that it is the policies of nationalisation, pursued by the Labour Party and strongly supported by the Scottish Left (and by the Communist-Socialist poet Hugh MacDiarmid) which had the result of handing over control of Scottish Industries to bodies outside Scotland, so that by the 1970s, all the Clyde shipyards were part of consortia run from London or abroad. So when it came to it, these distant economic blackboards could be wiped clean by monetarist-leaning Labour governments which Scotland had voted for, just as later by Thatcherite governments which had never received a majority vote in Scotland.

'Glasgow Sonnets', then, seems to register the watershed of that realisation of powerlessness which produced the much more separatist, devolutionist Scotland of today. And what, to come back to it, could the poet do? Write an elegy? Wish that 'a less faint, shaky sunup/ glimmered through the skeletal shop and shed', as heavy industry rapidly became first *in situ* industrial archaeology, and was then tidied away into open-air 'heritage' museums, outsold by 'Mitsubishi or Krupp'. As the poet says of these ruins, 'The images are ageless but the thing/ is now'. Again, the poet is powerless to intervene, for 'Without my images the men/ ration their cigarettes, their children cling/ to broken toys, their women wonder when/ the doors will bang on laughter'. Sonnet *vii* looks wearily at the attempts to 'Splint the dying age' by 'Environmentalists, ecologists/ and Conservationists'. The familiar cityscapes are transformed by pedestrianisation, by making riverside walks where now-demolished shipyards had been, sandblasting old buildings to 'multiply pink piebald facades', a process which seems to make a theatre-set out of something which had once been solid and real, so that the city becomes 'The gutted double fake'. The process of demolition and rebuilding continues in sonnet *viii*; the clean modernist shapes of the looping flyovers are beautiful (as even 'ravished tragic Toshy' – Glasgow's turn-of-the-century architect Charles Rennie Mackintosh – would have recognised, says the poem) but the sudden opening up of swathes of landscape is brutal and disturbing ('Vistas swim out from the bulldozer's bite'), as when the stars now come right down to a horizon which used to end at the tops of the intervening buildings. The decanted central areas are meant to revert to 'leaves or larks or sploshy/ lanes' but this de-urbanification is paid for by the 'dead boarded site – the life that overspill is overkill to'. The supposed 'garden cities' of the 'overspill' townships on the outskirts are built in the confident modernist style celebrated in the Mies Van der Rohe slogan 'Less is more', which is indignantly denied in this poem, and the notion of the garden city is denounced as 'the flimsiest oxymoron'. Again, then, the poem protests at powerlessness, at solutions conceived elsewhere being imposed *here*; at cities which are treated like liquids which can be poured into any desired container – they can be 'distilled', and can have an 'overspill' population. Sonnet *ix* sees the city as undergoing the pain of its own transformation ('It groans and shakes, contracts and grows again./ Its giant broken shoulders shrug off rain'). The city may express an impotent rage ('It sometimes tears its smoky counterpane/ to hoist a bleary fist at nothing, then/ at everything, you never know'), but the restoration of what has now been reduced to a landscape of 'barricaded windows' can only be imagined as a kind of apocalyptic judgement day, when 'the shops, the ships, the trust/ return like thunder'. The 'seeing eye' at this point seems to retreat to a vantage point which is at a panoramic distance and accepts that the geological and economic forces which create cities are not to be resisted: 'Give the Clyde the rest./ Man and the sea make cities as they must.' In the final poem of the sequence the necessity of looking away, which is considerable, is yielded to: the vantage point is that of a 'schoolboy reading *Lear*' in a high-rise block of flats. The poet's highly literary sensibility sees the multi-storey building as like 'a sonnet stretched to ode' and presumably there is some hybridisation here of the narrator's voice and percepts, so that these are partly transferred to the boy, who is acquiring the education which will be his personal ticket out of this environment. *He* will have choices, and won't be used up by forces elsewhere which he will never

see, and which will never see him. Yet such remains the all-too-general
fate of the lives depicted here, and the sequence ends with the focus
on them:

> But stalled lives never budge.
> They linger in the single-ends that use
> their spirit to the bone, and when they trudge
> from closemouth to laundrette their steady shoes
> carry a world that weighs us like a judge.

'Glasgow Sonnets', then, is a remarkable set of city poems which
keeps the poetic idiom low-key and intact, so that the medium itself
takes very little attention. It makes no attempt at multi-registered
linguistic hybridity, nor does it strive for earthy vernacular realism,
absorbing its narrated voices (as in sonnet *iii*) into the standard
contemporary poetic register of the narrating voice. It sees and
comments in a public mode of poetry, speaking for the disempowered
and the silenced without embarrassment and without any obsessive
examination of its own motives for doing so, or any showy agonising
about the style of address it should use. The sequence is untroubled by
its own vulnerability to the charge that the expert deployment of
rhyme, pentameter and literary allusion sits oddly in the context of
showing lives which suffer grievous retribution for their failure to
acquire the skills needed to analyse *King Lear*. However ambivalent
we ourselves might feel about our own acquisition of such skills, it is
undeniable that they do seem to provide a pretty effective personal
windbreak in the face of the 'mean wind' of economics whose effects
are shown in the sequence. Peter Reading, traversing similar territory
in *Perduta Gente* seems more aware of the danger, and adopts a differ-
ent strategy from Morgan, as we saw. Yet Morgan does seem to accept
the Audenesque view that 'poetry makes nothing happen', whereas
Reading (and Harrison, I think) would not do so and would believe
that poetry can have an impact on opinion if it can find a way to make
the form as shocking as the content. This difference in belief has, I
think, something to do with the formal choices the poets make. But a
more internally troubled register might have been less able to express
the horror at the urban transformations which were so widely experi-
enced in the 1970s, and so little registered in literature, art or music.
   It should be added that my view here of Morgan's attitudes to
urban change is at odds with that offered in Geddes Thompson's *The*

Poetry of Edwin Morgan (Association for Scottish Literary Studies, 1986) where we are told:

> The sheer consistency of his attitude is well-revealed when he wrote about the massive redevelopment that has taken place in his native Glasgow over the last two decades: the demolition of the older tenements and road systems and their replacement by high-rise flats and ring-roads. It is fashionable to criticise these developments, to lament the passing of an older way of life based on a supposed close communal spirit engendered by tenement living. Morgan will have none of this. He sees the changes as necessary, indeed inevitable. (p. 12)

But this upbeat reading of the sequence seems to involve, first, reading the bulldozers, rather improbably, as bringers of enlightened change and new possibilities ('Vistas swim out from the bulldozer's bite', sonnet *vii*), and second, a heartless dismissal of those who cling to the tenements, seeing them as people who wilfully turn away from the light, and from enlightenment ('stalled lives never budge', sonnet *x*). As I indicated, the penultimate sonnet expresses the futility, ultimately, of resisting the change ('Man and the sea make cities as they must'), but this is very far from the bluff figure of a Morgan who 'will have none of this', and expresses hackneyed views of the 'We cannot go back – we must go forward' variety. Indeed, there *were* choices available, and wrong choices were made and their consequences imposed on others right through the 1970s as that process of 'decanting' population into high-rise 'overspill' estates went on. Eventually, community groups were formed and resistance began, and it turned out that what people actually wanted was either that the old housing be renovated and brought up to modern standards, or else that communities be kept intact and people be re-housed in newly built properties in the same location. This is not a story of refusing to 'budge', or embracing the past rather than the present, but of not wanting to end up as the duster for some distant body's blackboard. Surely, the poet who coined that image (in the end line of sonnet *x*) could never entertain a single-minded 'commitment to the present' (p. 13) in the terms envisaged by Thomson.

W. N. Herbert

Morgan's fellow Scottish poet of a later generation, the Dundonian W.N. Herbert, expresses broadly similar social attitudes, but in a looser poetic framework. The quotation in the chapter title is the opening line of Herbert's 'Port Selda' (*The Luarelude*, Bloodaxe, 1998, p.116). The first two stanzas of the poem (which amount to about a third of the total) evoke the three successive waves of urban-destruction which have transformed most major British cities within living memory, that is, Second World War bombing, 1960s 'urban renewal' and the de-industrialisation of the 1970s and 80s. The lines fuse this triple-layered process into a single apocalyptic visitation, a scar on modern memory which is different, of course, and less intensive than that left by the First World War (as recounted in Paul Fussel's *The Great War and Modern Memory*, Oxford University Press, 1975), but is at the same time just as pervasive, and perhaps all the more traumatic for being generally repressed:

> I remember when all these fields were factories,
> when an industry was the limitation beyond which
> the city couldn't think. Before
> our shorefronts needed to know
> what their former yards had built
> to fill in the information boards.
> This was before the bomb, the bomb,
> the modernist bomb,
> the bomb that cleanses.
>
> picture a Heinkel, thrown into a himmelwarp
> by passing over Bonnybridge in 1942,
> emerging to continue its mission in the mid-
> 60s and blow Dundee, blow
> all your cities backwards.

The specific localisation here is Dundee and its environs, but the subject is 'all your cities' and what has become of them. The opened vista of shoreline where the mills, or factories or warehouses, have been demolished remains a visual shock long after the hoardings and information boards have come down, and the citizen's helplessness in the face of the onslaught is suggested here (in the quasi-comical mode favoured by Herbert) by the 'Dad's Army' grandfather ('his helmet gleams like a pie-dish on the drainer') who rushes about trying to catch the incendiary bombs while 'only the buildings of historic or/ architectural interest are struck;/ only the quarters of any character are hit'. As the fantasy of urban resistance reaches its climax, 'the bomber is felled by an indignant bottle/ cast from Lochee' and a policeman 'like a column of oatmeal' points his gun at 'the jute-coloured head of the survivor'. Here the 'jute-coloured head' is metonymic of Dundee's '3Js' past, that is, its sentimental self-image as the city of 'jute, jam and journalism', and the grandfather's exploits have an improbable élan which belongs in the pages of *The Dandy*, the Dundee-produced home of comic-strip epics like 'Desperate Dan' or 'The Broons'. But the policeman is smooth-talked into inaction by the philosophical musings of the downed pilot ('The question here is where to put the muzzle?' his speech begins), and bamboozled, we must presume, by the ending of that speech, and of the poem, which quotes a question but calls it an answer:

> Through such compelling darknesses
> its answer always comes:
> 'What is looking for us in all these means?'

If it is indeed an answer then it is, of course, one to which there is no question. Yet the effect of ending the poem thus is to enclose the social processes of urban change within an aura that is ontological and apoc- alyptic – whatever actually caused the urban changes we see, and whether they are ultimately for good or ill, it feels exactly as if the horsemen of an incomprehensible apocalypse have simply chosen to visit plagues of destruction upon us.

The result of the triple-layered urban destruction mentioned above is something like collective trauma, but its effects have largely been repressed. The bookshops of virtually every city in the country show symptoms of the trauma in the shelves of 'Local Publications' which represent a nostalgia industry now bigger than the residual industries whose decline they meticulously record. Likewise, there is a booming market in local-nostalgia fiction, usually composite sagas charting the rise of working-class heroines from heaving terraces and tenements to success and respectability in suburbia and beyond. These books love the now-demolished working-class enclaves of major cities and their long-vanished industries, like Scotland Road and the passenger liners in the Liverpool stories of Helen Forrester, Anne Baker and Lyn Andrews. But the trauma is little represented in higher-brow fiction, and there is an evident gap between the new-realist tales of the working-class affluent apogee in the 1960s – *Billy Liar*, *Saturday Night and Sunday Morning*, and so on – and the rise of writers like James Kelman in the 1980s. But my main point here is that the urban trauma and dislocation of our times *is* registered in the often-neglected urban poetry of the post-1960s period, though the manner is often that blend of local-realism with pervading surrealism that we saw earlier in the case of Sean O'Brien. And, of course, it is not generally registered in the most prominent poetic figures of the period, a fact which cannot be surprising, given the belated 'Georgian' tendencies of British poetry. The effects of those tendencies have contributed to the cultural marginalisation of poetry, as witnessed by the inability of key prestigious publishers to sustain poetry lists, and the widespread reluctance of students to opt to study it. But this is where we came in.

Notes

1 For an enjoyable, leisurely read on the topic see *Loiterature*, Ross Chambers, Nebraska University Press, 1999, especially Chapter 8, 'Flaneur Reading'.

2 'One step forward, two steps back: Ciaran Carson's *The Irish for No*', in *The Chosen Ground: Essays on the Contemporary Poetry of Northern Ireland*, ed. Neil Corcoran, Seren Books, 1992, p. 216.

3 *Comparative Criticism, 18: Spaces: Cities, Gardens and Wildernesses*, Cambridge University Press, 1996, pp. 91–105.

4 The term 'Butskellite' conflates the names of the two main political leaders of the time, the Conservatives' Rab Butler and Labour's Hugh Gaitskell. The post-1945 'Butskellite' consensus, lasting through the 1950s and into the 60s, saw wide agreement between the two parties on the essentials of social and monetary policy as regards running a mixed economy, maintaining the welfare state and striving for full employment,

5 For example, we say 'I wake at seven', which in conversation means that this is my habitual practice, whereas the same line in a poem designates an action in the past performed once only, and now about to be imaginatively re-lived, as in Gerard Manley Hopkins's opening line 'I wake and feel the feel of dark not day'.

Select bibliography

Acheson, James and Romana Huk (eds), *Contemporary British Poetry: Essays in Theory and Criticism*, State University of New York (Albany) Press, 1996.

Adams, Anna (comp.), *Thames: An Anthology of River Poems*, Enitharmon Press, 1999.

Atkins, Marc and Iain Sinclair, *Liquid City*, Reaktion Books, 1999.

Barnie, John, *The King of Ashes*, Gomer Press, 1989.

Barnie, John, *The City*, Gomer, 1993.

Barnie, John, *No Hiding Place: Essays on the New Nature and Poetry*, University of Wales Press, 1996.

Bertram, Vicki (ed.), *Kicking Daffodils: Twentieth-Century Women Poets*, Edinburgh University Press, 1997.

Bush, Clive, *Out of Dissent: Five Contemporary British Poets*, Talus, 1997.

Caddell, Richard and Peter Quartermain (eds), *Other British and Irish Poetry Since 1970*, Wesleyan University Press, 1998.

Carson, Ciaran, *The New Estate*, Blackstaff Press, 1976.

Carson, Ciaran, *The Irish for No*, The Gallery Press, 1987; Bloodaxe, 1988.

Carson, Ciaran, *Belfast Confetti*, Bloodaxe, 1990.

Carson, Ciaran, *The Ballad of HMS Belfast: A Compendium of Belfast Poems*, Picador, 1999.

Corcoran, Neil, 'One step forward, two steps back: Ciaran Carson's *The Irish for No*', in *The Chosen Ground: Essays on the Contemporary Poetry of Northern Ireland*, ed. Neil Corcoran, Seren Books, 1992.

Corcoran, Neil, *English Poetry Since 1940*, Longman, 1993.

Crawford, Robert, *The Savage and the City in the Poetry of T.S. Eliot*, Clarendon Press, 1990.

Davie, Donald, *Thomas Hardy and British Poetry*, Routledge and Kegan Paul, 1973

Didsbury, Peter, *The Butchers of Hull*, Bloodaxe 1982.

Didsbury, Peter, *The Classical Farm*, Bloodaxe, 1987.

Didsbury, Peter, *That Old-Time Religion*, Bloodaxe, 1994.

Dun, Aidan, *Vale Royal*, Goldmark, 1995.

Dunn, Douglas (ed.), *A Rumoured City, New Poets from Hull*, Bloodaxe, 1982.

Dunn, Douglas (ed.), *Two Decades of Irish Writing*, Carcanet, 1975.

Edwards, Ken, *Drumming & Poems*, Galloping Dog Press, 1982.

Ellin, Nan, *Postmodern Urbanism*, Blackwell, 1996.

Fairer, David and Christine Gerrard (eds), *Eighteenth-Century Poetry: An Annotated Anthology*, Blackwell, 1998.

Fanthorpe, U.A., *Selected Poems*, Penguin, 1986.

Farley, Paul, *The Boy From the Chemist is Here to See You*, Picador, 1998.

Fisher, Allen, *Place Book One (I – XXXVII)*, Aloes Books, 1974, republished by Truck Books, 1976.

Fisher, Allen, *Place Book Two (Unpolished Mirrors)*, Reality Studios, 1985.

Fisher, Allen, *Place Book Three (Stane)*, Aloes Books, 1977.

Fisher, Allen, *Place Books Four and Five (Becoming)*, Aloes Books, 1978.

Fisher, Roy, *Poems 1955–1980*, Oxford University Press, 1980.

Fisher, Roy, *A Furnace*, Oxford University Press, 1982.

Fisher, Roy, *Birmingham River*, Oxford University Press, 1994.

Fisher, Roy, *The Dow Low Drop: New & Selected Poems*, Bloodaxe, 1996.

Gifford, Terry, *Pastoral*, Routledge, 1999.

Gregson, Ian, 'An exhausted tradition', *New Welsh Review*, no. 27 (Winter 1994), pp. 22–3.

Gregson, Ian, *Contemporary Poetry and Postmodernism: Dialogue and Estrangement*, Macmillan, 1996.

Griffiths, Bill, *The Book of Split Cities*, Etruscan Books, 1999.

Hampson, Robert, *Seaport*, Pushtika Press, 1995.

Hampson, Robert and Peter Barry (eds), *New British Poetries: The Scope of the Possible*, Manchester University Press, 1993.

Harrison, Tony, *Continuous: 50 Sonnets from 'The School of Eloquence'* Collings, 1981.

Harrison, Tony, *Selected Poems*, Penguin, 1984.

Henri, Adrian, *Tonight at Noon*, Rapp and Whiting, 1967.

Herbert, W. N., *The Luarelude*, Bloodaxe, 1998.

Houston, Douglas, *With the Offal Eaters*, Bloodaxe, 1986.

Kennedy, David, *New Relations: The Refashioning of British Poetry, 1980–1994*, Seren, 1996.

Kidd, Helen, 'The paper city', in *New British Poetries: The Scope of the Possible*, ed. Robert Hampson and Peter Barry, Manchester University Press, 1993

Kingsley-Weatherhead, A., *The British Dissonance*, Columbia University Press, 1983.

Lucie-Smith, Edward, *The Liverpool Scene*, Rapp and Whiting/André Deutsch, 1967.

MacSweeney, Barry, *The Boy from the Green Cabaret Tells of his Mother*, Hutchinson, 1968.

MacSweeney, Barry, *Hellhound Memos*, Many Press, 1993.

McMillan, Ian, *Selected Poems*, Carcanet, 1987.

Morgan, Edwin, *From Glasgow to Saturn*, Carcanet, 1973.

Morrison, Blake and Andrew Motion, *The Penguin Book of Contemporary British Poetry*, Penguin, 1982

O'Brien, Sean, *The Indoor Park*, Bloodaxe, 1983.

O'Brien, Sean, *The Frighteners*, Bloodaxe, 1987.

O'Brien, Sean, *HMS Glasshouse*, Oxford University Press, 1991.

O'Brien, Sean, *The Ghost Train*, Oxford University Press, 1995.

O'Brien, Sean, *Deregulated Muse: Essays on Contemporary British and Irish Poetry*, Bloodaxe, 1997

O'Brien, Sean, *The Firebox: Poetry from Britain and Ireland after 1945*, Picador, 1998.

Penguin Modern Poets, *The Mersey Sound*, Penguin, 1967.

Raban, Jonathan, *The Society of the Poem*, Harrap, 1971.

Reading, Peter, *Perduta Gente*, Secker and Warburg, 1989.

Rees-Jones, Deryn, *The Memory Tray*, Seren, 1993.

Robinson, Alan, *Instabilities in Contemporary British Poetry*, Macmillan, 1988.

Robinson, Peter (ed.), *Liverpool Accents: Seven Poets and a City*, Liverpool University Press, 1996.

Simpson, Matt, *An Elegy for the Galosherman: New and Selected Poems*, Bloodaxe, 1990.

Simpson, Matt, *Catching Up With History*, Bloodaxe, 1995.

Sinclair, Iain, *Lud Heat*, Vintage, 1995.

Sinclair, Iain (ed.), *Conductors of Chaos: A Poetry Anthology*, Picador, 1996.

Sinclair, Iain, *Lights Out for the Territory*, Granta, 1997.

Sinclair, Iain, *Dark Lanthorns*, Goldmark, 1999.

Sinclair, Iain and Rachel Lichtenstein, *Rodinsky's Room*, Granta, 1999.

Smith, Ken, *The Poet Reclining: Selected Poems 1962–1980*, Bloodaxe, 1982.

Spears, Monroe, *Dionysus and the City: Modernism in Twentieth-Century Poetry*, Oxford University Press, 1970.

Tafari, Levi, *Liverpool Experience: Collected Poems*, edited by Cristian Habekost, Michael Schwinn, 1989.

Thomas, R.S, *Collected Poems, 1945–1990*, Phoenix, 1995.

Tindall, Gillian, *Countries of the Mind: The Meaning of Place to Writers*, Hogarth Press, 1991.

Index